SHOOTING POLARIS

SHOOTING POLARIS
A Personal Survey in the American West

JOHN HALES

≈

UNIVERSITY OF MISSOURI PRESS
COLUMBIA AND LONDON

Library of Congress Cataloging-in-Publication Data

Hales, John, 1952–
    Shooting Polaris : a personal survey in the American West / John Hales.
        p.   cm.
    Summary: "Memoir of surveying for the BLM in the Utah Desert. Reflects
on man's relationship to nature and work, the Mormon Church and the settling of the West, the idealistic legacy of the sixties, the controversy over
Glen Canyon Dam, and the often antagonistic relationship of American
capitalism to ecological management"—Provided by publisher.
    ISBN-13: 978-0-8262-1616-8 (alk. paper)
    ISBN-10: 0-8262-1616-1 (alk. paper)
    1.   Hales, John, 1952- 2.   Surveyors—United States—Biography. 3.   Sur-
veying—Utah—History—20th century.   I. Title.
    TA533.H35A3 2005
    526.9'092—dc22
                                                                                    2005021970

♾This paper meets the requirements of the
American National Standard for Permanence of Paper
for Printed Library Materials, Z39.48, 1984.

Designer: Kristie Lee
Typesetter: Crane Composition, Inc.
Printer and binder: Thomson-Shore, Inc.
Typefaces: Veljovic Book, Cronnos MM

For Connie
and for Jodi and Jason

CONTENTS

CHAPTER EIGHT

CHAPTER NINE

CHAPTER TEN

CHAPTER ELEVEN

CHAPTER TWELVE

EPILOGUE

ACKNOWLEDGMENTS

This book owes much to many people. My friends and colleagues at California State University, Fresno, especially those teaching in the creative writing program, have provided support and encouragement: Linnea Alexander, Craig Bernthal, Lillian Faderman, Tim Skeen, Liza Wieland, Steve Yarbrough, and Deans Luis Costa and Vida Samiian. My nonfiction workshop students have taught me a lot more about writing than they will ever learn from me. Jerry Thomas, Dan Mates, Eric Stahlke, and Don Buhler provided useful information concerning surveying practices; any errors or gaps that remain are completely my own. I'm especially grateful to Corrinne Clegg Hales, my first and best reader, for her careful ponderings of numerous drafts and her consistently good advice.

Portions of this book have appeared in different form in these publications, to whose editors I am deeply grateful: *Ascent, Fourth Genre, Georgia Review, Hudson Review, Southern Review, Weber Studies,* and *The Pushcart Prize XXVII.*

Although I've neither invented nor conflated landscapes and individuals, and have attempted to recount accurately the settings, experiences, and feelings of half a lifetime ago, this book is ultimately a work of memory and imagination, and as Tobias Wolff reminds us, memory has its own story to tell. I'm certain that my narrative differs to some extent from the recollections of those with whom I shared these experiences, and I've given most of these individuals different names in the book out of respect for their privacy and in recognition of the integrity of their own stories.

SHOOTING POLARIS

Talk of mysteries!—

Think of our life in nature,—

daily to be shown matter, to come in contact with it,—

rocks, trees, wind on our cheeks!

the *solid* earth!

the *actual* world!

the *common sense!*

Contact!

Contact!

Who are we?

Where are we?

Henry David Thoreau, "Ktaadn"

PROLOGUE

Orientation: The Front Chainman
Loses His Bearings

No one could remember a government surveyor actually going crazy, especially while on the job, out in the field running line. I'd heard stories about surveyors who were sadistic, alcoholic, unhygienic, or incompetent (although there were fewer incompetent-surveyor stories than you might think), but Jim Williams was the first to enter the annals of the Cadastral Survey as having crossed that boundary line into the condition we referred to uncharitably as *mental*. He was also one of the first surveyors in anyone's memory to get lost, lost seriously enough that we had to stop work and redeploy our survey crew as a search party.

Like me, Williams was a summer temporary, hired back for his second year, having done well enough the year before to be promoted from flagman to front chainman. Pulling the long measuring chain through the desert and mountain landscape of southern Utah was a difficult job, one that he'd been learning quickly and managing pretty well, and so we had been puzzled that morning when he'd hiked out dragging the chain behind him and had just kept walking, not stopping to pull the chain tight against Larry's pull long enough to take the measurement.

At first we didn't connect his failing to stop with the odd behavior he'd been demonstrating for the couple of weeks we'd been on this particular job, the first one of the summer. It wasn't unusual for an inexperienced front chainman, focusing too much on the difficult terrain through which he was supposed to thread the chain, or distracted by a hawk circling picturesquely overhead, or made dizzy by the first symptoms of sunstroke, to walk too far and have to back up a little. But even Larry's shouting "Williams? *Williams! Far enough!*" didn't slow him down, and that *was* unusual. Besides being the rear chainman, Larry Daniels was the party chief—our boss—and his yell generally had enough force and credibility to freeze us in our tracks until he was able to explain how we'd screwed up and what we needed to do to get it right. Instead, Williams just kept going, still walking a pretty straight line and still dragging the long steel measuring tape we continued to call a "chain" because its ancestor two hundred years earlier had actually *been* a chain—and by the time we all realized something was wrong, he'd disappeared into the tall sagebrush, leaving us with the dawning understanding that this could be serious: a crazy guy taking off fast into some of the steepest, driest, and most chaotic landscape in southern Utah.

Larry sent Matt back to the truck, telling him to loop downhill in Williams's general direction along the dirt road we'd bounced in on that morning, and Larry, Tim, and I set out following the tracks Williams had left in the soft sand. The waffle print of Williams's boots and the odd linear scrape of the chain he pulled left a trail that looked a little like the tracks lizards leave in soft sand, only human-sized, and made him pretty easy to follow, at least until we came to a wide bulging expanse of bare sandstone slickrock, and lost him. That's when we started to get worried.

I'd met Jim Williams just two weeks earlier, at the orientation meeting that began each surveying season in early June. My girlfriend, Karen, had dropped me off in front of Salt Lake City's federal building, near the large plaza that had been the setting for marches and rallies I'd attended faithfully over the preceding several years protesting the war in Vietnam. The drive had been quiet and a little awkward, the result of our not having finished our discussion the night before concerning when I'd be back, and whether or not we were actually living together—I'd sort of moved some of my belongings to her apartment for the summer but wasn't really sure *where* I actually lived, whether in the apartment that I'd just sublet to a fellow student until September, or in Karen's apartment, or even in the government bunk trailer in which I'd actually be spending most of my nights that summer. It was dawning on both of us that, unlike the summer before when I'd made it back to Salt Lake just about every weekend, much of this summer I'd be spending weekends as well as Mondays through Fridays residing at the survey's base camp at the other end of the state. "So you'll be back this Friday, right?" she said, and I said, "Sure," worried that we hadn't understood each other as we'd made our plans—the first job of the summer was just outside Richfield, an easy three-hour drive; the Kaiparowits job wouldn't begin for several weeks. We kissed with a reassuring degree of sincerity; I grabbed my duffle from the backseat of her Volkswagen and headed inside to be oriented. As I walked past the decorative fountain, I remembered—as I always did when entering the federal building—one evening a few years previously when I'd soaked my bandanna in this very fountain in preparation for what we were sure would be a tear gas attack. We'd all been a little disappointed that it hadn't played out that way, and I regretted sometimes that I would conclude my career as a war protestor ungassed and unarrested, and worried a little that my life might well follow this pattern of anticlimax and inconsequence.

After signing various forms in the personnel office, among them a pledge that I wouldn't overthrow the government while in its employ (the summer before, I'd actually taken a moment to consider the loyalty-oath implications, but a year later I'd been so worn down by the compromises required by my job I signed without much thought), I found a chair in the tenth-floor conference room that provided a clear if distant view of the pointy roof of the Salt Lake Temple. During breaks between lectures by various division heads concerning truck maintenance and payroll paperwork, surveying methods and procedures, and helicopter safety, I met the people I'd be working with for the summer.

I already knew I'd been re-upped with Larry, for better or worse. I had to admit to being encouraged by the fact that he could have bumped me to another crew and hadn't, and after enduring his routine, mostly good-humored insults about the likelihood of vermin in my beard and long hair, which I wore in the style of the times—the mid-seventies—tied for work in a ponytail (Larry kept his face clean-shaven, his hair trimmed carefully above his ears, in the style of small-town southern Utah, which dated from the Eisenhower administration), I was relieved to hear him confirm what I'd already heard, that we'd be heading south that afternoon for Richfield, spending the first three weeks on a school-section job near Koosharem Peak before joining the other crews for the summer's big project, the original survey of three townships on the Kaiparowits Plateau. Matt Shaw would continue as crew chief and instrument operator, doing his work quietly and efficiently and whispering out of the corner of his mouth information that might help me avoid fucking up in front of Larry. I was introduced to the other summer temporaries, an obviously Mormon guy named Tim—whom I hadn't met before, but having spent most of my twenty-two years as one of the faithful, I felt confident of my ability to sniff one out—and Jim Williams.

I'd heard a little about Williams. Mostly, what I'd heard was that in his nonsurveying life he was a Harvard student. This had been explained to me in a tone of mock reverence and with rolling of eyes, as accompanied nearly all discussions of university education among the survey crews. The full-time surveyors, the party chiefs like Larry, were none of them educated beyond degrees from rural Utah high schools and the occasional college-level courses the BLM required them to take in specific surveying topics. Those of us who were there only for the summer—"temporaries," we were generally called, or "seasonals": the chainmen, flagmen, instrument operators, and crew chiefs—were nearly all college students, and good ones, too. To even get on the list you had to score in the upper nineties on the civil service exam or have a near-perfect grade-point average that could be translated, using a formula I never quite understood, into a near-perfect civil service exam score. The temporaries on my crew were all Phi Beta Kappa bound; we knew how to get A's. And A's from Harvard? That was something else, something the state-university rest of us pondered.

After a long morning of lectures, during which we were counseled against snakebite, poison ivy, late paperwork, and decapitation (walking into the helicopter's spinning rotor blades would "ruin your day," we were told), our big boss, Woodrow Sylvester, the fast-talking chief deputy surveyor for Utah, walked our crew a few blocks north and treated us to a fancy lunch in the Skyroom. The restaurant occupied the top floor of the Hotel Utah, which positioned us slightly above the architecturally complicated battlements of the Salt Lake Temple just across the street. As usual,

Woody did most of the talking, praising the civil service scores we temporaries had managed to attain, as well as Larry's precociousness (in his early thirties, Larry was the youngest, and newest, of the party chiefs), and repeating his mantra from the morning's orientation, which was "there are no stupid questions," reprised sometimes as "the only stupid question is the one you don't ask." We listened to Woody, nodding our heads as we ate our club sandwiches and eyeballed the Angel Moroni, who stood barely balanced on one foot atop the highest tower of the Temple, and pondered the all-seeing eye of god carved into the granite of the Temple's east facade.

There's much to observe in the architecture of the Salt Lake Temple. Leaving the church hadn't made me any less curious about the various images and signs carved into its otherwise blank gray granite, and I was inventorying it all—what I could see from that particular window, and what I couldn't, but remembered from dozens of trips to Temple Square over the years—as Woody talked: the foundation buttresses, for example, into which are carved representations of the earth; the columns, marked by decorations that track the phases of the moon and capped by elaborately carved depictions of the sun. I couldn't see my favorite of all these mysterious details because it occupied the far west tower, but I remembered the day I'd finally made out the subtle bas-relief array of stars in the shape of the Big Dipper, the stars at the far edge of the dipper lining up exactly with the position of Polaris, the North Star, also set in stone on the Temple's west facade.

After we'd finished lunch and walked back to the federal building, the less important members of the crew had an hour to kill while Larry and Matt checked out some of the new high-tech equipment we'd be trying out later that summer. Tim sought out his fellow Mormons—about half the summer temporaries were returned missionaries, many of them students at Brigham Young University, and they took every opportunity to reinforce their faith as a group before being split up and sent off to whatever meager southern Utah temptations they'd be facing on their own—so I found myself with Jim Williams searching for a map of the moon, a quest that only later, in hindsight, seemed ominous.

Williams had heard that the government had recently printed a complete and topographically accurate moon map, including the side we'd never seen as well as the side on which we'd recently landed a dozen or so serious-faced American astronauts. He had to have it. We started with the BLM offices, then headed for the elevator, from which we searched from floor to floor, from government office to government office. It wasn't in the Geological Survey office that retailed more earthbound topographical maps to hikers and developers, and we learned, not to our surprise, that no one in the Bureau of Indian Affairs office knew much about it either, but with me in tow Williams roamed the hallways until he found an office that handled public relations. Yes, they had a map.

I'm still not sure what a surveyor is supposed to look like, but I knew from the start that Williams wasn't it. He combed his brown hair into a style embraced by neither party chief nor summer temporary, straight forward into bangs that were trimmed just above his eyebrows in the manner of a middle-aged liquor salesman trying to camouflage a receding hairline, or a sixth grader whose mother still dressed him for school. His skin was pale, verging on wan. From the first day under the unrelenting Utah sun until his last, as the rest of us went through the sequence of burning, peeling, and eventually tanning into various protective shades of brown, whatever color he picked up never really took. The best he could manage was a kind of blotchiness, his lips flaking scales white with Chapstick.

Even so, I wasn't sure I looked much like a surveyor either, and it turned out that Williams and I had a lot in common, Harvard vs. University of Utah notwithstanding. We quickly learned that we approached surveying in similar ways, a mix of the academic and the anthropological. We thought a lot about what things *meant*; were both self-consciously in wonderment at the means and ends of surveying, the cultural and vocational mix the BLM had thrown us into, the combination of arcane science, centuries-old land-use legislation, and just plain gut-busting labor with shovels, axes, digging bars, and chainsaws. We speculated elaborately on the ambition of the Jeffersonian project that provided us with summer employment, and focused on the meaning of surveying minutiae as well. On that first day driving south, Williams and I analyzed the speeches we'd been subjected to; we wondered together what it meant, for example, that the BLM's state safety officer had been introduced to us by Woody as having been a hell of a machine gunner in World War II, with body counts you'd need one of those new electronic calculators to enumerate properly.

Later, I discovered that, like me, Williams had been touched on some nonsurveying level by the complex ritual that was the star shot, the set of astronomical observations by which Cadastral surveyors determined their position and bearing, a process that first surprised, and then somehow amazed me. I don't know what I had expected—I suppose I'd understood that any survey would have to depend on some accurate sense of where you were and what direction you were going—but I sure hadn't been prepared for the fact that something as practical, something as literally down-to-earth as a survey line derived its identity from a point as distant and exotic as Polaris, the North Star, which you somehow sighted on in the *daytime.* The summer before, on our first day working an all-too-interesting township just north of Vernal, Utah, I had watched, intrigued and a little suspicious, as Larry and Matt went about first deriving a set of numbers from several sights on the sun (somehow without blinding themselves as they looked sunward through the transit's scope) that were translated by means of sines, cosines, and tangents taken from a small red fieldbook, and exact hours, minutes, and seconds taken from Larry's wristwatch, into a long mysterious equation yielding yet another set of coordinates that told Larry exactly where to look in the bright morning sky for Polaris, which he claimed to have found, neatly centered in the transit's crosshairs.

When I finally said something—Matt had advised watching, as opposed to asking, as the best approach to learning the ropes—it was to the effect that this must be some kind of snipe hunt, a traditional means of messing with the heads of beginning surveyors. I mean, the North Star? In the daytime? But after Larry had recorded his final set of numbers from the transit and was willing to take a chance on my knocking the tripod over, he let me look, and I'll be damned if Polaris wasn't there, tiny but bright and undeniable.

I'd understood only a fraction of what had taken place that first time, and was only later, after observing a dozen more star shots over the course of the summer, beginning to understand how it all added up, but it was enough that first day to dazzle me, leaving me not just impressed, but more than a little moved. I think I began to understand myself in relation to the universe that morning I first saw Polaris, in daylight, as an actual fact of earthly life, and if Williams's reaction hadn't been as personal as mine, it was along the same lines. For Williams, as for me, the step-by-step process of shooting Polaris had come to mean something more than the sum of its parts.

During the drive to Richfield, when we weren't critiquing the orientation, catching up on how the off-season months had gone, or being instructed by Larry—"Woody told you there isn't such a thing as a stupid question," Larry said, looking in the rearview mirror at the three of us temporaries in the GMC Carryall's backseat. "He's wrong."—Williams studied his moon map. He entertained us with narratives of government surveyors on the moon, laying out township and section lines on the moon's dark, less familiar face. Which, he pronounced, was his favorite side.

When did I begin to figure out that all was not right with Jim Williams? I guess I should have known that first week, during which his craziness revealed itself slowly, if in retrospect pretty clearly. But this was after all the seventies, the less-easily-pigeon-holed decade assigned the task of mopping up after the sixties, and I wasn't any more confident than anybody else as regards what constituted normal behavior. I remember that Williams carried the moon map with him everywhere he went, folding it in various geometrical shapes and patterns. The map gradually took on the texture of papyrus from constant folding and close examination, inscribed with the straight lines of its creasing. He soon added two new perspectives on the meaning of the map involving a dollar bill and a stopwatch, which he wore on a bootlace lanyard around his neck, apparently in place of his wristwatch, which he'd stopped wearing. Williams spent hours folding the dollar bill in various triangular shapes designed to reveal the significance of the pyramidal all-seeing eye, the Masonic emblem that had found a place on American currency, as well as on the facade of the Temple we'd checked out from the Hotel Utah's Skyroom the day we'd been oriented. Then he'd place this artifact at an exact spot he'd located on the dark side of the moon, a point marked with pencil lines that connected it with other points he'd traced with a ball-point pen, or a magic marker, or with pinholes meticulously pierced into the gray surface of the moon, constellations of his own design that shone through when he'd hold the map up to the sun, lining up sunrays, pencil lines, and folds in the gray lunar surface.

He timed everything with the stopwatch, not trying to keep track of how long things took, but seeming instead to parcel out a specific number of minutes and seconds, an interval of time he'd arrived at in his head. Pressing the button, he'd watch the hand sweep the face, then mark times on a piece of paper, stopping the watch when the lines' convergence indicated time was up. We'd be bouncing along in the backseat of the stiffly sprung Carryall, hanging on to the seat, the armrests, and ourselves to keep from crashing our heads against the truck's ceiling, and Williams would be arranging maps and pyramids and making pencil notations and keeping it all in rough order while the watch's hand made its sweep at his command, keeping track of a chronology the rest of us didn't even try to understand.

The first time he'd done this—the first few times, actually, during the first couple of days on the job when we'd shot Polaris for bearing, and then driven around finding the necessary roads, discovering which gates required which keys, learning what dubious chiseled rocks were accepted by local ranchers as the legal boundary markers—no one seemed to mind. Williams had earned a reputation the summer before for eccentricity, but he'd proven himself to be dependable and quick to learn. As I said, he'd been promoted to front chainman, a position that required concentration and diplomacy. The party chief was by tradition also the rear chainman, and Larry wouldn't have worked with Williams if he'd thought he was crazy, or at least measurably crazier than the rest of the summer temporaries, many of whom he regarded as more than a little strange anyway, what with our long hair, majors in such useless subjects as American literature, and a preference for pot over Coors at the end of the workday.

But Williams *was* crazy—maybe schizophrenic, probably obsessive compulsive, certainly bipolar, I understand now. We should have figured that out the first week, when he'd begun folding the bill, and lining up the craters he'd picked out bordering the dark-side counterpart to the Sea of Tranquility and the position of Polaris, and the staring, all-seeing eye of god, and the bright silver stopwatch. More than anyone else, I should have understood. We shared the motel room the BLM rented for us in Richfield, so I knew something no one else did: Williams wasn't getting much sleep. The first week he was out maybe a few hours every night, but by the second week Williams wasn't sleeping at all, outlasting Carson and Snyder and the national anthem, waiting apparently for the test signal, which he'd study with some interest.

That Thursday night, the night before what would turn out to be his last day on the job, Williams was unusually hyper, trying his best to let me sleep but having a hard time keeping still. I finally nodded off, and woke a few hours later to see the arrangement Williams had laid out on the motel room wall, just above the TV. He'd taped the moon map across the wall, thumbtacked the folded dollar alongside, and strung the stopwatch lanyard in a web that looped around the channel dial and the volume knob, then back to the dollar bill, from which the stopwatch dangled over its precisely assigned spot on the moon. Looking at me intently as I rubbed my eyes open, he pointed over his shoulder toward what he'd constructed on the room's wall, saying, "Do you see it? Do you *see* it?"

That last day—Friday of the second week—was supposed to be a relatively short workday. Larry wanted to finish what was left of the east boundary, the first line we'd run in preparation for running the much higher and more difficult line westward over the flank of Koosharem Peak. Williams had been unusually quiet during the jolting ride to line—I guessed that his week of no sleep had finally caught up with him, and I was encouraged to see that he was wearing his wristwatch again—but then he walked off, pulled the chain out to its full length and kept going, and before we knew what was what, he was out of sight. We followed his prints as far as we could, but he was moving fast and mostly downhill, and we lost track of him on that broad swell of sandstone that rose like a coral reef out of an ocean of sagebrush.

We fanned out a little, tried to figure out where he was headed, but we hadn't been very successful in figuring him out before, and we couldn't make much sense of this either. It helped a lot when Larry found the chain. Williams had pulled it at least a mile before dropping it, the last thing that connected him to the work of the Cadastral Survey, and to us. It was still stretched out in a line that was pretty straight, so we walked more or less in the direction the chain pointed.

I couldn't help noticing that Williams was still walking like a surveyor, not in the way of a spooked deer trying to escape, or a backpacking tourist finding the easiest, most efficient way through difficult terrain. He wasn't exactly following the bearing we'd been running that morning, the one we'd calculated according to the observation of Polaris we'd done the week before, but Williams was still moving in a more or less straight line, not detouring to avoid the obstacles of buttes and ravines, but rather following line, walking over and through, not around or alongside, and although he was moving fast, I somehow understood that he wasn't trying to hide.

After an hour of finding, then losing, his trail, running ahead and circling back, just as Larry pulled out his walkie-talkie and began telling Matt to drive to the nearest phone and call out the troops—sheriff's deputies, search-and-rescue teams, the highway patrol helicopter—we found Williams's tracks again, and then, a chain length away, we found Williams.

He was flushed, smiling, breathing hard, pouring the last of his canteen water on the ground in a circle around the pattern he'd arranged on a flat spot in the middle of a small redrock amphitheater: concentric circles of damp sand; the map, showing the round orb of the moon's far side; a dollar bill folded in a new, more elaborate shape of his own design (he'd finally given up on the pyramid, the all-seeing eye); and his stopwatch counting the minutes and seconds as he parceled them out. Rows of small rocks in various lines linked the objects, bisecting perfectly the dark circles of wet sand. As we approached, Williams sat down carefully in the middle of all this order, alternately rubbing sand into the cloudy crystal of his wristwatch and pushing the start/stop button on the stopwatch. He smiled happily, not worried, not surprised to see us, and completely exhausted, sunburned, and starry-eyed.

He said, looking me straight in the eye, what he'd said that morning: "Do you see it?"

Then he said: *"This is where I am."*

CHAPTER ONE

Where I Surveyed, and What I Surveyed For

I worked summers as a government surveyor through most of the 1970s, an employee of the Utah office of the Cadastral Survey, an obscure arm of the federal government responsible for extending and maintaining the rectangular subdivision of America. Our mandate had been spelled out in Thomas Jefferson's Land Ordinance of 1785, legislation that (among other things) determined that settlement of the vast American West would take place amid ranks of perfect square-mile squares called sections, bounded by straight lines that ran according to the four points of the compass. It was our job to resurvey and remonument some of the earliest surveys (whose original stone markers had eroded into ambiguity over the intervening years) and, less routinely, to survey those rare miles of American acreage that had somehow managed to escape being corralled by Jefferson's straight lines. During those summers, I proceeded slowly upward through the ranks, beginning as a lowly flagman doing little more than pounding in flagged markers where he was told, and concluding my career as a crew chief and instrument operator, the person who actually looked through the scope and instructed the flagman where to pound in the flags.

In my memory, those eight summers have largely melted into one surrealistically long summer during which I surveyed a thousand perfectly straight and precisely intersecting miles of desert and mountain, with some specific landscapes of contorted sandstone leading into vaguer, more generic obstacle courses of rock outcrops and mountainsides of ponderosa pine and desert juniper. Some individual townships—our assignments were generally organized around one or more of these collections of thirty-six square-mile sections—come more specifically to mind, of course, being more memorable by virtue of natural beauty exceptional even by the high standards that define most Utah landscapes, others memorable as a result of who I was that particular summer, and the way in which that identity was clarified or complicated by the specific landscape in which I worked. Two summers—my first, through which I stumbled incompetent and often tragically disoriented; and my last, over which I more successfully prevailed as the professional surveyor I had more or less become—of course stand out.

It is my second summer, however, the summer of 1974, that has located itself most firmly in my memory, in large part because that year provided what would turn out to be my only experience working on an original survey. Government surveyors have labored conscientiously (if mostly invisibly) since 1785, and as a result Jefferson's goal of an American landscape lined, gridded, numbered, and known has been achieved: very few unsurveyed acres remain, and those in areas so isolated or devoid of commercial value—lacking the barest potential for mining, grazing, farming, or urbanizing—that no survey is likely to be required. As a consequence, most of the Cadastral Survey's energy is directed toward reestablishing surveys that have already been run, following the notes of surveyors long dead in order to restore the integrity of their lines and replace their eroded rock markers with more enduring steel ones. That summer, however, we'd been assigned the rare unsurveyed township, a thirty-six-square-mile portion of the Kaiparowits Plateau, a tumultuous landform in southern Utah that rises from the canyons of the Colorado Plateau just west of Lake Powell.

The summer of 1974 was notable in other ways, a summer of beginnings and conclusions, of firsts and lasts, particularly for surveyors. That summer the microchip finally caught up with the Cadastral Survey, which meant that long established surveying habits would yield painfully to new electronic ones, enforcing a revolutionary break with instruments and procedures that had evolved slowly and steadily since the Sumerians began laying out survey lines in order to reestablish fields after annual floods. And the following year's more enlightened hiring practices would determine that 1974 would be the last summer that government surveying would remain an all-male world.

It was also the summer Richard Nixon lost his final battle with the House Judiciary Committee and waved the nation goodbye from the door of the helicopter whisking him to retirement in the comfy BarcaLounger of America's short attention span, a preview of more abashed helicopter evacuations of Americans from Saigon nine months later. Less nationally and more personally, it was the summer I began to realize that I didn't love the woman I'd been with for several years, the summer I began to understand that my connection with nature was more conflicted than comforting, and the summer I came finally to accept that I would never believe in god. As I climbed into the helicopter that flew us to work each day, it often felt like I was leaving behind something more substantial than mere solid ground.

That summer I began learning the advanced skills necessary to becoming a surveyor, which included completing my first observation of Polaris in order to determine my bearing, as well as my exact position on earth. It was also the summer I began to grasp where I stood in the universe, a discovery as profound as it was unexpected, an understanding that has served as the scaffold—however rickety—upon which I would construct the rest of my life. This understanding was the unanticipated result of the way I spent my workweeks—surveying the Kaiparowits Plateau—and the result of the way I spent my weekends, working my way less formally around much of the same landscape.

The year 1974 was also crucial for the Kaiparowits Plateau. Located along Utah's southern boundary, where the Colorado River swings westward assertively enough to indicate its lack of enthusiasm for the tangled water politics of Arizona and California to the south, the plateau's roughly triangular shape is bounded on two sides by landforms nearly as linear as the state line. A fifty-mile-long thousand-foot-high dropoff, identified with rare literalness on maps as the Straight Cliffs, neatly separates this high desert of junipers and pinions from the dry red-rock chaos of the Escalante River drainage. Another unusually undeviating formation, a thirty-mile line of upthrust sandstone plates called the

Cockscomb, runs almost due north and south to mark the western boundary.

The southern boundary of this triangle, however—part state line, part river meander—is complicated by history as much as by the contortions of its landforms. For millions of years (indeed, until less than forty years ago), the southern escarpment of the Kaiparowits Plateau dropped a mile straight down into the Colorado River, which flowed with uncharacteristic peacefulness at the bottom of Glen Canyon, a deep narrow channel carved by the river's abrasion against a thick blanket of orange sandstone called the Navajo Formation. Today those riverbanks lie buried nearly a thousand feet beneath the surface of Lake Powell, which slinks through the narrow gap between the long wedge of the Kaiparowits's south buttresses—the southern end of the Straight Cliffs—and the round swell of Navajo Mountain. Geologically, the plateau and the mountain seem related, as if they were uplifted simultaneously in the distant past by the same geological forklift that elevated a triangular block to the north and raised a blister to the south. Together, they form a kind of exclamation point, Navajo Mountain serving as the dot.

Because Navajo Mountain rises three thousand feet above the highest corner of the Kaiparowits, its summit provides a useful overlook from which to really see the plateau, a better bird's-eye view even than the helicopter provided as it flew us to work each day, and one weekend that summer I hiked to the summit in order to finally see just what the Kaiparowits was made of, how its parts fit together. I'd been experiencing the plateau up close all summer, foot by foot, mile by mile; I was hungry for the long view, the big picture.

Nothing, of course, is what it you expect. In the first place, you can see very little in any direction from the actual summit of Navajo Mountain, a place too flat and too wooded to allow much of a view. But if you walk a half mile or so through the woods in a northwest direction, things open up, the orange sandstone brought to light by the slow volcanic blistering that created Navajo Mountain falls away suddenly beneath your feet, and you find yourself staring into what's left of the narrow gorge carved by the Colorado River over the last several million years, and seeing as though from an airliner the intricate web of the Escalante River and its tributaries. You can make out the Henry Mountains far to your right, the Aquarius Plateau (with bright pinkish national-park blotches of Bryce Canyon and Cedar Breaks) on the distant horizon, the swell of the North Rim of the Grand Canyon fading away to your left, and at center, the broad angular expanse of the Kaiparowits Plateau, jutting toward you with the flattened aggressiveness of an aircraft carrier.

I'd like to say that the scene is dominated by the Kaiparowits, but it isn't. Although its 1,600–square-mile girth takes up most of the view, its blank flatness, the tableland colored blue-green by the blended shades of juniper, piñon, and sagebrush, falls away to the northeast into the Straight Cliffs with a drama you can't quite see from here, and to the west, the disorganized system of lesser plateaus and mesas and canyons blurred by pale smoke blown from several of the region's coal-fired power plants and rendered featureless by the flat light of midday, the area around Nipple Bench I'd been surveying all summer, fades into beige ambiguity. None of this can compare to the geological drama that surrounds it: the delicate latticework of the Escalante and its side canyons to the north, those narrow slots and wide sandy bottoms through which I'd march high school students the next spring in search of spiritual reasons to postpone dropping out of school long enough to actually graduate; and closer, on my side of the reservoir, the sandstone escarpments that literally fall away beneath my feet in a series of steep twisting canyons I can barely follow with my eyes.

Most insistent, however, is Lake Powell, that unnatural fact separating me from the benches and canyons in which I spent my workweeks that summer. You can't quite see to the southwest that spot where the gorge narrows sufficiently to allow its plugging by the Bureau of Reclamation, and so you can't see that graceful arc of steel and concrete called Glen Canyon Dam; and you can't quite see to the north and east the miles of mudflats laying themselves down where the Colorado and its vital tributaries—the Escalante, the Dirty Devil, the San Juan—meet the stagnant water of the reservoir and drop their load of silt. Between these extremes of cause and consequence, however, you can see about a hundred miles of what looks to be an impossibly broad and blue river bisecting the desert landscape like a jagged tear, a blank boundary not only between near and far landscapes, but also between what's exposed and what's concealed, between the dynamic processes of uplift and erosion and the static facts of flatness and opacity.

On that blue unrelieved surface of Lake Powell itself you can just make out the narrow V's of speedboats and the broad, flat wakes of houseboats threading their way up the main channel and into far narrower side canyons—some impossible to see into, even from this elevation. If you keep looking, following the turns of the off-shoots on your side of the lake, the canyons that drain the ridges and arroyos beneath your feet, you might eventually locate Rainbow Bridge, from this distance tiny, graceful, its actual size impossible to imagine.

Looking all of this over, you get a sense of extent and expanse, and you can see a lot of water, a lot of sandstone, and even a lot more forest than your desert experience has led you to expect, but you don't get scale. From here, you don't gain much in the way of useful understanding of how all this compares to the size of the human body, or the depth of the canyon below the water's surface, or even the comparison an astronaut might comprehend from space, a body of water—easily traceable from one hundred miles up—that was created by human hands.

Part of the scale problem involves what you *can't* see. Along with the dam itself and the flyspecked mudflats that mark the downstream and upstream boundaries of the lake, you don't see, from here, the narrative, the story behind this particular meeting of the natural and the human. You can't hear the arguments that surrounded the decision to create this particular landscape—the contentious compromise that saved another stretch of river upstream at Glen Canyon's expense; the regret and recrimination that followed immediately after passage of the fatal legislation. For example, you can't see the glowing cigar of Floyd Dominey, the Bureau of Reclamation czar, whose ambition and political acumen spurred the creation of the scene before you; neither can you see the only slightly less luminous conscience of David Brower, the then-president of the Sierra Club, whose neglect and strategic miscalculation allowed the project to steamroller over the too-late and too-little objections of the nascent environmental movement. You can't see Edward Abbey just out of sight upstream in Moab, completing that summer the final draft of *The Monkey Wrench Gang,* the book that first recommended the draining by any means necessary of all that unnaturally detained water. In fact, you don't see any human beings from here. You know that those wakes follow boats loaded with people; you understand that Rainbow Bridge is crawling with tourists, individuals who can compare the expanse of the bridge with their own short reach, can imagine, as the tourist guides tell them, Utah's capitol building fitting easily within the gigantic space created by the thrust of the arch.

So you probably know about Lake Powell, and there's a good chance you know what was gained and what was lost by its construction. The flooding of Glen Canyon has become less history than myth, a paradise actually lost in my lifetime, a morality tale demonstrating the consequences of pride and ambition, distraction and ignorance. But you probably don't know about the Kaiparowits Plateau, and how close it came to being lost.

I became a surveyor—more accurately, I became a flagman on a survey crew; opinions vary concerning whether a flagman can call himself a "surveyor"—for several reasons. It was partly the result of my not wanting to participate in anything remotely connected to the Vietnam War. I was a college student, and I needed a summer job, and as a result of that GPA equation loophole I had pretty good civil service test scores. Although a high lottery number protected me from the draft, I was left vulnerable to other opportunities for moral capitulation to the war machine, in particular, offers of employment at a series of Utah's ubiquitous defense installations, jobs I turned down with a series of increasingly strident and self-righteous letters proclaiming my opposition to the Vietnam War and my desire to keep some moral distance. I finally managed to get my name on the right list and was offered a job with the Bureau of Land Management, working on a survey crew. One of my college roommates had worked as a surveyor, and he told me it was a great job: it's the kind of work you take turns doing, he said; you work your ass off for an hour, then you wait for the next guy in the crew to do his job and work his ass off, and you do all this amid some of the prettiest landscapes in Utah, which has a lot of world-class scenery. You make okay money by the hour, and you get paid per diem, a twelve-dollar daily stipend, most of which you can pocket by eating cheap, and it's not even remotely like forklifting crates of napalm into cargo planes headed for our clients in Vietnam.

Much of this turned out to be true. I spent my first summer—

the summer before the Kaiparowits Plateau—working in a beautiful township just north of Vernal, Utah, and although the surveying we did was much more difficult than had been described, it was varied and, to my surprise, *interesting.* We'd spend a morning hacking our way through a juniper forest, establishing our survey line, and after lining in a lath marked with a length of orange surveyor's ribbon, I'd relax while the chainmen measured the corridor we'd established and the instrument man measured the angles we'd turned. Then I'd be off to the next ridge, trying to line in a flag as close as possible to the old corner, the rock left by the government surveyor who'd been the first to work his way through these parts, who had chiseled in such a way as to hopefully distinguish that particular rock from the hundreds of other rocks scattered across the desert landscape.

That first summer was spent carrying out "dependent resurveys," projects intended to reestablish lines surveyed nearly a hundred years before, usually in order to resolve disputes regarding boundary lines between private and public lands. We'd begin with copies of the original surveyor's handwritten notes, which described the bearings and distances he'd traveled, as well as a rough description of the topography he'd traversed—ridges, washes, plateaus—and the rocks he'd marked and the bearing trees he'd blazed. It felt a little like archaeology, and it felt a little like public service, and although the idea of using a shovel and an ax to draw straight lines across nature conflicted with much I'd come to understand about post–Earth Day approaches to appreciating and protecting the natural world, I felt fortunate to be paid so well for spending time in places I'd previously backpacked into at my own expense. After all, I reasoned, if the work of the Cadastral Survey were morally suspect, I would certainly have rejected with an angry letter the presumption of its offer of employment.

The second summer of my surveying career, however, presented a slightly more complicated set of ethical circumstances. We'd be doing an original survey, which meant that the lines we'd be inscribing would be our own. The Kaiparowits Plateau featured some of the few unsurveyed portions of American landscape to be found outside the state of Alaska, the result of its near-total isolation and heretofore economic uselessness. High, dry, and distant from railhead, river port, or highway, the plateau was surrounded by cliffs and canyons that would not easily permit roadbuilding (only a few precariously situated dirt roads traversed its expanse, passable only a few months a year, and then only by vehicles with high ground clearance and four-wheel drive) and vegetated mostly by scrawny piñon and juniper trees and scrub grass of interest only to the few cows the BLM permitted local ranchers to graze. As surveyors worked through the nineteenth century and into the twentieth to complete Thomas Jefferson's project of inscribing a neat square-mile grid onto the geography of the North American empire he'd envisioned, they'd taken a critical look at the Kaiparowits Plateau, understood this barren place to be neither farmland nor timber claim, and surveyed greener pastures elsewhere. BLM surveyors had established the outlines of some townships on the Kaiparowits in the fifties and sixties, but the thirty-six square miles of the interiors of those townships remained unsurveyed. We'd be the first to fill in the blanks, to finally inscribe Enlightenment ideas of order onto some of the most chaotic natural landscape in America.

We were doing this because there was coal to be mined and electricity to be generated. It had been known for some time that coal resided deep in the sedimentary rock that stacked itself in layers to form the Kaiparowits Plateau. Some of that coal had been burning underground for centuries; early Mormon cattlemen had felt the heat rising out of cracks in the sandstone and named one prominent rise "Smoky Mountain" for reasons neither metaphorical nor nostalgic. I mean, it was actually kind of *smoky*. But the deposits had remained a "reserve," reserved for some time in the distant future when coal seams closer to the surface and more convenient to railheads would be exhausted.

That hadn't happened yet—in fact, I'm as surprised as I am relieved to say that it *still* hasn't—but history was rushing things that summer. Americans were coming to understand that the high sulfur coal of Appalachia might be easier to mine, but it was rougher on the environment we'd recently begun worrying about; and more abruptly coming to understand that America had made itself too dependent on foreign energy sources. Suddenly the reserves that lay sleeping smokily under the plateau became the object of courtship by energy companies, and the federal government found itself considering bids on mineral claims that hadn't been surveyed and hence had no legal description. Suddenly, completing the survey of the Kaiparowits Plateau had become a national priority, which meant, among other things, the Cadastral Survey could budget money for helicopters in carrying out work so suddenly necessary to the national interest.

It also meant that, if I wanted to place my situation in the worst light possible, I might as well be surveying for the Peabody Coal Company, the same evil corporation whose coal train had hauled away the town of Paradise, a tragedy of fall-of-man proportions recorded in the John Prine song I'd been singing to myself for years, often when backpacking in pristine wilderness. Having had its way with western Kentucky, Mr. Peabody's coal train was currently hauling away a good chunk of northern Arizona; now Mr. Peabody was laying tracks toward the Kaiparowits Plateau. As if it weren't bad enough that I'd be preparing the way for coal mining, it turned out that I'd be laying the groundwork for the *burning* of that coal, and the consequent mucking up of that deep blue southern Utah sky I loved so much. Understandably hesitant to add the smoke of huge coal-fired power plants to the already toxic mix that floated above Phoenix and Los Angeles, the powers-that-be planned to build their generating station close to the source of its fuel, on one of the heretofore undeveloped benches of the Kaiparowits Plateau.

All this gave me pause. After all, as anyone who knew me would tell you, I *loved* nature. As the antiwar movement wound down in response to Nixon and Kissinger's all-too-successful efforts to sneak out of Vietnam without actually admitting either defeat or culpability, I'd been inclining my political efforts more toward environmental concerns. The last politically charged event I'd attended was an Earth Day rally in a Salt Lake City park, through which Karen and I had sustained a nature-loving high boosted by the many joints being passed among the rallied. Not only did I hike routinely in wilderness areas; I advocated for *more* of them whenever the opportunity arose. I'd taken the moral high ground when offered the opportunity to work for the Pentagon, and I'd long since embraced the Thoreauvian exhortation to be a counterforce against the machine. I could have written an eloquently outraged letter telling the energy-industrial complex, and specifically its craven lackey the Bureau of Land Management, where to stuff their smokestacks.

But after an embarrassingly short period of moral agonizing, I decided to take the job for a second summer, and even when I'd realized the full extent of my complicity, I hadn't quit in protest, and to be perfectly honest, I've done a lot more soul-searching in the years since than I did that summer, when I was caught up in the excitement of surveying, too distracted by the process to consider the product. Simply put, I loved surveying. More to the point, I *needed* surveying, needed it in ways I've spent years trying to understand.

CHAPTER TWO

Running Line on Nipple Bench

Three survey crews shared quarters at Wahweap City that summer, fourteen men distributed among seven trailers. The permanent, full-time surveyors had their own trailers, streamlined aluminum tubes built for tourists in the forties and fifties, each of which had been converted into something part living space and part office, a bed and small kitchen wedged in between drafting tables and file cabinets and bulky wooden boxes containing transits and other equipment too valuable to leave in the pickups and Carryalls overnight. The rest of us assigned ourselves places in two blocky bunk trailers, each one crammed with a half dozen surveyors ranging from GS-2 survey aides to GS-5 technicians. I was a GS-3, but firmly in the "aide" category.

One bunk trailer we called the "missionary trailer," segregated according to religious belief and populated mostly by summer temporaries who were not only Mormons in good standing but had completed two-year Mormon missions in the service of spreading the faith. In this trailer, some standards were agreed upon, including keeping profanity to a minimum, no drinking or smoking, of course, and no joking about the sacred undergarments required for advancement in the priesthood and admission to the Temple. The other trailer, the aluminum box in which I'd claimed a bunk, was called, well, the *other* trailer. Although I carried more than a little residual guilt for having flaked on the mission (I'd always expected that the year I turned nineteen I'd fly off to preach to the unconverted of the world, but instead I drove deep into Wyoming, where I spent the summer washing dishes in a tourist resort on Jackson Lake), there was little doubt into which trailer I'd be placed, although the truth be told, I didn't really belong in either one, being neither comfortable with the saints, nor as content in my disbelief as my other-trailer trailermates. In any case, dress codes and other rules were more relaxed in our trailer: we profaned prodigiously, and mostly wore boxer shorts as we waited in the late afternoon heat for our turn in the shower stall, a dark, narrow enclosure in which fungus peeled off the walls in gray sheets.

The crews themselves were pretty well integrated in terms of religious leanings. As a party chief, Larry was spared having to make the decision about trailers, but although he had been raised a Mormon and had become in recent years more dependable in his church attendance (marrying Suzette and having a couple of kids had calmed him down a little from his more adventurous early years in the army and the field), I don't think he'd have been comfortable living in the missionary trailer, just as he complained sometimes about the way his garments itched in the heat and said not quite under his breath *fuck me!* when his calculations didn't add up. Besides Larry and myself, and minus Jim Williams, who would be trying out various medications while commuting back and forth between a Salt Lake City hospital and his parents' house for the remainder of the summer, our crew included Matt Shaw, the crew chief and instrument operator who when not running a transit for the government taught math at Salt Lake City's lone and lonely Catholic high school. A dark, handsome guy who'd attracted the most attractive of the small-town waitresses we'd encountered the summer before, Matt was aiming for a career as a full-time surveyor and was not remotely interested in Utah's predominant religion, and hence less interested than you'd think in most of those cute, usually blonde, southern Utah waitresses. And replacing Williams as front chainman was Tim Johanssen, a returned missionary who nevertheless wanted to be thought of as somehow different from the other returned missionaries with whom he shared the missionary trailer.

Tim was an unusual kind of Mormon, utterly conventional, completely pious and obedient, but with an unaccountable, almost anthropological interest in other ways of life. He was one of the only returned missionaries to sport facial hair, in his case just barely, a narrowly trimmed hedgerow that ran across his upper lip. On Errol Flynn it looked rakish, but on Tim it looked kind of halfhearted, rendering an already forgettable set of features even vaguer and more anonymous.

Tim loved to talk, and he was full of questions, especially for me it seemed, but he liked hearing stories from the other side wherever he could find them. He'd felt honored the summer before when several of the surveyors he was working with in Mexican Hat, Utah—none of them Mormon, all of them the kind of pseudo-mystics the sixties had produced in droves—had invited him to witness a weekend of peyote eating, the mushrooms allowing them to experience something in the desert around their trailer not partaking of their weekday Jeffersonian project, a very different brand of Enlightenment. Tim enjoyed telling the story: the eating of the buttons with chips and refried beans, the resulting choking and heaving, and then the hazy peacefulness, a bright-eyed restfulness that was to his surprise anything but frightening to behold.

He explained the experience to me several times that summer, the first time in a cafe in Richfield, while we were eating bad chicken-fried steak dinners after a long day on Koosharem Peak. It was odd to hear him tell it; as he spoke, Tim's tone shifted from the safely ethnological to the nearly envious, and he wanted me to understand several things. First, he said, he thought it was *interesting;* he didn't think it was necessarily *immoral,* and yet he found it *troubling to him personally.* He'd searched the scriptures for an answer to the question of peyote eating. Although peyote was clearly off limits to the faithful, as well as the law-abiding (the hat Tim wore to work each day was decorated proudly in the stars and stripes of our nation's flag), it wasn't proscribed specifically in the Word of Wisdom, and he found himself thoroughly enjoying the part of the ritual he'd allowed himself to take part in. He'd joined the circle around the bowls of chips and beans and the plate of buttons and had partaken of the food that helped the others get the peyote down their not completely cooperative throats, and he'd tried to stay with his fellow surveyors even as they departed into transcendence. I formed a picture in my mind of Tim walking alongside a departing train, waving goodbye as it left the station, understanding that he'd chosen to not buy a ticket but feeling just a little abandoned just the same.

The experience hadn't changed his life—Tim knew better than anybody where he stood and the direction he was headed; from a devout Utah family that rivaled my own in the venerableness of its pioneer ancestry, the degrees, minutes, and seconds of Tim's bearing had been set on the day he was born, a straight line that might as well have been measured by means of a star shot. His first twenty-four years had proceeded smoothly through a mission and the prebusiness degree he would complete the following spring, thence directly to an okay MBA program, and Temple marriage (he currently lacked a girlfriend, but checking off this item on his list felt like a formality, a simple inevitability). Of course he'd get married, have kids, work comfortably in middle management, drive home to a house in a nice suburban northern Utah neighborhood. But observing peyote eating hadn't been on his checklist, and it seemed to have modified his view of the way he wanted his life to be understood by others, especially, that summer, by me, with whom he had long discussions prompted by questions about why I'd left the true church, and what it felt like to be, well, *outside.* Unlike the other Mormons, who saw in me, as an unapologetic (if sometimes confused) former Mormon, either a potential prodigal son in need of gentle guidance back to the flock or an apostate deserving condemnation, or at least refutation, Tim never argued with me, and he never tried to persuade me to return. He'd ask questions like: if you're glad you left, why all the agonizing? "I'm sure your family understands," he once said. "Why so much guilt?" But these questions weren't intended to undermine my newfound lack of faith. Instead, he seemed genuinely interested in the theory, if not the practice, of the unthinkable.

Tim carried his puzzled, envious conventionality with him on his back that summer along with a huge Nikon he'd bought a few years before on his mission to Japan, a beautiful instrument protected from the elements by its thick leather case, wrapped in a blanket of foam rubber, and bundled carefully into a rucksack. Tim's fantasy was to be a photographer for *National Geographic,* but this was of course a deviation from the line he'd been assigned, a bearing not prescribed in his personal *Manual of Surveying Instruc-*

tions, and so he unwrapped this treasure only once or twice a day to take a shot that seemed worthy of all that expensive equipment. I believe he exposed only one roll of film the entire summer.

A straight line goes where it goes. I learned quickly that this was the essence of the government surveyor's work, the source of hard consequences for both the surveyor and the landscape he surveys. Hikers, road builders, even infantry soldiers, knowing that a straight line is not always the shortest distance between two points, can negotiate with the terrain, accommodate its impositions and irregularities when necessary or convenient, but after the bearing is calculated and the correct angle is turned, the scope of the surveyor's transit points the only direction it can, and the crosshairs don't equivocate. They tell only one simple truth, and that truth is straight, narrow, and uncompromising.

In addition to determining that the settlement of the vast American West would take place amid ranks of perfectly square square-mile sections, bounded by straight lines that ran according to the four points of the compass, Thomas Jefferson's Land Ordinance of 1785 spelled out in remarkable detail just how those lines would be run. In specifying the means by which this mandate would be carried out, the ordinance transformed the simple job of surveying a straight line into a two hundred-year project representing perhaps the most aggressive imposition of human will on natural landscape seen in the history of the world.

Although land had been parceled out along straight lines for millennia—surveyors like to call theirs the *second* oldest profession—never before had those lines been extended with so little regard for natural landscape, nor on so grand a scale. Before 1785, land surveys were generally carried out according to the practice of metes and bounds, an approach that limited surveyors to running crooked lines that followed natural contours and avoided the obstacles inevitably served up by the landscape, establishing boundaries that outlined tracts of land that were topographically logical. A typical surveyor might run a necessarily contorted line that followed the twisting bank of a river, extend it straight for a distance until fertile bottomland met less economically useful cliffs, and then designate an immovable boulder or sizable tree (the "witness tree" of Robert Frost's New England) to serve as a boundary marker upon which ownership would depend. Because the survey was based on relatively permanent physical points of reference, the orientation of the compass bearing and the straightness of the line were less important than general agreement concerning the objects and markers that determined the boundaries of one's property.

Although it would be overstating things to argue that surveyors running metes and bounds surveys worked in harmony with the natural world, the basic theory embodied a healthy respect for nature as it stood. Even when boundaries were surveyed in advance of settlement, and in grids—as in the venerable New England township surveys—the grids were oriented in deference to the lay of the land, and rectangles were preferred because the math was easier, not because linearity was next to godliness.

To Jefferson, and others of like mind on the committee of the Continental Congress he chaired, metes and bounds surveys represented abject surrender to the caprice of topographical nature. His plan was to straighten up the dangerous clutter of wilderness by surveying the West into a grid that connected the nascent American empire with the mathematical equations and underlying linearity that defined true, universal, capital-N Nature, while at the same time inscribing an actual grid on the American landscape, a net of intersecting straight lines that would partition the wilderness into orderly square-mile sections. These lines and squares would be established well in advance of settlement, giving the first settlers the assistance they required in keeping the degenerating influence of wilderness at bay long enough to inscribe their own straight lines of private ownership, lines that would parallel and reinforce the section lines that connected adjacent sections to form lines that connected the Alleghenies to the Pacific. Jefferson's goal—of his many plans for America, perhaps the one that has remained most faithful to his intention—was a continent perfectly squared, gridded, and aligned, north-south lines running straight from pole to pole, east-west lines stacked in pure alignment with the equator, the squared and abstracted landscape of America one sees best from the window of an airliner flying from coast to coast.

Achieving Jefferson's ambitious scheme became the job of generations of obscure government surveyors. As descendants of this long, hardworking, and little-acknowledged lineage, my crew and

I had to resurvey and restore the old township and section lines and run new ones. Put another way, our job was to follow line where it went and make that line tangible and material, to translate the pure language of mathematics into the vernacular of actual landscape, to carve straight lines into the slopes and curves of nature, and to mark with an iron pipe and a rock mound each point where lines intersected, ultimately creating a formal garden the size of a continent. Through the eight summers I worked for the Cadastral Survey—summers that didn't quite mesh with my non-summer life as a college student and English teacher—I learned the equations and practices that define the theory and application of linearity, witnessed over and over again the intersection of mathematical order and topographical randomness, and came to understand that this was an uneven contest: line, undistracted by the conflicting agendas of the natural world, always prevailed.

The first few weeks of my first summer as a surveyor can best be understood as a crash course in linearity. My crew had been assigned a township just north of Vernal, a small oil and ranching town in eastern Utah. This thirty-six-square-mile concentration of chaotic desert landscape straddled the geological boundary where the rise of that vast monolith of granite called the Uinta Mountains begins to disturb rock formations reclining comfortably to the south; for miles in each direction, layers and layers of sandstone, shale, limestone, and some ugly black rock I never could identify were pushed skyward, their backsides levered into ramps and cliffs that ran all over the map.

Although this township served as a pretty good geology textbook, what I needed was a text in elementary *surveying,* and this daunting collision of order and chaos, of desert and swamp, of ramps and domes and deep canyons, included far too few bunny slopes for the beginning surveyor, far too many opportunities for incompetence and embarrassment—a learning curve as steep and rocky as the terrain. This was, after all, my first summer, long before I'd begun to understand what Jefferson and the Enlightenment had to do with all this. What I needed to understand that summer—and quickly—was simply *line.*

The first thing I learned was that government surveyors drop the article when talking about line. We didn't say, "Where does the line hit that cliff?" or "Now we'll project a line across that canyon."

It was just "line." At some point in the Old Testament, The Lord God becomes simply God, and like Moses, I learned that there was only one true line, and that government surveyors would have no other lines before them.

This was because our line was different from the lines of other surveyors. Our line followed its mathematical imperative, not the wishes of a client, or the legalisms of a deed, or the whim of a river's meander. Our line arose from the pure world of mathematics, from calculations derived through observations of the sun and distant stars. It ran not just according to the cardinal points of the compass, but according to those cardinal directions made perfect, north-south and east-west bearings more exact than the trembling pointer any earthbound compass could hope to deliver. Line was literally handed down from the sky: line running north aimed straight at Polaris, the North Star, and drew its identity from this otherworldly connection; at least once a week we'd spend an hour or two checking the accuracy of line by nailing Polaris in the crosshairs of the transit (not the easiest thing to do in the bright sunshine of the desert) and recalculating our exact position in the great scheme of things. Line was real, at once transcendent and tangible, the Enlightenment's most visible and enduring legacy to the landscapes of America.

I spent my first week, while assigned the lowly job of flagman, completely lost. They'd tell me: line goes across that ridge; hike over there, tie a couple of feet of red flagging around a four-foot lath—a splintery, rough-sawn stake flat and skinny as a yardstick—sharpen its end with your ax, and hammer in the flag exactly where we tell you to. Of course, I'd see where Larry was pointing, I'd nod my head, and I'd hike off in the general direction, appearing finally on a ridge a half mile north of where I was supposed to be, waving hopefully with my T-shirt—we had no radios that summer—until they saw where I'd wound up, waved me over and over and over until I'd hiked back the errant half mile and finally appeared alongside the transit's crosshairs, ready to pound in the lath. That spot I now knew was line, but how did it get from there to here?

I took weeks to learn the practices of lineation, and then a few weeks more to understand—and many more weeks to feel instinctively—how it all fit the insistent reality of the Utah landscape. I was learning the theory, even the meaning, of running line; like

Jim Williams, the guy with whom I'd had a number of deeply the-
oretical discussions leading up to the Friday he'd walked purpose-
fully off into craziness, I could spout forth a pretty impressive
dissertation on the ideological and aesthetic implications of linearity. I was, after all, an English major. What I wasn't learning was
line. I wasn't getting what every good surveyor needs more than
theory or even context: I wasn't getting the *feel,* the sense of *line-
ness.* My duty as a flagman was to pound in a flag on line. Problems involving direction were up to the guy who looked through
the transit and measured the angles, and questions involving distance were up to the crew members who pulled the long measuring chain. But my job involved a great deal of hiking to the
next ridge, or up a mountainside, or into the depths of a canyon,
to pound in a lath on line. I needed to be where the others were
looking before they could fine-tune my position, line me in on
the exact bearing.

This is what they did to make something useful of me, to transform me into a surveyor. Matt, the transit operator, would take
me aside—protecting me whenever he could from Larry's impatience—and point out the ridge he wanted me on. He'd suggest a
way for me to get there; it wasn't necessary for the flagman to walk
exactly on line, which is nearly impossible anyway once you're in
the forest or the rockslide or the arroyo. He'd focus my task: put a
flag *there,* he'd say, pointing toward a specific spot on a distant
ridge. Then he'd have me look through the transit, pick out a foresight, a rock or tree that I'd recognize when I got up close. I'd find
a tree with a bent trunk or a lightning scar, a feature that distinguished that tree from every other tree on the ridge. Then I'd carefully plan my route, figure out which path to descend, and where
to begin my climb to the top of the ridge where the tree I'd picked
out awaited me.

I'd have two things in mind: I'd focus on where line ran, that
ideal vector running straight and pure above my head; and I'd
focus on where I needed to place my boots, one after the other, to
arrive at the exact place where line crossed a particular ridge. The
problem was that things look very different up close. In the desert
landscape of eastern Utah, what looks like a plausible trail turns
out to be an extended detour among rocks the size of boxcars, and
those carefully differentiated clearings, clearly triangular or circular or the shape of a duck when seen from a distance, look pretty

much alike—or don't seem like clearings at all—when you're finally tramping through them. Even a ridgeline, a dimensionless
outline from a mile away, might be as wide as a football field when
you're walking along it, looking for that one tall cedar tree with the
lightning scar that twists just so.

But after a week or two of complete incompetence, I began to
understand how it worked. I learned the way a tree or a cliff changes
as you shift your perspective. I did this at first by keeping my eye
constantly on my foresight, noticing the change as it happened
gradually, keeping track of its evolution from distant blur to an individual piece of topography next to which I could stand securely
within the bright magnified circle of Matt's transit. I slowly developed an ability to see how terrain changes, to visualize how a
ridgeline might look from a vastly elevated point of view, from a
position alongside that transcendent ideal of a mathematically
perfect landscape. I was finally able to picture myself as if from
a distance, a person who was simultaneously an employee of the
federal government and a point of mathematical definition, de-
scending one ridge to ascend another, departing momentarily from
line when the terrain forced him to, reattaching himself to line in
order to place that necessary flag.

It's difficult to explain the profound change that took place in
me during those first few humiliating weeks, when I'd gotten lost
routinely enough to change the look on Larry's face from amuse-
ment to disgust to resignation: how can a person be so *lost?* his face
would say. How can you head off in the direction we send you,
and then land a mile up the wrong mountain, facing the wrong direction?

My disorientation had to do with placement—my own, the rocks
and trees, even the stars, the movement of the sun. I was learning
to locate myself in natural terrain; I was figuring out how to discover my place, to keep track of my position as it changed in response to the angle of a hillside or the turn of a tree's shadow.
Before, as a child growing up in a familiar landscape, this had been
easy: there had always been the customary rock faces of the
Wasatch Front to the east, the distinctive islands of the Great Salt
Lake to the west. But in unfamiliar landscapes, you discover other
ways to orient yourself. For some, instinct serves, a sense of sun
and shadow, a feel for the wind-bent arc of salt grass or the growth
patterns of lichen—a sense you'd cultivated since you were born,

an intuitive understanding of nature that is at least as cultural as it is personal. For me, a white boy raised in Eisenhower's America, the tepid flowering of Western Civilization—a nation for whom intuition was suspect, circles indecisive, an unmowed lawn evidence of flawed character—it was line.

We had a week before the helicopter was scheduled to arrive in Wahweap City, so we began surveying the corner of the township that was closest to the only dirt road that entered this side of the Kaiparowits Plateau, the one that began at the end of the town's graveled main drag, dipped hub-deep into Wahweap Creek, and then angled up a spooky dugway carved into the banded cliffs. Each crew had been assigned a single township; ours was the nearest to town, about ten miles as the crow flies, and the other two were immediately north and east, each one that much farther from the lone dirt road. It became clear the first day that the road was going to do none of us much good; it ran the only place it could run, along the base of a series of cliffs split by deep canyons and buttes separated by clefts and fractures that would make running line a nightmare—maybe an impossibility—without the helicopter that would arrive the following week.

On the other hand, I had learned already, and would continue to learn over the next decade of surveying with and without helicopters, that *no* line is impossible, even if the placement of an actual corner monument sometimes is. I came to know this a couple of ways. The first was with a statement that embarrassed me with the obviousness of its truth, a measure of how much I had to learn about surveying. Just after my first orientation, when I'd heard that we might be getting helicopters the following summer because the townships we'd been assigned were too isolated and rugged to survey any other way, I'd asked Craig Sylvester— Woody's less antic older brother who also worked for the Cadastral Survey—for details about what they'd referred to as "helicopter surveying."

Craig had a reputation for pure uncomplicated competence; his sections always closed tight, and he explained things in the fewest possible words always to the greatest possible effect. In his early sixties, he was craggily handsome, his sunburned face lined with worry and wisdom and, I learned later, pain, the result of the wear and tear that was the legacy of his forty-plus years in the field. I said, a little worried about this glimpse of terrain so daunting we'd have to dangle from helicopters to even get a foothold: "How often do we actually *do* helicopter surveying?"

"We do helicopter surveying all the time," he answered. "But we hardly ever get helicopters."

I learned these truths about surveying slowly, the set of circumstances that defined the danger and difficulty of our work: Utah contains some of the most rugged, untraversable, fractured-into-chaos landscape to be found on the well-wrinkled face of the earth. The work of a surveyor involves inscribing civilization's most prized invention—the straight line—into the landscape regardless of the degree to which that landscape rejects linearity, refutes mathematics, and mocks the idea of order. Combine this inevitable collision with the rule that has governed national survey practice since the Ordinance of 1785—that these lines must *actually be run*—and you understand something of the challenge faced by the employees of the Cadastral Survey.

Perhaps that goes without saying: of course you have to run line. How else does line get there? But most land surveyors—almost all of those who don't work for the government—don't always *run* the actual *line*. As inheritors of the metes and bounds tradition, they are allowed to substitute math for linearity. If a surveyor's job is to establish two points and then determine the bearing and distance of the boundary line that spans those two points, he'll run line directly if it's convenient. But if it's not convenient, and it often is not, he can run a traverse; that is, he can survey a crooked line that takes him around inconvenient rock outcrops, alongside difficult forests, and then back to the next corner. The miracle of trigonometry then allows this canny surveyor to compute all the angles and distances of his traverse—his crooked line between the two points, a neat sequence of triangles—and create a fictional straight line that, on paper at least, connects the points that are important, the corners of the boundary line he's responsible for establishing. This line will have a correct bearing, and it will have a specific and accurate distance, and it will go straight through impossible cliffs and pierce tree trunks three feet thick, and this line will constitute a legal boundary. And the surveyor, a person fortunate enough to be employed by a private surveying company, will not have broken a sweat.

But surveyors who worked through the seventies for the U.S.

Cadastral Survey were still required both by custom and by the imperatives of the canonical *Manual of Surveying Instructions* to actually *run* line: to go where the transit directs up that mountainside, to physically occupy the crumbling edge of that cliff. It was allowable to triangulate a distance if it couldn't be measured directly—for example, if line shot out into space across a canyon so vast and deep that the front chainman would be swallowed up before he could hold a tight measurement for the rear chainman to record. In such extreme cases, surveyors were granted permission to lay out a baseline along the canyon's rim, and the instrument operator could turn angles to the flag the flagman planted across the gap, and the party chief could calculate the distance. But line must be followed exactly; the lath lined in across the canyon must be a direct reflection of the exact bearing line actually follows. If that one spot on the ridgeline across the canyon is occupied by a tree, the tree must be cut down, or at least trimmed until the transit operator can see clearly to a spot that can be physically occupied by the transit's tripod. For Cadastral surveyors, there is no traversing. There are no crooked lines.

There are a number of reasons for this, a few of them practical, the others philosophical and cultural. Basically, the fact that we continued to run the actual line is testimony to the enormous momentum of the Enlightenment. The intention of the men who conceived the rectangular survey was as straightforward as it was arrogant: the United States would be the first nation in the history of the world to be surveyed *reasonably,* a utopia where the hidden order of nature would be recognized and revealed, brought to the surface, and then physically inscribed into the disorderly costume of rocks and trees that constituted the great unsettled West. In the same way that the bleeding, thorn-bound Sacred Heart of Jesus is displayed outside his ribcage in Renaissance paintings and inexpensive plaster statues for the purpose of bearing witness to the otherwise invisible truth of Christ's Passion, the invisible truths of the Enlightenment—the earth's mathematical essence, its clock-driven movement, its perfect sphericity—would be made visible by means of the exacting lines of latitude and longitude, of equator and poles, of meridians, parallels, azimuths, and tangents, which cross and recross to form the web of intersecting lines that threaten to obscure everything else on eighteenth-century maps of the world. This national mission would assure that the perfection of true nature would be made manifest through the inscription of the square-mile grid upon as much of North America as Manifest Destiny could corral.

According to this vision, the United States would be more than a nation: it would become the actual meeting place of the ideal and the real. Just as its citizens' unruly passions would be ruled by the triangulated stability of the three branches of government, the unruliness of its wilderness would be ruled by the actual inscription of the straight line. (It's not for nothing they call that straight-edged instrument a *ruler.*) In order to insure that these lines would be drawn on the ground just as surely as they would be traced on maps, the Land Ordinance of 1785, and the several ordinances and instructions that followed, required that as surveyors established each line, they were to make it *real,* to actually carve line into the landscape, to blaze the trunks of those trees whose branches brushed line, to dig trenches, mound rocks, and otherwise chisel linearity into the very face of America.

· The plan worked. Those markers and blazes eventually became fencelines, windrows, county roads; over time, the rocks and mounds that marked intersections of section lines became fence corners, crossroads, and intersections of state highways that continue today to model the straight and narrow for dozens, often hundreds, of undeviating miles. Those survey lines were made manifest as irrigation canals and county lines, and as freshly plowed furrows and rows of ripe corn—precise parallel echoes of century-old surveys run according to the cardinal points of the compass, an endlessly replicated grid that has given us the checkerboard aspect of America our astronauts can trace from outer space.

In following these first-generation surveyors in order to re-establish their lines and replace their rock markers with more permanent monuments, it made sense—both genealogically and practically—to replicate their methods, to follow their practices as precisely as possible; to run the actual line, just as they did. But the practices of these first surveyors were also determined by something more immediate than Jeffersonian utopianism. Simply put, their instruments were not capable of maintaining the integrity of a long traverse and achieving the accuracy Jefferson's vision required. They knew the mathematical equations—the traverse is simply a sequence of math problems, a series of triangles to be calculated and solved—but their magnetic compasses and short measuring chains weren't sufficiently accurate to yield useful numbers. They could read angles only to within a degree or so, and chaining a mile meant at least eighty different pulls, each pull fraught with overlaps or gaps; to plug these numbers into a complex trigonometric equation would only magnify the already considerable error. These surveyors could survey a *straight* line, however; they could pick out a foresight and chain their way to it, cutting a reasonably straight line in the process, and after they'd measured a mile, they could manage a ninety-degree angle to the east or west, check it against their compasses and, when more precise instruments became available, the position of the sun, and carve out another straight line. Basically, they surveyed the actual line because they had to.

But we *didn't* have to. Even measured against the higher standards established by the more evolved instruments making their appearance through the 1970s—theodolites that could measure an angle to less than a second, and laser-powered distance meters—our transits and 500-foot measuring tapes were certainly accurate enough to traverse with, which is why most land surveyors not working for the government traversed routinely. The occasional surveyor who found his way onto a government survey crew with the significant disadvantage of having studied surveying in college was invariably shocked that we weren't using the traverse, that we actually stayed with the actual line in the face of swamps, trees, and dangerous rock faces. They spent their first weeks on the job asking, "Why don't we traverse here?" Or, "Wouldn't it be better to traverse *around* this cliff?" Eventually they'd stop asking and accept the practice, if not really understand the reason.

Not burdened by preconceptions or even the barest understanding of how surveying was done in what we called the "private sector," and assisted by the reading I did during my school months in psychology and anthropology and literary theory, I eventually figured out some of the reasons. I slowly came to understand that we continued to run the actual line for reasons that were esoteric and arcane, perhaps even religious. Line itself was sacred. Line was what we followed, what we spent our days honoring, what we cleared safe passage for, what we left engraved into the face of the planet. We did it *because* it was difficult and inconvenient. We did it because we were human beings operating in the world of the Enlightenment, the uncompromising and cruel world of applied perfection.

Much of Utah's landscape cannot be physically occupied by a human being. Sometimes the space is already taken by a century-old ponderosa pine; sometimes by a forty-five-degree hillside of shale fragments slippery as marbles. Sometimes it's a perfectly flat spot, wide enough to pitch a tent, but atop a sandstone tower tall as a city skyscraper. Line projected by a survey crew inevitably grazes or intersects such difficult landscape, and our measurements often required that we occupy some of it. At minimum, we needed a spot to pound in a flag on line, with room for the transit operator to erect the transit, and a place for him to stand while he extended line or measured an angle.

In spite of all this famously rugged Utah topography, I can't remember more than a few points on line that couldn't actually be occupied somehow. I *thought* I had found such a spot one afternoon early in my career, that first summer when we were surveying the rugged township north of Vernal. Our last line of the day shot from Matt's transit across a shallow wash, over a broad loaf of a sandstone ridge, beyond a deep but hikable gap, finally bisecting a rock fin, a thin sandstone formation nearly two miles away. Larry wanted a flag placed on each high point, three flags in all; he wanted the last flag, the one from which we could eventually shoot line directly to where the map showed the section corner to be, on the relatively flat spread of sagebrush just the other side of the fin, a narrow uplift of sandstone that looked from a distance like the highest blade on the backbone of a half-buried stegosaurus. I said, as I always did once I'd gotten past those first weeks of total confusion and had developed a provisional sense of where line went and how to get there, "sure."

Larry loved those shots, for reasons of elegance as well as accuracy. The more mileage you could cover, the more flags you could line in from one point—especially if the transit operator had a good foresight on the horizon (for example, a distant peak that stood in the crosshairs)—the more perfect would be line. The worst place was a jungle, where you shot only a few dozen feet at a time from flag to flag, forced to depend on the accuracy of the bronze bearings that held the scope true as you flipped it from the flag behind you to line in the next one. The collimation—the inevitable blip in the instrument as it flipped 180 degrees from back to front—added up to measurable inaccuracy. The best situation was what we faced today: the transit operator sat at one point with miles of visibility and a great foresight while the flagman, me, set up a row of flags, close to where each corner would be found and reestablished, on line for as many miles away as possible.

The first couple of flags were no problem. I hauled myself to the high points, found myself close to line each time, and mounded in flags—this was bare sandstone, so I stacked rocks around each lath until it was solid. But the fin was another matter. I was able to climb without too much trouble onto its crest, which was a couple of yards wide, and although the drop was significant on each side, it seemed possible at first to get in a flag. I waved at Matt to tell him I was ready to be lined in, and he started waving back, waving me with his white T-shirt farther and farther to the west.

It was like one of those jokes one inevitably hears at Grand Canyon overlooks: a photographer gestures to his wife, saying, "a little to the left, a little more to the left. . . ." Matt waved me farther along the fin than I'd hoped, farther west as the slope steepened and the sandy surface of the eroding sandstone felt increasingly unsteady under my boots. The fin grew steeper and steeper as I walked west until I was certain I couldn't go any farther. Line, I believed, ran where human beings couldn't go. Matt waved; without a radio, I waved back. I had pretty good eyes back then, so I could see Larry and Matt confer. I knew that my getting a flag in there would save us a lot of time and hard work, but if it couldn't be done, I hoped they were saying, it couldn't be done.

I hiked back, met them at the truck, and Larry seemed to accept my judgment. "We'll figure out something else," he said, leaving me to wonder overnight just what that something else might be. The next morning I found out. After we hiked to the base of the fin and looked it over from below, Larry carried the transit up the gully to the head of the fin, and I watched, humiliated, as he walked down the crest and set up the transit, shifting it around until he could line up the flags I'd set yesterday with the foresight he could still make out on the horizon. He'd not only walked casually to the spot I'd been afraid to approach on my hands and knees the day before; he'd done it balancing a tripod over his shoulder, and he'd set up the transit over the spot, and he'd lined us in to the north, where we found the old rock marker we were aiming for.

Even today I feel the need to point out that by then I'd climbed some difficult mountains. Although I was still a beginner, I'd proven on peaks in the Tetons and the Wasatch that I was capable of some pretty good moves on rock. I wasn't especially coordinated or agile, but I had balance and what I thought was a good sense of friction, a sensitivity to just how sticky my boot's grip was on a specific piece of rock. I remember thinking the day before that I'd probably go a little farther down this spine of sandstone if I had the rope belay I'd come to depend on in my more recreational climbs. What I learned watching Larry was that I'd have probably gone there if somebody had shown me that it was possible. Or if I'd known how necessary, how *important,* it was.

I had plenty of time to reflect on my failure. Larry had a habit of only rubbing it in if it was a minor screwup; he'd quickly learned that I was harder on myself than he could ever be, and he let me stew in my own juices the rest of the day. I made no excuses. I did resolve, however, from then on to go wherever line went unless *Larry* told me it was impossible. I resolved to think of establishing line as something profoundly different from what I did for sport: I was willing when climbing a mountain recreationally to say no to a pitch that was beyond my competence, but I'd let the party chief make that call for me as a surveyor. I worried that I might get hurt some day thinking like this, but I knew rather than come back to the crew again saying it couldn't be done, I'd push myself as far as I needed to go, as far as line took me.

The area of mountain-driven uplift contained within the borders of our township was made even more chaotic by Ashley Creek, a large stream that flowed south from the Uintas, wandering through the township according to gravity and geology, splitting the rock when necessary to pass through angled ramps of hard caprock. In the intervals between these narrow canyons, the stream slowed and spread, meandering through swampy floodplains, lush overgrown counterpoints to all that dry, ordered chaos thrown up by the distant rise of the Uinta Mountains.

We eventually found ourselves surveying line that ran across the flattest and swampiest of these openings. This was an unusual line for us to survey: the southwest boundary of a long-defunct but still legally significant military reservation, the enduring legacy of a fort that had been established in the last century to address what Americans referred to then as the "Indian Question." The terrain was awful: boggy meadows, mosquito-infested swamps, tangled underbrush, and we had to cross and recross the cold knee-deep stream over and over again. It was bad enough that we had to clear line through all this muck; chaining for distance would be a nightmare, and because the floodplain was both flat and wooded, there seemed to be no way to get the clear shot we needed to triangulate.

We knew we weren't fighting our way through a Vietnamese jungle only because we could see through the trees pinkish glimpses of the canyon walls that confined the flat swamps and willows of the floodplain: high sandstone ramparts stood to the east and west, and on one perfectly flat wall someone had lowered himself on ropes to paint a huge war memorial, a red, white, and blue American flag the size of a troop transport with—we counted—forty-seven stars; and beneath, in six-foot-high black letters, REMEMBER THE MAINE.

This kind of display wasn't unusual. The Utah landscape has always been regarded by its colonizers as an insufficiently stretched canvas upon which to paint the outlines of the New Jerusalem, and every mountainside above every Utah town is still marked with an oversized capital letter representing the local high school. The Wasatch Front has become one long billboard proclaiming the civic identities of the citizens who lived in its shadow, and if a local Mormon imperialist had chosen to stir up Spanish-American War fervor (after routinely threatening war *against* the U.S. government for a half century, this was after all the first opportunity for Mormon boys to fight *alongside* the Feds), who would stop him? The canyon walls were already crowded with pictographs painted and chiseled by citizens of the long-departed Frémont culture, themselves probably not the first inhabitants of our township, markings that, in addition to representing the sun and moon, might well be translated as some kind of Neolithic call to arms, an indigenous version of the stars and stripes, a pre-Columbian statement of nationalistic fervor, perhaps even the prehistoric equivalent of a survey marker. The porous sandstone walls had allowed the natural pigments as well as America's best lead-based paint to establish their messages for perpetuity; pictographs and the American flag were there for keeps, and I knew that archaeologists a thousand years in the future would ponder with equivalent curiosity the ambiguous markings left by the ancient Frémont, nineteenth-century American imperialists, and U.S. government surveyors.

Larry came up with a plan to get us through the swamp without chaining. First, we cut an eight-chain path (about two hundred yards) on line through the brush, measured the distance, and measured it again—whatever Larry's idea was, it required an especially accurate initial measurement. Larry then had Matt pick a specific star on the flag painted half a mile away on the sandstone face, move his transit to the lath at the end of the segment we'd just chained, and turn a second angle to the star. Using this side of the triangle as a base, Larry then calculated the measurement for another side, the line between the star and our first lath. This line, at the same time imaginary and serviceable, became the base from which we'd triangulate our distance, measuring our progress through the next difficult mile and a half without chaining another inch.

It was at least as accurate as trying to pull a chain through all that wilderness, and it was elegant. I was so impressed I could hardly stand it, and at the end of the day, back at the motel, I asked Matt to explain how it had worked.

"Okay, I give up," I said. "How did Larry *do* that?" How, I asked, did Larry create a baseline in the air, a transparent, intangible line measured by calculation alone, by turning only one base angle and directly measuring only one side of the triangle? How did he keep track of where we were? "It felt like we were pulling ourselves up by our bootstraps," I said, tugging off my wet boots and wringing out my soggy socks, at the same time mystified and impressed.

"It's all triangles," Matt said patiently, trying hard to reach one of the slower pupils he'd faced in his dual careers as government surveyor and high school math teacher. As long as we had a clear view of the American flag and could read the angle that defined his relationship to the star he'd picked, Larry could calculate the distance we'd run from each flag I'd pounded in, and to make sure line remained absolutely straight from flag to flag, we'd stopped halfway to recheck our line with a quick shot of Polaris, refining the line's accuracy by locating ourselves in this broadest of contexts. As Matt talked, I was able to picture in my mind a series of triangles connected like links in a tight length of chain, angles and distances anchored on one end by the American flag, connected on the other to line that ran unimpeded through the narrow corridor we'd clearcut through the trees and underbrush with axes and chainsaws and marked with our own flags, me serving as a kind of guidon bearer.

Looking back over our shoulders at the stars and stripes that waved inertly above our heads, and renewing our alignment with Polaris—creating a neat web that somehow connected the Spanish American War, a star on the American flag, a less metaphorical star that burned white with nuclear fuel a thousand light-years away, and a defunct but persistent cavalry outpost established a century ago—we forced our march with axes and machetes the distance necessary to reinforce the military boundary, to run line where it led.

The map of this corner of the Kaiparowits Plateau we'd been assigned, prepared a decade earlier by the USGS, told us that our township included part of Nipple Bench, a relatively flat square mile or so that was presided over by Nipple Butte and watered to little apparent purpose by Nipple Spring. All those nipples. I don't think I've surveyed or backpacked in any area of southern Utah where there was not to be found a rock formation called something like Brigham's Prick or Molly's Tit, so obsessed with virility and/or fertility were the early Mormon settlers, even though those names seldom made it to the USGS maps. But Nipple Bench was the real thing; the United States Geographical Survey said so.

We managed to drive to within a mile of our starting point in the township, and we hiked the rest of the way, carrying our Gurley Mountain transit, our Gunter chain, our collection of axes, shovels, lath, and fieldbooks to our starting point, which was easy to find: a brass-capped iron pipe, surrounded by a mound of stone, that had been placed there in the late fifties by the survey crew that had run the skeletal survey, outlining the townships but not venturing inside the thirty-six-square-mile interiors except to identify school sections. This marker, the brass cap that recorded the intersection of sections 1 and 2 of the township to the south and sections 35 and 36 of the township to the north—the township we'd be surveying over the next two months—was where we'd begin.

While Tim and I rested in the shade of a juniper tree against the midmorning sun and in anticipation of the long day ahead, Matt set up the transit over the brass cap and collaborated with Larry first in carrying out a sun shot, and with new figures in hand taking on the more complex and ambitious observation of Polaris, turning the angles and timing the intervals necessary for the calculation that would yield the bearing we'd follow as we surveyed our new line northward. As I watched the drama unfold, I thought about Williams, and about the wonder we'd shared in considering the mysteries of celestial orientation, then reminded myself that he'd followed his own peculiar wonder into levels of bearing and placement that had landed him finally in the psychiatric ward of a Salt Lake City hospital.

It took Larry about an hour—this year with the assistance of a new electronic calculator—to determine line, the bearing to which Matt would turn with his transit, and Tim and I prepared to set out, Tim more slowly dragging the long metal tape while Larry, the rear chainman and keeper of the numbers, kept the coiled chain straight as it unraveled, holding it in outstretched arms the same way a husband might hold yarn for his wife's knitting.

I looked through the transit to see where line ran—I'd finally learned to squinch my eyeball up to the scope without steadying myself by grabbing the tripod or transit, and the fact that for once Matt didn't seem nervous as I approached his finely oriented instrument I took as a compliment. After memorizing the view through the scope and backing away from Matt's setup with the necessary grace I'd lacked the summer before, I hiked line northward—passing Tim, who was more slowly threading the chain across the difficult ground—thinking both consciously and intuitively about line, deciding the best way to intersect that point where line would reach forty chains (a half mile), where we'd eventually plant a quarter corner pipe (so named because the half-mile points divide the section into four quarter sections), and finally remembering from my view through the crosshairs of Matt's transit where line crossed the ridge that rose to meet Nipple Butte, the swollen sandstone dome topped by a suggestive cap rock, the rounded western side of which blocked the transit's view to the north.

I pounded a lath into this westward swell of Nipple Butte, exactly on line about halfway between the butte-woman's armpit and the rough stone tip of her nipple. We accomplished this task without joke or irony—Williams would have appreciated the implications and provided witty commentary, but he was no longer with us—lining it in according to Matt's instructions over the radio I carried in a pouch on my surveyor's belt that sagged with two canteens, pouches for a signal mirror, surveyor's tape, and a paperback book, his words directing me.

"A few feet east," he said over the radio, giving me the first rough directions, then laughing: "Hey, John—the *other* east."

I shed a little of the smugness I'd felt in succeeding as a surveyor by not knocking over Matt's tripod. *Okay,* I thought, *the sun rises over there, not over here; I need to keep that in mind.* "An inch west," Matt radioed, "a little more, a little more. That's it." I hammered the lath in as gently as I could so as to keep it on line, the point (which I'd shaved sharp with two swings of my ax) finding its way through the hard desert dirt that had eroded from the more consolidated swell of the nipple-shaped formation that rose above me.

Then Matt's voice again over the radio, specifying ever finer increments of measurement as I tapped the lath closer to alignment with the transit's crosshairs, toward its intersection with pure linearity. "Close," he said, reaching now for units of measure not exactly prescribed in the *Manual,* but nevertheless part of the exclusive boy's-club world of the Cadastral Survey. "Bump it a little west now, a hair more, a cunt hair now . . . a *red* cunt hair . . . *good.* That's it." And that *was* it: line.

I sat beside the lath with the morning sun on my back and watched as Tim and Larry pulled the chain tight, measuring their way north along line, three, four, five times pulling the eight-chain tape taut, marking what they'd measured with red and white chaining pins, Larry measuring the vertical angle while Tim pulled the chain loosely ahead, giving Larry time to record the distance, to calculate the triangle provided by the vertical angle, to translate this raw and distorted earthly measurement into the sublime distances of the grid that hovered perfectly flat above the tortured imperfection of the Kaiparowits Plateau. I watched as Matt folded the legs of the transit, swung it carefully over his shoulder, and started making his way toward his next setup over the flag I'd just pounded in. As they began hiking up the flank of Nipple Butte to measure the distance and extend line, I walked slowly ahead in what I hoped was a true northerly direction, sliding in sand that grew increasingly soft as I descended from the hardpanned round summit of the butte.

That day we extended the line almost two miles, some of the easier mileage we'd manage that summer, the one line that ran along something flat enough that we could sight in from a spot with sufficient altitude, in sand soft enough to easily bury the pipe. From our flag on Nipple Butte, we surveyed our way to the quarter corner just down the north side of the butte, dug a deep narrow hole in the hardpan, inscribed the necessary numbers into the marker's brass cap, buried twenty-two inches of the thirty-inch iron pipe to which the cap was attached, built a two-foot-diameter mound of stone to the north, and proceeded another half mile to our first section corner of the summer, the corner that marked the intersection of the boundary lines between sections 25, 26, 35 and 36; then another half mile to the next quarter corner, the halfway point on the line that separated sections 25 and 26. By then, the sun had warmed into noon, burned us from directly overhead for several long hours, and then made it clear with its shadows that if we hiked back to the truck now, we'd be back to Wahweap by 5:30, a little earlier than the 6:00 we'd more or less decided on as quitting time. As we finished tamping down the dirt and placed the final rock in the mound, we looked hopefully toward Larry.

"Let's head in," he said.

I surveyed a total of eight summers and didn't get killed; I put in flags that risked the transit operator's life, and I lived to see Larry back down before I would. Okay, maybe once. But none of this prepared me for the experience I encountered one afternoon during the last summer of my surveying career. I was working then with Bob Richardson, a tall, skinny man in his early forties with an incongruously full beer gut and a blond redneck flattop. When I'd first met him a few years earlier, he was a happy crew chief, a full-time career surveyor, neither overly burdened with responsibility for the accuracy of the survey nor accountable for the crew's rate of progress. He neither signed the notes as party chief nor filled out paperwork for the state office. Instead, he operated the transit with quiet skill, dug holes efficiently and happily, and chainsawed line across a cedar-choked plateau quicker than anybody.

By the time I'd been assigned to Bob's crew, I'd progressed from flagman to crew chief/instrument operator, and he'd advanced—against his deepest wishes—to the position of party chief. Bob had been promoted during a time when surveying was changing dramatically, requiring a lot more book knowledge and technological training than he'd been exposed to in his fifteen years of no-longer-valuable experience; he looked at his fancy new Hewlett-Packard programmable calculator with suspicion and fear, and held it as if it would bite him, never quite trusting, and not always even recognizing, the numbers that blinked red in its readout. He'd been surveying all these years because he'd loved it, and surveying had loved him; now he looked worried, even mournful, worn down by a year of party chief responsibilities, drinking less beer than he'd like each evening because of all the calculations he'd need a clear head to complete.

We were surveying a particularly precipitous section of the Wasatch Front above Provo, Utah. We'd been provided with a helicopter, but it didn't help much in these mountains. There was literally no place level enough for the helicopter to land between the line of peaks at eleven thousand feet and the base of the mountains six thousand feet below, which meant that workdays typically involved being dropped off on a summit or high ridge, hiking several thousand feet down, getting in a few hours of surveying, then hiking down the rest of the way, either to a residential street where we'd parked a truck that morning, or to a foothill clearing where the helicopter would give us a quick ride back to the Provo airport. It was brutal work, no less dangerous for being within a few miles of a sprawling city; we were working only the downhill muscles in our legs and ruining our knees in the process. We spent that summer struggling through thick oakbrush, climbing down fierce rock outcroppings, shooting line up and down impossibly steep talus slopes—and averaging less than half a mile a day.

A narrow canyon cut its way through a corner of the township we'd been putting off all summer. On the USGS map it was called Deep Creek Canyon, but we'd renamed it Deep Shit the day we first flew over it and checked what we saw with our eyes against the ominous preview the map had provided. The map's contour lines ran so closely together in describing the near vertical steepness of the canyon that it looked like a dark, ominous amoebic splotch, a black hole. Even the elements feared this chasm: an intermittent blue line on the map indicated that a seasonal stream (presumably Deep Creek) entered from above, but the map showed no stream emerging below, even seasonally. The notes recorded by the surveyor who had run the original survey a hundred years before claimed that a rock quarter corner would be found at the very bottom, which meant that there was no way of avoiding Deep Shit Canyon, and sure enough, when we finally ran line, followed it right to the brink, and peered over the edge into the place line went, we understood that our procrastination had been justified. It was an ugly hole, choked with rockslides, ledges sharp as teeth, metamorphic rock tortured and cracked beyond the possibility of any apparent trail or place to put your feet without being twisted and thrown, and we couldn't just shoot line over the canyon because there was a corner to be established, a specific intersection that we needed to tie into our survey, a point we'd have to monument with an iron pipe and a rock mound.

The original survey had been completed by a man motivated more by self-preservation than courage or honesty; we'd learned by now that he simply hadn't gone into many of the places he'd claimed. He had done a pretty good job of leaving well-marked corners where the surveying had been easy, but we never did find one of his markers on a steep rock face or deep in a ravine, and we knew we wouldn't be finding one at the bottom of Deep Shit Canyon, where he said he'd placed it a hundred years ago. We understood that he'd observed the same combination of steepness, narrowness, and rock ledges that could tear your body apart, and had said *No way.* Our job was to rectify this act of cowardice, to plunge literally into the breach, to plug this gap in the line that separated order from chaos, to reinforce the invisible wall that kept nature from hindering the advance of American civilization.

The cleft was so narrow that we couldn't see to the very bottom, which meant that we'd have a hard time shooting line exactly where it needed to go. The only way we figured we could get line in there was to carry a transit into the maw of all this rock. We settled on this plan: the flagman and I would climb down the cliff, passing the transit and tripod and the pipe and ax to each other from ledge to ledge. Bob would line us in from the edge of the canyon with the theodolite, and then I'd use the transit to extend the survey into the part of the canyon we couldn't see from above, a shaded rockslide where we figured the marker would go, and where we'd look for, but knew we wouldn't find, the old rock corner. After setting the pipe, we'd hike into the narrow exit through which even water feared to run, down one more ledged face, and meet up with Bob, who would have clambered down the hillside with the theodolite and found his way to the truck.

By then I'd learned a lot about biting the bullet and doing what had to be done. I was apprehensive, but mostly I just wanted to get it over with, to do a good job of running line and placing the corner, and come out without injuring myself. Then Bob said something to me I've never heard one surveyor say to another: he took me aside just as I was about to go over the edge and said quietly, almost whispering, "If it's too rough down there, just chuck the pipe and get the hell out. It's only surveying."

"Sure." I answered Bob confidently, relieved but also feeling odd, at once a little confused and deeply moved. There was a professionalism to surveying that I both admired and worried about, the complete inability of any of us to say no. Perhaps it wasn't professionalism, but it wasn't machismo either. After all, we were surveyors, not mountain climbers or big game hunters or gunfighters. We never used words like *courage* or called each other pussies, as did some of the guys I climbed with on weekends; we were driven by trigonometry, not testosterone. And some days it was fun. We'd hike for miles, leaving newly marked section corners in our wake, rejoicing in the blue Utah sky and taking in all the beauty and sublimity that part of the world has to offer. We were being paid to spend our days in the same landscape national parks were built to celebrate.

But many other days involved some of the hardest, most dangerous work human beings are called upon to do, and it was never okay to just stop, to take more than a minute's rest, or to say *I can't do this.* There were a lot of things we couldn't say. For example, we couldn't say to each other, Are you crazy? Carry a transit up that cliff? *No way.* Cross this river without a rope? *Forget it.* Cut our way with axes through all this timber? Get *real!* Those words would never escape our lips. Occasionally over the years we'd get a summer worker who would complain or goldbrick, but he'd never last through June. My first summer, the day I decided I couldn't plant a flag on the sandstone spur, was the one and only time I said it couldn't be done, said *I can't do it.*

That assumption about surveying left me no alternative but to descend into Deep Shit Canyon. We slowly crawled downward through the ramparts of ledges, and after a search that left us scrambling up and down a rockslide that made it pretty clear the original surveyor had only observed this spot from afar, we calculated where our marker should go—based on the rock corners we'd already found along this north-south line—and mounded the pipe with rocks, of which there were plenty, and pulled our way back out, suffering scratches and bruises but no lasting damage either to ourselves or (more important) the transit. As we stumbled out of the narrow divide and through the last set of rock ledges, finally sliding down the first actual dirt we'd encountered all day, Bob was there with the truck and a cold Coors and an actual handshake, the kind of gesture I'd grown accustomed to going without for just doing what the job required.

As I said, by then I'd come to accept the motivation for our work, our routine belief in the ultimate importance of line. But I hadn't realized just how *heartless* was the unexamined obligation of going everywhere line went, until that day when Bob told me: *it's only surveying.* His words were so unexpected, so unprecedented in all the years I'd been a surveyor, that I felt a little jolted, even disoriented. Bob was telling me that I was more important than line. It felt a little like love.

A pretty good first day on the Kaiparowits Plateau: my first line on an original survey, even with all the buttes and ravines the flattest mile we'd see for a couple of months, and what turned out to be both my first and last drink of water offered up by the landscape, and not from my canteen. Just the other side of the flank of Nipple Butte where our straight line had run its course, I hiked past what must have been Nipple Spring, marked by a rusted stock tank, a pipe dribbling water into a murky pond, and some dispirited but nevertheless green mesquite. I remember just making out a few petroglyphs carved dimly into the varnished sandstone near the spring, indistinct yet distinctly human outlines of geometrical forms, circles and triangles, rough intersecting lines, and a few stick figures representing humans and animals, rough by the standards of the best-known inscriptions, the artful walls tourists are directed to, the figures fenced off from the touch of vandals and admirers alike. It's always been difficult for me to keep from touching things I shouldn't, and I reached forward and placed my hand alongside a particularly intricate arrangement of lines and squares, understanding that this spring had been flowing off and on for hundreds, perhaps thousands of years, that human beings long dead from cultures long extinct had sipped this same warm water. I wondered if they'd thought of breasts as they'd walked around the formation and found water at this spring, and I wondered just what those shapes in the rock meant, why they'd chiseled their precise angles and circles and rough representations of themselves into the rock of Nipple Butte.

I placed my cupped hand into the pipe's drizzle, watched my palm slowly fill to overflowing, sipped a little of the slightly bitter water, and returned to walking as close as I could to the actual line, the bearing of which we'd determined that morning to within a half minute by sighting on a star a thousand light-years away, counting steps to help me estimate the distance that would mark one mile, keeping my mind on the invisible grid hovering just above my head, paralleling the natural topography of Nipple Bench and touching earth only at those points marked by a thirty-inch iron pipe, an inscribed brass cap, and a mound of stone to the north.

CHAPTER THREE

The Polygamist's Bar and Cafe

Wahweap City was situated just north of the Arizona border on a 100-mile stretch of Highway 89 that connects the lonely desert outposts of two empires, one nostalgic and religious, the other boosterish and secular. The outpost to the west is Kanab, a small community established in 1864 by Brigham Young to consolidate the southern reaches of the kingdom he ruled from Salt Lake City's Temple Square. Kanab's early years had been insecure and inter-mittent—abandoned during periods of war between Mormons and Paiutes, briefly prosperous during the 1880s as a ranching center and refuge for Mormon polygamists chased southward by federal marshals, followed by a half century struggling through the economic doldrums that define most small Mormon towns located in the marginal landscapes of southern Utah. Then a slow, steady boom fed by Hollywood and the National Park Service: Kanab's surroundings have provided authentic desert backdrops for uncounted westerns, and the town began serving the burgeoning postwar tourist industry as a base of operation for families visiting nearby national parks. This recent identity has succeeded in lining its main street with coffee shops and motels, but the town's early purpose still speaks clearly through its collection of large brick houses built along New England lines a hundred years before by Mormon elders made prosperous by logging, cattle, and polygamous marriage.

Drive east from Kanab long enough, you'll cross the Colorado at

Glen Canyon Dam to arrive at Kanab's secular doppelganger, Page, Arizona, a town constructed by Bureau of Reclamation utopian visionaries in the late fifties to house workers building the dam and to stand forever as the antithesis of boomtown irresponsibility. Page was scrupulously laid out on a bluff overlooking the dam's construction site, on land traded from the Navajo Nation, and by 1974 had grown into a pint-sized utopia of carefully curving streets, orderly plantings of trees, a convenient number of strip malls, and (along Lake Powell Boulevard) a row of church buildings housing a baker's dozen of distinct denominations, a collection of theological alternatives that underlined the contrast between Kanab's Mormon monopoly and Page's free-market religiosity, but nevertheless seemed far out of proportion to the needs of the small community of Bureau of Reclamation employees who would remain in Page after the smoke and dust of construction settled.

Standing like a poorly negotiated compromise between these extremes of theocracy and bureaucracy stood what was left of Wahweap City, part trailer-park ghost town, part would-be embryo of the New Jerusalem. Like Page, the town had been built to house workers constructing Glen Canyon Dam, although the word *built* doesn't really describe a hasty graveling of dirt streets that still somehow adhered to the founding father's Enlightenment ideal, a city plan laid out according to the cardinal points of the compass, an orientation Thomas Jefferson would have recognized, but an execution that would have horrified him: the careless pouring of small concrete slabs intended to serve as porches for trailers, the stringing of electric wires from poles already bent and weary from service elsewhere, the bulldozed gashes of roads that persevered irrelevantly to outline residential areas planned, surveyed, and even numbered, but never actually occupied. There had been no Brigham Young to pronounce this the right place, as he had done so famously in viewing the future site of Salt Lake City in 1847. Here the right place was merely the intersection of Highway 89 and the rutted road that wound its way toward the gravel pit on Wahweap Creek that provided grit for the concrete stacking up in layers to finally accomplish the plugging of the American southwest's biggest river.

I'd actually witnessed the pouring of some of that concrete, when I was about six years old, in the middle of the night, under circumstances so dreamlike I've turned to my parents for reassurance that it actually happened. My family spent a week or ten days each summer exploring the West by car, and that particular summer we were headed for scenic attractions in the Four Corners area. My parents liked to drive through the night when we had a lot of miles to cover, and as a consequence I remember many times waking early to find myself in the middle of vast wastelands of western desert, watching the sun rise behind distant blue mountains, peering over the shapes of my brothers in sleeping bags stretched across the folded-down expanse of a series of station wagons—Fords, Mercurys, Pontiacs—at flat dusty expanses of sagebrush and alkali, broad sandstone mesas and eroded shale hills.

My memories of those nights are probably more vivid than memories of the days we spent touring national parks. We'd find a gas station at dusk and park under insect-clouded floodlights near the restrooms, where we'd brush our teeth and wring out our bladders for the night. Dad would fold down the station wagon's backseat, roll out luxurious four-inch-thick pads of foam rubber he'd bought by the foot at a war surplus store in Salt Lake City, and lay out sleeping bags and pillows, strapping everything else onto the roof rack, and we'd be off, Mom and Dad in front taking turns driving, my sister small enough to sleep between them on the bench seat, my two older brothers and me fighting for territory in the back.

It was always hard for me to fall asleep—part unfamiliar surroundings, part persecution by my brothers, part excitement of travel—and Dad forbade reading by flashlight for reasons I still don't entirely understand, so I'd watch the moon shadowing the desert, the flash and fade of headlights, the fleeting neon colors of motel signs and the glowing windows of cafes in the occasional small towns we'd drive slowly through in these years before the interstate, listening to the reassuring hum of our car's tires on pavement, my parents' calm voices subdued by the night and by their common purpose, and the muted conversations on the late-night radio call-in programs my parents preferred for their night driving. I'd finally fall asleep feeling a part of an adventure, knowing that I'd wake up in an exotic landscape before everybody else, a place I'd never seen before or even imagined, always empty, vast, a little scary in its blank wildness, but made safe by the colonizing presence of the highway over which we sped. That night I'd fallen asleep warm, comfortable, and looking forward to waking up in whatever part of the wide unknown world awaited me.

My parents saw this as a comparatively painless way to cover two hundred miles without the daytime heat of desert driving, as well as the fights, the bathroom stops, the Dairy Freeze lunch breaks that complicated vacation travel. It was unprecedented, therefore, for them to wake us up at 3 a.m. to view a construction site, and I can only imagine that it was my father's idea, that he saw something important in the construction of Glen Canyon Dam that his children should bear witness to. I remember him carrying me half asleep from the parked station wagon to a viewpoint on what must have been a bridge, the graceful arch that carries Highway 89 over the Colorado River and above the dam they were building to contain it. I don't actually *remember* the bridge, or any other details of parking the car, or my parents dressing us against the cool night. What I do remember is hovering in space above the most awesome thing I had yet seen in my few years as a conscious human being.

My father held me as I slowly awakened in the chill desert air and looked down, seeing, as my eyes focused and adjusted to the overwhelming glare, a series of gray squares the size of football fields lit up like a stage far below my dangling feet, hearing the muffled sounds of diesel engines, giant turning wheels, shouts of men who moved, tiny but purposeful, in the floodlights far below, at the bottom of the canyon. Glen Canyon Dam must have been less than a third completed; I remember it filling the bottom of the deep canyon, barely climbing the sandstone walls on each side, and at that point it was a mass of cement, just beginning the gradual taper that rises slowly to become the thin curving structure sweeping gracefully from wall to canyon wall the tourist sees today.

Today, we see only the fragile curve of the dam's crest, the concave arc of the sloping downstream side that slides like a neat geometrical equation into the perfect cubes of the power plant below. Viewing the dam today evokes faith in mathematical formulas and principles of engineering. It's easy to believe in the eggshell principle of the arch dam, to forget the mass of concrete, the sheer tonnage of cement required to stop a river. As is the case with Glen Canyon itself, the rising water hides what's most true about the structure: mass. That June night in what must have been 1958, however, mass is exactly what I saw, and scale, and extent. The expanse of concrete squares filled my vision: everything was cement, dam, construction. There was no night sky, no river, and precious little canyon wall. Cables, trucks, men, and concrete—the spotlights erased everything beyond the glare, beyond the boundaries of the construction site. The air was heavy with the smell of curing cement and the sounds of machinery and my father's voice in my ear, teaching me, telling me what was necessary to make something like this possible: the refrigeration lines that drained the dangerous heat generated by curing cement, the enormous bucket that was filled with concrete from a tower standing precariously on the canyon rim, raised from its loading and hurled swinging at the end of cables to the workers below, where it released its load, filling a square with the dark gray of fresh concrete but adding nothing discernable to the bulk rising from the canyon floor.

As usual, I understood only a portion of what my father told me, but my eyes and ears took in exactly what I could apprehend: a proudly unnatural force making an undeniable mark on the world. Only later did the mechanical details add up, as I toured Hoover Dam on another vacation, posing for pictures beside a concrete bucket the size of a small house similar to the ones I'd seen at Glen Canyon, but that night I understood instinctively what it all meant, and it thrilled me, made it impossible for me to sleep after we were replaced in our sleeping bags. I positioned myself in the back of the station wagon where I could look straight up through the slanted rear window and watch the stars reappear, shyly at first, gradually retaking the night sky as we drove away from the overpowering glare of the construction site, stars finally assuming the reassuring shape of the Big Dipper, the only constellation I recognized, and the North Star, the only star I knew by name. I was still awake when the sky changed with the more subtle light of early morning, pondering my new and inarticulate understanding of what it meant to be a human being, as we sped toward our destination, the ruined cliff dwellings of Mesa Verde National Park.

The crews—at least we summer temporaries—would have preferred to set up our bunk trailers in Page or even Kanab, towns with a movie theater, a grocery store, and a public park, and alternatives in the way of food and drink (safely over the Arizona state line, Page's bars actually served *liquor*). But we were placed distant from such comforts in Wahweap City, a dismal spot with few trees, no grass, and one bar and one cafe, both run by a man who believed himself to be the spiritual and entrepreneurial successor to Brigham Young. Warren Knowles and his several wives had entered this Promised Land just a few years before we'd brought our bunk trailers and our twelve-dollar per diems and the promise of a summer of prosperity. The town site hadn't been much more than a ghost town then, its population dwindling toward zero following its boom years as a low-rent alternative to Page for housing construction workers, leaving a collection of cracked concrete slabs and sagging power lines, acreage too hardpanned and graveled-over to be reclaimed by even the most persistent desert vegetation that grew just beyond the city limits. Because his labor costs were low—his wives worked the kitchen and the counter, and served up $1 beers (an outrageous price for a bottle of Coors in 1974) past midnight to thirsty surveyors—Warren had managed to hang on until the energy crisis brought not only government surveyors but representatives of energy companies and (as if I hadn't felt guilty enough) college students who worked summers cataloging ecological and archaeological details in order to determine possible environmental impacts, gathering the data that would ultimately fill the thousands of pages of the environmental impact report, the anthropological, historical, floral, and faunal specifics that provided some hope of stopping the development for which our survey was preparing the way.

Wahweap's revival was the result of a potentially lucrative confluence of geography and highway. The road that connected 89 with the abandoned gravel pit intersected another, more important dirt road, the route we'd followed that first week as it twisted its way toward a treacherous but passable dugway onto the Kaiparowits Plateau, the only breach in the rampart of cliffs between the Cockscomb and the Colorado, and therefore the only practical access to the planned mines and the several provisional sites for the power plant.

Among other things, this meant that, like Brigham Young's own empire a hundred years before, Warren Knowles's empire would be financed with government money, and with something of the same irony. Federal troops sent west in 1857 to arrest Young and his fellow insurrectionists in what became known as the Utah War established their fort a few miles from Great Salt Lake City, more than a thousand miles from their source of supply at Fort Leavenworth on the Missouri River, and so they found themselves buying their food and supplies with hard U.S. currency at vastly inflated prices from their erstwhile enemies. When things quieted down and the troops departed Utah, the army sold its excess stock and wagons to the locals at war-surplus prices, providing the Mormons with the equipment they needed to import increasing numbers of newly baptized immigrants and push the borders of their empire outward from its Salt Lake headquarters. Warren Knowles had been experiencing cash-flow problems, and once again god (this time by means of the energy crisis) had brought the federal government—Warren's sworn enemy—within fleecing range.

Like the Mormon pioneers a hundred years earlier, Warren regarded his humble beginnings as the foundation for earthshaking things to come, and the sorry appearance of his town was merely a measuring stick against which his later triumph might be measured, an ambition noted by the government bureaucrats charged with preparing the way for the vast construction project on the horizon. In the seven thick volumes that constitute the environmental impact report the Department of the Interior was compiling the summer we surveyed the Kaiparowits Plateau (one of the first required under new environmental protection legislation for something as impactful as a multimegawatt coal-burning power plant), perhaps the only sarcastic note can be found in the report's description of Wahweap City, a town ". . . composed of mobile homes in various conditions of upkeep. There are no sidewalks, lawns, paved streets, or public recreational facilities in the community. Public services are severely limited. This is not to convey that some residents may not be contented and/or optimistic about the future prospects for the community." Warren Knowles's contentment and/or optimism was based on the reasonable assumption that a significant percentage of the several thousand construction workers and, later, miners and power plant employees would want to park their trailers—and perhaps even build their homes—in the closest existing community, and Wahweap offered by far the shortest commute to any of the several sites being considered.

What Warren didn't know that summer was that Wahweap City had already been excluded from the federal government's overall design. Department of Interior planners apparently considered the town a lost cause, and the environmental impact report released the next year included not just recommended sites for the power plant, and its accompanying mines, roads, and power lines, but plans for a brand-new community that would be constructed a few miles up the highway from Wahweap, a fully conceived array of gracefully curving residential streets, a modest but comprehensive commercial district, a couple of nicely landscaped parks, and your choice of the usual churches. A kind of mini-Page.

In the meantime, Warren was doing pretty well financially, and he appreciated the irony in the government's underwriting construction of his independent nation. Warren *hated* the government. *Any* government—the United States of America, the State of Utah, even Kane County—and he took chest-puffing pride in his belief that each of these governments hated *him*. It was probably true that various local and national law enforcers wanted to arrest him for being in flagrant violation of any number of laws. He'd taken plural wives—a crime still quaintly listed under the criminal heading "cohabitation"—and he was undoubtedly in violation of countless EPA, OSHA, and local zoning ordinances. As far as Warren was concerned, this was still the Wild West, and he spread out his makeshift compound any direction he wanted, using whatever materials he was able to pull from older structures, which might or might not have belonged to him, or to haul in from the surrounding public land, which certainly didn't.

During one of our many late-night discussions that summer, Warren reminded me proudly that he was being shadowed by government agencies ranging from Utah Fish and Game to the Central Intelligence Agency, and he'd made elaborate plans to protect himself against the inevitable raid. He must have finally decided I wasn't the kind of government agent he need concern himself with, because that night he leaned over to me and whispered, "Want to see something?"

I guess I did, because I followed him to the parking lot outside his bar, where he opened the trunk of his dusty black secondhand Lincoln Continental Mark III, and as bats swirled in erratic zigzags around the streetlight shining bleakly overhead, Warren let me handle the weapons arranged on the trunk's carpeted floor ranging in size and firepower from a sleek Uzi and a brace of various assault weapons to a World War II–era Browning Automatic Rifle, a weapon that nearly toppled me with its heft as I aimed it at imaginary feds watching his compound from afar.

This was long before Waco or Ruby Ridge, but Warren's fear of governmental interference and betrayal was as old as Mormonism itself, perhaps as old as the United States of America, a distrust that I had grown up learning alongside the more superficial patriotism that Mormons had taken on in order to achieve statehood. I grew up understanding that the federal government had failed to protect my ancestors from persecution in Ohio, Missouri, and Illinois, had chased them all the way to their sanctuary in the mountains of Utah, and had jailed my great-grandfather for the simple crime of obeying god's commandment to marry multiple wives, one of whom turned out to be my great-grandmother. As I got to know Warren better through the summer, I'd argue with him on topics ranging from the theological to the political, and I'd generally find the usual reasons to dismiss his pronouncements out of hand. But there was something about his view of the world I understood too well, and something about his sureness I envied in spite of myself.

Warren Knowles was well aware of his connection with Brigham Young and the circumstances of the early Mormons, and he cultivated a resemblance that was already a little eerie. Warren had Brigham's blocky head, abbreviated neck, and muscular shoulders and arms, and he wore his hair in the manner of the nineteenth century, which (this being the midseventies) was back in vogue nationally: Warren wore his straight hair long, covering his ears, just about touching his shoulders. During one conversation, we figured out that the two of us had the longest hair in town, not counting a couple of his younger wives. He'd recently grown a thick moustacheless beard in the style of Brigham Young's later years; framed photographs hanging on the wall of a clean-shaven Warren documented the fact that he'd also been a dead ringer for Brigham in *his* similarly beardless early years. Like his role model, Warren Knowles had postponed letting his beard grow until he'd assumed the mantle of the prophet and commenced building the New Jerusalem.

And like Brigham, Warren was straightforward, articulate, and—I have to say it—almost credible. However bizarre many of his views (he had learned from conversations with god, for example, that Jesus was Anglo-Saxon and had spent those mysterious miss-ing years amassing a fortune as a tin-mining magnate in England), Warren spoke them with quiet certainty, and a tonal quality nei-ther hysterical nor theatrical. Warren's wives were straightforward in describing the energy and skill he brought to their nights of one-on-one cohabitation, which were determined by a schedule of ro-tation; he came off a little like the characters Nick Nolte has played for years, smart and strong and virile beyond question, and usu-ally a little over the edge.

Warren not only patterned his ambitions after the Mormon ex-ample; he believed that his personal kingdom was a fulfillment of their theological revolution that had lost its way. He believed that the keys to the Mormon priesthood had been handed directly from Brigham Young to himself; according to Warren, the keys were withdrawn and held in escrow during the period the church stopped marrying off its teenage girls to the same doddering patriarchs and caved in, compromised, achieved statehood, and assimilated, its elders leaving Utah's territorial prisons to join the U.S. Chamber of Commerce and take part in harvesting the fruits of the American century.

Warren's plans were grounded in the theory that had worked so well for the original Mormon pioneers. Settle in a part of the coun-try nobody else wants, preferably on the border to another juris-diction (Kanab had been placed only a few miles away from the Arizona town of Fredonia, and nineteenth-century Mormon po-lygamists commuted regularly back and forth to evade marshals sent from either direction); do everything you can to propagate, to multiply and replenish the earth; and push outward the bound-aries of the empire by establishing satellite colonies. Claiming his right under the Homestead Act of 1862, perhaps the most prolific offspring of the Ordinance of 1785, Warren had begun the con-struction—on BLM land—of a settlement just off the road that ran alongside the Cockscomb, a clear demonstration of his under-standing that popular perceptions aside, the Homestead Act pro-moted the agendas of empire builders more surely than it nurtured the dreams of those fabled hardworking Little-House-on-the-Prairie farm families.

Perhaps most important of the assumptions he followed was this: don't entertain any sentimental notions about the landscape. Brigham Young understood that his predecessor, Joseph Smith, had gone to nature to find god, but Brigham also understood that the barren topography of the mountain west was something vastly different from the fecund Edens of Missouri and Illinois from which they'd been driven, and that the Utah landscape was, pure and simple, the raw material by which the New Jerusalem would be built. It was that straightforward, and that successful. The people who built the Utah version of Zion believed that canyons were for damming, rivers for irrigation, forests for clearcutting, and mountain granite for the construction of temples and for strategic defense—the mountains served nicely to protect the saints against outsiders. It was a practical Mormon settler, after all, who provided the first description of the beautiful Technicolor formations of Bryce Canyon: "a hell of a place to lose a cow." Even when outsiders finally convinced locals that they could *make money* as a result the fact that they lived amid some of the most scenically interesting landscapes in the world, the inevitable conflicts that arise in choosing between preservation and development were apprehended slowly, and even today, Utah is a state that celebrates Rainbow Bridge, the Salt Lake Temple, and the world's largest open-pit copper mine as partners in its appeal for tourist dollars.

I spent many hours talking with Warren Knowles that summer, and over the years since I've come to understand that few of those hours were wasted. Among other things, Warren helped me understand the depth of my disbelief, just how irrevocable was my swing from Mormon to whatever it was I had become. In one of our earlier discussions—Warren held court nearly every evening in the cafe, sitting in a booth by the cash register and welcoming passersby to sit and converse—he found my leaving the church perfectly understandable, but my agnosticism (I'd recently decided I possessed neither the commitment nor the courage it required to become an atheist) harder to fathom.

"Of *course* you'd leave the Mormon church," Warren said. "They haven't been right about anything since Brigham Young, and you don't have to be a genius to understand that god doesn't change his mind about things like polygamy."

What he *really* couldn't understand was my uncertainty, my unwillingness or inability to find an alternative. "You've got to believe in *something*," I remember him saying one night. "Leave the wrong religion, sure, but find yourself one that's right, even if it's one you make up yourself." I had to agree that *not* believing was a tenuous position to hold, negation having, by definition, not much to offer in the way of structure or prop, but that's where I seemed to stand, or at least the empty space I limped around in.

I'd been thinking vaguely that this difficult-to-describe yet firmly held belief in disbelief might somehow be related to my love of surveying, and I think my conversations with Warren helped me understand that too. His placement—and if anybody was placed, *he* sure was—was profoundly different than mine. For one thing, he *had* a place, was reinforcing its boundaries brick by brick, and he seemed to know where he stood with regard to the natural world, which was basically on top of it. Me, I'd grown up confused about nature. Maybe a lot of people do: the more I read and teach the literature of wilderness, the more I recognize the uncertainties that color the conflicted space humans inhabit in the natural world. On one point we all seem to agree—all of us, including Thomas Jefferson, Ralph Waldo Emerson, the author of *Gilgamesh,* and even Warren Knowles, to name just a few—that our individual selves exist in some kind of profound relation to the specific landscapes, the rocks, trees, and dirt, in which we anchor our lives: not quite connection, but not quite disconnection either. Cultures differ mainly according to whether they emphasize the connection or disconnection angle. The Greco-Roman, Judeo-Christian tradition saw this particular glass of water as mostly empty, possibly in order to explain why human beings seemed so *unhappy,* and its Mormon descendants made a home for this chronic sense of alienation in the canyons and mountains of the American West.

But of course it's more complicated than that, especially for somebody like me, who'd been raised a Utah Mormon. On one hand, I'd grown up in a culture rooted in romantic, even transcendental, beliefs concerning the natural world. Joseph Smith went into nature to find god; he left the fenced pasture of his family farm to enter the farm's woodlot, what Mormons continue almost Druidically to call the "Sacred Grove." Smith was a romantic, perhaps even a mystic; if not a full-blown transcendentalist, he was at least a fellow traveler. He grew up on the same nascent romanticism that prompted William Cullen Bryant to pen such neopagan tracts as "Thanatopsis" and "A Forest Hymn," and Joseph Smith founded his Church of Jesus Christ of Latter-day Saints only

a few years before Emerson published "Nature" and officially put
the Enlightenment on notice in America. Both events heralded the
beginning of something natively and uniquely American, two ide-
ologies connected by their belief that godliness pervaded the very
molecules that made up nature, a belief in a deity transcendent in
both humans and the landscape they occupied.

For me, nature—at least as it was manifested in the landscape—
had always come across as comforting. The house I grew up in
stood a few short blocks away from the steeply rising rock face of
the Wasatch Front, and from the time I was a child, that's where
I'd go for relief from whatever troubled me. It never occurred to
me to be afraid of nature as embodied in physical landscape. I suppose I knew about flash floods and earthquakes, and I was aware
that the mountains I loved so much rose from a vastly undependable foundation called the Wasatch Fault, a geological quality-
control lapse that would eventually tumble the houses of my
foothill neighborhood down the hillside and into the Great Salt
Lake, but Mormon geologists had assured me in church that this
would happen long after the millennium had run its course and
we were all presiding over worlds of our own, worlds presumably
with less dramatic tectonics. If I'd bothered to sit down and actually calculate the death toll visited upon my neighborhood by our
foothill playground—three friends killed in a fall from an icy cliff,
the skier who'd crossed over Mount Ogden only to be buried in an
avalanche a few blocks from our homes, the teenage girl beaten to
death one night by her boyfriend on a dirt road that curved through
the foothills just up the street—I might have managed a more accurate understanding, but the vocabulary of my Mormon youth
always connected "mountains" with "safety" and "refuge" and
"home."

On the other hand, Mormonism embodied all the usual suspicions of the body, of the animal, of the basely physical that define
much of the Western tradition. These suspicions led the first Mormons to attack nature on two fronts: they worked to channel, if not
always subdue, the natural animal within by means of the ideol-
ogy of guilt and permission (nobody ever had less fun with multiple sex partners than nineteenth-century Mormon polygamists),
and they worked with great success to transform the chaotic Utah
landscape into something ordered and profitable. Mormonism had
prepared me well for the contradiction, confusion, and outright

hypocrisy that defined my own life in nature, especially that summer. It was true that I loved the forests, the mountains, even the stark, waterless desert. It was also true that I feared that other face of nature, the chaos of landscape not yet made useful, the disorder of sexual urges not yet brought under control, the incompetence of human biology, our bodies easy prey for the tiniest predator. Biology, in Mormonism, was not exactly destiny; it was more often the enemy, and the face the enemy presented most clearly to me was the polio that struck down my oldest brother the year I was born. I mean, I *loved* nature; however, I wasn't quite sure how I felt about *nature.*

Although I alternate between blaming myself and blaming my upbringing for this confusion, maybe it's *nobody's* fault—maybe it's just history that's to blame, the broad sweep of Western civilization in general, and more specifically the peculiar shift in perspectives prompted by the Mormons' exchanging one landscape for another. After Joseph Smith was murdered, his followers fled in famously epic style to the mountains and deserts of the Great Basin. They took on a new leader at the same time they occupied a new landscape, a man who was as well suited to the transparent aridity of Utah as Joseph had been to the murky and mist-shrouded hill country of the Susquehanna Valley, where he had conversed routinely with angels and figures from the New Testament; and the upper Mississippi Valley, where he had gone so far as to declare a hillside pasture in Missouri the *actual* site of the Garden of Eden. Brigham Young was no mystic, however, and in the same way some theologians have interpreted the fall from Eden as felicitous, Young turned exile into empire.

It's difficult to imagine a greater contrast between the geography the Mormon pioneers escaped and the geography in which they found relative safety. The Wasatch Mountains provided physical protection from the enemies that had driven them from wetter, greener, more Garden of Eden–like terrain, but this view of refuge quickly became more metaphorical than actual. This was difficult country from which to scratch a living, let alone create an empire. Water gushed from inaccessible mountains to dead salt lakes without having much effect on the soil in between; potentially fertile valleys were few and inconveniently placed, occupying a narrow band between the alkali of the Great Basin to the west and the sandstone wasteland of the Colorado Plateau to the east. So right away, Mormons stopped praying in the landscape (abandoning a habit they'd cultivated in deference to their first prophet's affection for what Bryant called "God's first temples"), and started reshaping it into something that they'd recognize as friendly. They built dams and carved irrigation ditches; they hauled away mountain granite and transformed it according to the right angles of Western architecture and architectural iconography into *actual* temples, putting up the pointed and castellated walls of buildings that refuted the landscape against which they stood. If the Salt Lake Temple mocked its mountain backdrop by maintaining with some irony the granite-gray colors of local nature, in St. George, Mormonism's redrock outpost to the south, Mormons constructed a temple of red sandstone, then immediately transformed it by means of stucco and whitewash into a gleaming white right-angled monolith that partook not one bit of the chaotic flaming cliffs and mesas that served as the colony's setting.

In other words, I grew up learning the theology of romanticism, but practicing the logic of the Enlightenment, the result of Brigham Young's not quite succeeding in his attempt to replace the flighty vestiges of transcendentalism with the more substantial principles of the eighteenth century. Joseph Smith had talked of plans for the City of Zion and had embraced the notion of the grid as the most ordered and utopian of urban arrangements; he'd been born into the metes and bounds confusion of New England, and had achieved his greatest empire-building successes amid the section lines of Ohio, Missouri, and Illinois, some of the earliest territories to be surveyed according to Jefferson's new rules. Nevertheless, to Smith, truth was not to be found in the grid. Truth was to be found in the woods, in the pure nature god had created, whose very molecules bespoke spiritual truth.

To Brigham Young and his chief surveyor, a strange amalgam of scientist and mystic named Orson Pratt, truth was to be found in straight lines and right angles, in perceiving the Platonic order *within* nature—the blocks of granite squared to form the Temple walls, not the fractured disarray that is Little Cottonwood Canyon from which the granite was quarried—as well as in imposing the order from without by means of Jefferson's rectangular survey. Mormon surveyors led this battle against nature in creating the setting for the next New Jerusalem, began inscribing straight lines radiating along the cardinal points of the compass, establishing a grid of square-mile parcels that determined a landscape of streets, fencelines, and irrigation ditches that contrasted dramatically with the fractured and eroded landscape Mormons arrived at in 1847, the project I worked each summer to complete. Zion would be laid out precisely according to the four points of the compass; each rural hay field would exist in mathematically calculable harmony with Temple Square, the squares within and upon squares speaking to an ultimate yet knowable truth recognizable as clearly to Brigham Young as it had been to Thomas Jefferson. Mystical connection with the transcendent intelligence that was nature according to Joseph Smith occupied less and less of the faithful Mormon's attention, which was increasingly directed toward more practical and calculable efforts to lay out a kingdom of sober rectangles and secure profit margins.

Joseph Smith went into the woods hoping the natural world would leave its mark on his soul. Brigham Young went into the wilderness with the goal of making his mark on natural landscape. Utah made the Mormons into *Americans,* ready to partition and use nature for what needed to be done. And during the summer of 1974, I fulfilled every possible destiny, having inhaled the romantic notions of the sixties in the same breath as the utilitarian imperatives of my life as a westerner, as a descendant of Mormon settlers who had struggled to survive in a harsh land; and as a surveyor, I daily acted upon the presumptively idealistic yet ultimately material assumptions of the Enlightenment, living in the Platonic grid hovering overhead, yet carving indelible marks into the undeniably physical fact of dirt and stone and wood. Confused? You bet I was. Warren Knowles sniffed that out right away, and because nothing offended him more than confusion, Warren devoted hours of conversation that summer to setting me straight.

This was the Wahweap City to which we had been delivered. That first day, after we'd positioned and leveled our trailers, hooked up electric wires, water hoses, and sewer lines, we headed in the direction of the only food-serving establishment in town in order to sample the menu we'd be ordering from for the next two months. It was there we slowly came to realize that the various women who cooked our food, brought it to our tables, and washed our dishes afterward were all married to the same husband, the guy who usually sat in the booth nearest the cash register, often with a child on his lap, a man who looked a little like Brigham Young except for the red headband he'd sometimes wear low across his forehead Cochise-style.

That first evening, after I'd learned just how little the trailer's swamp cooler contributed toward displacing the odors of mildew and ancient sweat, and after I'd learned that the food in the cafe was neither better nor worse than all the other food we'd eaten in small-town cafes the previous summer, I walked along the road that led out of town in the direction of Wahweap Creek and the Kaiparowits Plateau, checking out the bands of sandstone and shale now lit up in the reds and oranges of the sunset, the same colors as the beer sign that lit up the window of the polygamist's bar and cafe. I couldn't help wondering what Jim Williams would have made of all this—the strange theocracy that was Wahweap City, the bleak landscape that surrounded it, and the original survey we'd begin tomorrow. Walking back to town, I noticed once again that the only trees in the entire town were a few young cottonwoods that adorned the fenced sprawl of Warren's compound, and that there was only one streetlight, which had just switched on outside Warren's cafe. I surprised a tarantula, which, true to reputation, jumped straight up in a comical and pointless demonstration of fright and self-preservation.

The bunk trailer was empty when I returned to it, and I knew that the crews were spending their per diem checks in Warren's bar, buying overpriced beer from the most attractive of Warren's wives. Although I still hadn't developed the taste for beer necessary to becoming a real surveyor, I headed that way, sat down at his table by the cash register, and promptly got into an argument, the first of many that summer, with Warren Knowles concerning truth, knowledge, and the meaning of nature, and of god's intention for nature's use in the service of building his kingdom.

CHAPTER FOUR

Modern Methods

Our workdays that summer on the Kaiparowits Plateau would be instantly familiar to the surveyors who began in the last decade of the eighteenth century to implement the dictates of Jefferson's ordinance; indeed, you'd have to look back thousands of years to find survey practices that differed substantially from our own. The basic elements of land surveying have remained the same since humankind's agrarian beginnings—surveying has always depended on the line, and line has always been defined by bearing and by distance, the twin touchstones of the surveyor's craft. Because surveying practices have always been determined by the tools surveyors employ to measure bearing and distance, and because tools and instruments have changed slowly over the centuries, those techniques have evolved at the same slow pace, progressing toward increased accuracy and efficiency, yet remaining essentially the same in function and even in form.

This continuity, this connection between surveyors across uncountable generations, defined the profession until the seventies, the decade I learned to be a surveyor, the decade during which government surveyors switched from traditional to electronic instruments. By the end of the seventies, surveyors would find themselves practicing a different kind of craft. They would follow a set of procedures and assumptions disconnected from a tradition that until then had determined not only their practices, but also their view of the world. With these new instruments we surveyed a boundary line between the past and future, an untraversable chasm separating us from our history.

Although these new procedures made surveying somewhat easier and certainly more accurate, they also led surveyors inevitably into a more constricted, less profound understanding of the relationship between the ideal and real, between mathematical constructs and natural landscapes, that has always been at the heart of the profession, the change representing a small but nevertheless significant backcurrent in humanity's flow outward toward the cosmos, a return to that most dangerous of cosmic orientations, the earth-centered universe. As a result of the new instruments and the revolution in practices that followed, land surveying would become something less ambitious, more parochial, than it had after many centuries become. Simply put, by the end of the decade in which I became a surveyor, surveying would partake more of the microchip, less of the cosmos.

Our first week on the Kaiparowits Plateau, however, still belonged to the surveying tradition. Each day we'd rise at dawn, eat expensive but standard cafe-issue bacon and eggs at the polygamist's cafe, drag ourselves and our equipment to our trucks and Carryalls, then follow the gravel road down into Wahweap Creek, up the opposite bank, climb the steep narrow dugway onto and then across the sagebrush flats of Nipple Bench, the corner of the Kaiparowits Plateau destined (if the utility companies had their way) to be the site of an almost unimaginably huge coal-fed power plant. We'd follow the dirt road as far as we could across Nipple Bench, then make our own road to get as close as possible to line. We weren't afraid to hike, but one of the most prized of the Cadastral surveyor's core beliefs is that you get as close as you can by means of four-wheel drive before you start using your boots, no matter how slow or inefficient such effort is. We'd sometimes spend a half hour in compound low, the truck crawling a torturous, circuitous route into and out of washes and across sage-choked rubble to reach a point we could have hiked to directly in ten minutes.

The drill was by now familiar: we'd hike to the last flag we'd placed the day before, and start from there. Matt would thread the transit onto the head of the tripod, push each tripod leg deep into the sand, and drop pebbles from the short chain that dangled from the transit's base to the top of the flagged lath to assure that the instrument's horizontal axis was centered. Plumb bobs were considered dead weight, an affectation of private surveyors or those fancy-pants types who worked for the United States Geological Survey; we depended on gravity and what the *Manual* in other contexts calls "local materials," and upon the hope that there would be local materials to drop. In years to come, this assumption would drive me, as instrument operator, plumb bob-less amid occasionally stoneless terrain to other expedients, including dropping deer scat (I preferred *fresh* droppings because they were heavier), and a more personal variety of local material: one day, desperate for plumb, I dangled a heavy wad of my own spit off the end of my finger, a portable viscous plumb bob that I like to think would have sent a civil engineer into fits.

While Matt centered and leveled his transit, Larry and Tim would unwind the chain from its neatly coiled and folded figure eight, Tim pulling it ahead in the direction we believed was line, carefully draping it when necessary over sagebrush or the end of a juniper branch, both of them finally pulling it tight at each end and calling arcane numbers and directions at each other. *"Eight chains!"* Larry would yell, holding the chain by a scissorslike devise that clamped the chain tight and provided a secure grip.

"Cut three-tenths!" Tim would call, noting the exact distance the taut chain had inched past the chaining pin he'd stuck in the ground.

"Okay, three-tenths!" Larry would yell back, confirming the cut as he penciled the exact distance in his fieldbook then reading the vertical angle through the small clinometer all rear chainmen carried on their belts. I sometimes felt that I was overhearing a young Sam Clemens sounding the depths of the Mississippi on his way to becoming Mark Twain.

The skills necessary for effective chaining were subtle and not easily learned: there was a considerable degree of artistry involved in pulling a straight line across such crooked terrain, and the front chainman had to read the landscape in a way very different from the rest of us. The long Gunter's chain we used—more than five hundred feet long, one-tenth of a mile—was not really a "chain," although it had evolved from one. In the early days a chain had been just that, a string of interconnected iron links, each link about eight inches long. The chains-and-links terminology remained with us long after the chain had evolved into something without observable links, both as the name of the tool and the unit of measurement. We didn't talk feet and inches; we measured and recorded our distances in chains (sixty-six feet) and links (about eight inches, one hundred links to the chain).

There were several reasons for this. The first involved legal precedent—state and federal legislation, as well as the legal descriptions of most public and private property, are phrased in this ancient language, as were the survey notes we consulted during our resurveys. More relevant to surveyors, however, was the fact that the math was easier. That square-mile foundation of land-use democracy, the section, measures a mile on each side. We could divide this mile into 5,280 feet, each foot consisting of 12 inches, each inch divisible by $1/2$, or $1/4$, or $1/16$. Or we could divide the same mile into 80 chains, each chain made of 100 links, each link divisible by tenths. Even handier, for farmers as well as surveyors, was the fact that 10 square chains equaled 1 acre. Chains and links made our job easier, and if Jefferson had had his way, it would have been easier still: he argued for a slightly larger section, each side the length of what he called a "geometrical mile," 100 chains long, giving us another set of rounded numbers: an 1,000-acre section (instead of 640 acres), a 250-acre quarter section (instead of 160). But right-thinking Americans have from the beginning opposed across-the-board capitulation to the conveniences of the metric system, and so Jefferson was voted down in committee, depriving history of the slogan "$62^1/2$ acres and a mule."

Our "chain" was a single strand of flattened wire, eight chains long (I was not completely surprised to learn that the original chain had been only one chain long), forged from tough spring steel originally invented to provide a replacement for whalebone in women's corsets, a flat, narrow alloy (the cross section of a flattened soda straw) that loved a tangled coil at least as much as it loved the clean straight line. The front chainman had to drag this long skinny mass—176 yards, almost two football fields long—and hang it carefully on the highest points of vegetation he could find, making sure it didn't bind or pull with too much friction against a limb or rock.

It was humbling to see how quickly the chain transformed itself from a straight line moving with snakelike ease through the underbrush into a tangled bird's nest of wire loops that resembling nothing so much as a knotted and discarded Slinky. These tangles were difficult to unwind, and because this alloy could be as brittle as it was supple, a sharp bend, a knot, even too much friction against a rock would kink and snap the wire, necessitating a fix in the field that required the party chief to connect the two ends with a metal splint, pound the splint flat with the blunt end of an ax, then weld it tight with solder melted over a small brushwood fire, an hour-long procedure during which the front chainman stood silent and abashed, knowing that a better chainman than himself would have felt the difference between the weight of a long metal tape and a tangle of friction and knots. It was not good to bust a chain. During the next summer—the summer I worked as the last front chainman to practice that arcane art in the state of Utah, the last practitioner in a tradition that could be traced back in time to humanity's civilized beginnings—whatever my other sins and shortcomings, I managed to never tangle or break a chain.

So Tim's first responsibility was to keep the chain intact. His second responsibility was to read the lay of the land perceptively enough to understand what strategies would most likely result in a free pull. The chain had to be stretched taut; it could not bend against a branch or be deflected by a rock. Tim would move quickly ahead, taking care to drape the chain over sagebrush and from the very tips of tree branches, so as to leave the chain high and unencumbered enough that when the time came to pull it tight, the chain would spring from its zigzagged perches to pull taut and clear, conveniently above all that tangled clutter civilians call natural landscape. Again, this was an art, and the difference between doing it well and doing it badly meant the difference between chaining a mile in one short, efficient hour, or spending a day on that same mile retracing steps, untangling snags, and enduring the long-suffering silence of Larry, who waited not so patiently to get on with it so he could record the distance, measure the vertical angle, do the math, and measure the survey's progress.

By this time, I'd be hiking toward the next ridge, hopefully moving in the direction of the spot Matt had pointed me toward, a place I'd first examine magnified through the transit's scope, then contextualize the setting with my naked eye, nurturing my sense of where that exact point was and how I would get there. By this, my second summer, I was good at flagging, and relieved beyond measure when Larry decided that Tim would replace Williams as front chainman, and that I wouldn't be moving above the level of my flagging competence. I'd developed that necessary view of myself as a mathematical point moving through a landscape that somehow negotiated between the natural topography below my feet and Jefferson's platonic grid suspended like an office ceiling over my head; I had a sense of how I existed in three dimensions, watching myself traverse the floor of a canyon, climb a series of ledges to the top of a ridge, walk along the ridgeline until I found that exact juxtaposition of sage, juniper, and rock I'd mapped through the transit until I could practically see the dark lines of the cross-hairs marking the actual spot at my feet.

I'd shout *Wake up!* into the radio, watch the distant figure of Matt Shaw, napping in the shade of the tree closest to the transit, pull his hat back from where the brim had shaded his eyes, awkwardly stand up, adjusting his vision to the harsh reality of the midmorning sun, peer into the scope, and answer over the radio—as I knew he would—"*Jesus,* John, you're blocking the *view,*" which was his way of saying I was on line.

Tim, meanwhile, would be pulling the chain toward the flag I was pounding in. Tim was a talented front chain; I think Larry promoted him over me to replace Williams because he understood that Tim had a feel for linearity that I would never have, his straight and narrow view of the world only slightly distracted by our use of profanity and occasional peyote-eating and only slightly slowed by the weight of that expensive brick of a Nikon he carried on his back.

Matt's skillful work with the transit was the result of his being at home in worlds both ideal and real. His feel for the rocks and trees of the southern Utah landscape helped him to return to the same foresight over and over again, all the while keeping his bearings straight and consistent; every week or so we'd shoot Polaris to double-check, and he'd usually be within ten seconds of where he was supposed to be, far within the legal margin of mathematical and instrumental error, and, more important, securely within the narrower, more ambitious margin Larry had set for our crew. Matt's eyes worked equally well within the more abstract landscape of the transit itself, seeing easily through his magnifying glass into the instrument's small windows to read the obscure language of verniers and scales, a world contained within the transit that partook more of the grid that hovered invisibly above than the pebbles he culled from the dirt below, which he stockpiled in his pocket until they were needed to drop for plumb.

Larry knew strategy. It's easy to think of line as something less complicated than it really is, a matter simply of determining a bearing, then following where it took you, putting one boot in front of the other in a perfect march toward Polaris. That's what merely competent surveyors did. The best surveyors figured out ways to make the job easier and quicker. Although faithful to the imperative that line should be run directly whenever possible, Larry understood immediately which half mile would best be chained and which triangulated. He had a feel not only for which approach would be less work, but which would be more accurate: unlike some other Cadastral surveyors, he understood that sometimes a computed line was more true than one measured link by link. Larry also knew how to take advantage of work we'd already done—he remembered each of the flags we'd left on our north/south lines, so that when we encountered them when running east and west, he could confidently use them for bases, looking up in his yellow fieldbook the distances they marked and calculating triangulations through the more difficult terrain. He had a lot of what the older surveyors called common sense, which of course was greatly uncommon, even among the older surveyors.

Those were what came that summer to be called primitive methods, no different in kind from the methods employed by the first surveyors as they set out on their mission to subdivide the American wilderness, a work initiated by the obsessive-compulsiveness of Jefferson's Land Ordinance of 1785 and accelerated by the acquisitiveness of Thomas Hart Benton's Manifest Destiny. They followed north/south/east/west bearings, and so did we. They chained where they could, and triangulated when they had to, as we did. And like us, they followed line where it took them.

Even our instruments were similar—more evolved, more accurate, but not that much more sophisticated. The new Republic's first surveyors used an instrument called a "circumferentor," a kind of transit-in-embryo consisting of a magnetic compass the size of a dinner plate mounted flat atop a Jacob's staff, fitted with bubble levels and slitted metal gunsights across which the instrument man sighted according to the bearing revealed to him by the swinging of the compass's arm. Over time, the monopod sprouted two more legs to become a tripod; the gunlike open sights were augmented by the weak magnification of a telescopic sight (the first optical sights looked like peashooters, and were clamped inelegantly alongside the metal sights); and the compass vernier was supplemented by a second, parallel 360-degree scale that could be operated independently of the magnetic lines that run not always dependably in the earth beneath our feet.

The surveying rules and procedures that originated in legislation, and were communicated to surveyors by means of the official *Manual of Instructions* that was updated every couple of decades, eventually required that bearings be determined by observations of the sun, an improvement in accuracy made possible by such patented devices as the Burt's Solar Compass and, later, Burt's *Improved* Solar Compass, a Rube Goldberg arrangement of mirrors, verniers, levels, and lenses that after some extensive manipulation of clamps and knobs revealed a bearing uncompromised by the magnetic forces so easily distracted by pocket watches and iron deposits. Eventually, a more powerful scope was mounted on pivots that allowed the surveyor to see uphill and, later, farther still into the cosmos, and the vertical scales of the sextant—which had told mariners and explorers their position on earth for centuries—were grafted onto the telescopic sight, providing the surveyor with yet another vernier scale upon which to read the corresponding vertical angles.

This second dimension of usefulness arrived just as surveyors were leaving the flat landscapes of Ohio and Indiana to survey their lines over the mountains and into the canyons of the West. By the time the scope had evolved into something independent enough to flip from front to back, to connect where you'd been with where you were going, it became a transit, an American invention (some of the earliest were manufactured by W. and L. E. Gurley, the same company that built our transit) adapted to the surveying needs and traditions of the New World and hence much preferred over the English theodolite, which served its empire's global ambitions by pointing only ahead. Various contraptions—ever more improved versions of the Burt's Improved Solar Compass, for example—attached themselves like ornaments to this increasingly festive Christmas tree. The optics were augmented to provide the magnification and clarity necessary for the kind of miles-long shots western vistas made possible, and by the mid-nineteenth century the evolution of the transit design had slowed and stopped, having reached perfection, the form and function preserved faithfully in the Gurley Mountain Transit, the delicate-appearing but rugged instrument built in the forties and fifties we carried over our shoulders through most of the seventies.

Because progeny reflects ontogeny, you could see this remark-able evolution preserved in the structure of the Gurley. Although we never used it while running line—all our bearings were deter-mined by observations of Polaris—a large magnetic compass con-tinued to serve as the base from which the various scopes, scales, windows, and pivots arranged themselves. This was still a *compass*, enhanced and perfected, equipped for solar and astronomical fixes, but just *barely*; to release the arm of the compass and watch it swing into line with the earth's magnetic poles was to under-stand that this instrument was connected to the planet we surveyed at least as solidly as it was connected to the stars we observed. Our version of the Gurley transit had adapted nicely to the subtle ways surveying had changed since 1785. There was a little more accu-racy in the scale, which was readable to twenty seconds, a third of a minute (some instrument operators claimed they were able to make out a tenth of a minute), better optics—finally with suffi-cient resolution to allow a sharp-eyed transit operator to make out Polaris, if just barely—and yet the Gurley transit remained what it had been nearly two hundred years before, an instrument that, like the circumferentor, belonged both in the field and in the draft-ing office, a configuration of metal and glass that negotiated even-handedly between the ideal and the real.

The Gurley was rugged enough to sling over your shoulder still mounted on its wooden tripod, and would survive swinging on its central spindle miles of bumpy hiking; set up over a lath in the desert, it looked like it belonged there. Yet a glimpse into the thumb-sized windows protecting the delicate vernier scales that revealed angles with more accuracy than we actually needed re-minded us that this instrument was an integral subset of a long mathematical equation, the visible emblem of something tran-scendent and eternal, something not quite of the rocks and sage-brush that rubbed against its legs.

Because most of the Cadastral surveyor's time was employed in retracing lines run by the first generations of government surveyors, the fact that our instruments and our methods were not so different from those of a hundred years earlier gave us a profound advantage in running these resurveys. The first surveyors moved fast; the Founding Fathers intended that settlers moving west would establish their homesteads amid landscapes already crisscrossed and civilized by the rectangular survey. They feared the inevitability of contention and lawsuits that would result from settlement's preceding surveying, but they feared even more the effect raw nature had on that complex creature *Homo sapiens,* an uneasy combination of the animal and the spiritual that the American promoters of the Enlightenment trusted not one bit.

They'd seen the way civilized European immigrants reverted, regressed, became drunken and shiftless and violent as they occupied the isolated and wild country of the frontier. The Founding Fathers had also observed the way the straight lines of the farmer's furrows walked him ploddingly along the straight and narrow, making of him a citizen sedate enough to be responsible, yeoman enough to serve uncomplainingly the imperatives of American civilization. The theory was this: settlers who took possession of an already lined and gridded landscape would be soothed and encouraged by those lines and markers, stay sober, endeavor to become landed and prosperous. This ambitious goal required that government surveyors keep moving a step ahead of the flood of settlement.

So they surveyed fast. The instructions requiring that surveyors mark with pits and blazes the actual lines they surveyed had the effect of impressing upon the first settlers the outlines of civilization, the straight lines of correct behavior. Their instructions also required surveyors to keep careful notes on the topography they traversed, to identify species of timber and rate the quality of soil, the better to keep Washington informed concerning acreage for settlement and resources for constructing the world's next great empire.

The result of this dual responsibility was the creation of two gridded landscapes. One would take the form of plats drawn by draftsmen in the General Land Office, maps that translated the prose of field notes into graphic designs of rectangular order, an illustrated narrative of an ever-more-civilized and Enlightened west. The most comprehensive view Washington, D.C., had of the American West was provided not by the reports brought back by the heroic but geographically narrow expeditions of Lewis and Clark, of Frémont, Powell, Hayden and Starr, but by means of the millions of more pedestrian pages of Cadastral Survey notes, which served up vivid descriptions not of far-flung east-west swaths of the continent, but vast expanses of overlapping snapshots of townships, topographical descriptions set down on a scale that allowed the dots to be more usefully connected.

The other grid would be inscribed into the landscape itself. Surveyors were instructed to blaze trees, excavate trenches, and raise rock mounds along the lines they surveyed, and each quarter mile and each intersection of mile-long section lines would be marked by elaborate monuments of rock and sod. The sequentially updated editions of *The Manual of Surveying Instructions* printed throughout the nineteenth century included elaborate plates illustrating the prescribed method of marking section corners. These engravings resemble nothing so much as eighteenth-century depictions of Stonehenge, the pyramids of Egypt, and other then-fashionable monuments of ancient civilizations, an ordered array of rectangular pits and earthen mounds and towering rocks bearing inscrutable hieroglyphics translatable only through reference to the *Manual,* arrangements of earth, wood, and stone that finally appear more religious than utilitarian.

Of course, as we retraced our predecessors' steps, we never found anything even remotely resembling these idealized engravings. What we found—when we found anything—was a rock sticking out of the dirt at an angle that didn't quite look natural, distinguished by chips and notches that didn't quite look like the other chips and notches incurred by the less coherent processes of ice and wind and rockfall. We found scatterings of rocks that might have once been a halfhearted attempt at a mound built by a crew recruited for a month from a local Mormon hamlet and paid by the mile, not by the hour, and a pittance at that.

We occasionally found—especially in the ubiquitous desert juniper, a rugged tree slow to grow and even slower to heal—some carefully inscribed figures on a long clean blaze that pointed to where a rock corner might still stand erect, but more often we found an ambiguous scar, a puckered line in the bark that looked like a seam or a lightning strike or a healed gash where long ago a bear had sharpened its claws. The understandable haste of the surveyor who had submitted the low bid, combined with the slow yet brutal forces of erosion and the healing forces of living tissue, made it difficult for us to find these artifacts, let alone find them where they were supposed to be. We had copies of the surveyors' field notes, and we'd been provided with diagrams of the idealized landscape, the map drawn by a person who had drafted the plat two thousand miles from where the surveyors had worked; and we had the actual lines the surveyors had inscribed on the landscape, sometimes still clear and almost eternal—we could sometimes see where the line had been cut by axmen now long dead, and rock corners standing like headstones, carved with a skill and clarity that spoke of pride of workmanship—but more often the markers had returned to the dust from which they had been raised, requiring that we compute a new bearing and distance to reestablish the corner with our more durable iron pipe topped with a brass cap.

So some of what we did was running line—in order to tie in the old corners we found, we'd have to know the exact numbers that identified that point—and some of what we did was archaeology, and in this effort we were aided immeasurably by the fact that our instruments and our methods were very similar to those the original surveyor had used. After a couple of weeks of running a dependent resurvey, we had come to know the original surveyor. He would become a member of our crew, a shadowy presence. After the first dozen miles, we'd know whether he was scrupulous or sloppy; we'd know if—and by what amount—his transit had been off or his chain stretched long or kinked short.

Perhaps more important, we'd know just how trustworthy he was concerning the placement of his corners, and how diligent he had been in recording the topography his line traversed. Sometimes the notes would include (as the *Manual* required) a detailed description of the landscape intersected by his line ("at 22 ch. 3 lks. crossed small stream bearing NNW 30 degrees"), information that, if accurate, helped us a great deal in locating his rock monuments. Sometimes they'd include very little topography and suspiciously ambiguous information concerning the shape of the rock he'd placed and the number of bearing trees he'd blazed. Sometimes the notes would include copious amounts of topographical detail and marker description—most of it false, creative writing in the truest sense. It may be that the world's largest collection of unpublished fiction resides in the archives of the Cadastral Survey. One surveyor our crew followed recorded in his notes the placement of four bearing trees around an all-important township corner; re-running his original line and following photocopies of those exact notes in his own handwriting led us to a vaguely chiseled rock amid bare-rock sandstone formations, the nearest tree of any size a mile away. Some of the original surveyors were liars; some, we'd come to understand, like the guy who had not quite surveyed into Deep Shit Canyon, were just lazy or chicken.

"Don't bother looking up there," Larry told me one day. "Look over in those trees. This guy *hates* hiking up those rockslides." We referred to these surveyors in the present tense, as if they were still alive and perhaps facing charges of fraud.

It's important to understand how surveying had evolved from 1785 to 1974 in order to understand the trauma that accompanied the introduction of modern methods the summer we surveyed the Kaiparowits Plateau, when, in addition to the helicopter, we were provided with the first electronic measuring devices issued to BLM surveyors. Private surveyors had been using this technology for almost a decade, as had the minions of our great rival within the Department of the Interior, the United States Geological Survey; in the same way the government gave us four-wheel–drive vehicles only after other agencies had racked up the first forty thousand miles, we were the last to benefit from the electronic revolution, which was actually just fine with many of us.

Still, it's difficult to exaggerate the upheaval initiated by these new instruments. Over the years, chains had gotten longer, stronger, less prone to stretching or kinking; they had even lost the actual links that had defined an actual chain, but they still delivered measurements in the vocabulary they always had, so they had remained *chains,* even when they didn't look like chains any more. And they worked the way chains have always worked. One guy stood at one end, another guy at the other end, and they both pulled. If the terrain was flat and uncomplicated, you'd pull ten times, and you would have measured a mile. That was *measurement.*

Now, nobody pulled, and distances could be measured miles at a time. The new equipment—still first generation, big and heavy and clumsy—worked like this: the person formerly known as the rear chainman placed the measuring device—a flattened box about the size and shape of a briefcase—atop a necessarily huge, but unnecessarily flamboyant yellow-and-orange tripod (the Gurley's tripod legs were a more discreet oak patina, less a color than a texture). On the first day with the new equipment, Tim simply and with some awkwardness walked off into the desert dragging nothing behind him, reduced now to carrying not a chain but instead merely a small reflecting prism, a black cylinder the size and heft of a twelve-ounce Coors. When he'd reached the lath to which measurement was needed, instead of pulling and stretching and measuring the tenth-of-a-link cut, he limply held the prism over the lath I'd pounded in according to where line ran, making sure the clear glass end pointed in the right direction.

Larry's part in this exercise was similarly graceless. His job was to flip a switch, firing off infrared waves, then to wait for the electronic circuits to time the speed of their return. Instead of following the end of the Gunter's chain as it snaked deep into unsurveyed territory, Larry now stood alongside Matt, safely behind the machine (those of us at the other end who held the reflectors—usually at groin level directly over the flag—swore we could *feel* the electronic rays dissolving our prospects for parenting intact children) and skillessly turned knobs until the exact numbers of distance were indicated in neat square windows. He then turned off the machine, spoke a perfunctory "Got it" into the radio—no more colorful "cut six-tenths" call-and-response—and recorded the distance, the numbers in *feet* instead of chains and links, which seemed not just clumsy, but sacrilegious, and asked Matt for the vertical angle he'd measured through the Gurley, and computed the exact distance, converting through one last formula the embarrassment of feet into the dignity of chains.

The first day, it seemed strange, but okay. Except for that last feet-to-chains math problem, it was a *lot* less work, and it had to be more accurate. But in the days to come, we discovered a few complications, and—as in any paradigm shift—cultural disorientation.

In the first place, this much accuracy rendered the Gurley Mountain Transit the weak link in the surveying equation. Suddenly the Gurley looked very nineteenth century. And so we were provided with theodolites, instruments that looked like nothing I'd seen in the woods before. Appropriately enough, the theodolite we'd been issued was European, constructed in Switzerland by the oxymoronically named Wild Instrument Company; its laboratory-green enamel finish shone with competence and exactitude, its chrome knobs looked like they'd been appropriated from an expensive

German camera—and most disorienting of all, it had *no magnetic compass.*

Because the theodolite had an optical plumb (you looked through a tiny scope in the base that, when the instrument was properly leveled and centered, caught the lath in its crosshairs), pebbles were no longer necessary, obviating one more homey connection with local materials, and instead of the Christmas tree of exposed scales and bubble levels and the telescope-looking scope and delicately swinging compass we'd gotten used to—everything on a Gurley transit is hanging out—the theodolite *withheld,* kept its functions, its verniers, and especially its optics, concealed within its shiny, streamlined exoskeleton. I was struck dizzy with disorientation the first time I looked through the stubby scope, observing a circular slice of the Kaiparowits that was hugely magnified, unnaturally clear, and *upside-down,* making of nature something even more abstract and disconnected from what I began to doubt was really there.

Even worse, the theodolite needed pampering. We'd been careful with the Gurley, but carried it mounted on its tripod, the whole unit balanced and not uncomfortable on alternating shoulders as we walked from setup to setup. In contrast, we were forbidden to move the theodolite while it was still attached to its mount—the instrument went straight from the tripod to its protective case, a gleaming metal dome that snapped over the instrument like an army helmet, which was, in turn, enfolded in the padded compartment of a backpack custom made for the purpose.

This meant that for the first time in the history of the Cadastral Survey, we were required to labor under the burden of backpacks. Until that summer, government surveyors spent their long working days carrying everything they'd need on their belts. As I was assigned more responsibility and allotted more equipment, my own belt—webbed and grommeted and army-surplus—bulged that summer with an expanding collection of pouches and holsters. In addition to my two military-issue one-quart canteens, by the middle of the summer I spent surveying the Kaiparowits I carried a leather pouch that held pencils, a signaling mirror, and three rolls of surveyor's tape; another pouch containing a folded topo map, a fieldbook, a paperback novel, and a candy bar; a long thin pouch that holstered six chaining pins, a small ball-peen hammer, and a

file for sharpening my ax; and a smaller sheath containing the
scribe with which I'd mark bearing trees. A custom-made leather
case protected a set of numbered and lettered dies for marking
(with the hammer) the brass caps, and a thick, heavy, pre-
microchip walkie-talkie swung low in a black leather holster of its
own. I walked with the kind of bow-armed swagger associated with
steroid-addled weightlifters and overweight security guards.

These belts seemed silly at first, maybe even impractical: all
that weight around your waist squeezing your gut, chafing your
hips, and pulling down your pants (like the proverbial refrigerator
repairman, we flashed buttcracks whenever we stooped to add a
rock to a mound or scoop out a hole for burying a pipe). In my
other life as a hiker and a book-toting student, I'd comfortably
hauled similar weights in small rucksacks on my back, so it was
only because I was now trying to fit in—other than my ponytail, I
wanted to at least *look* like a surveyor—that I didn't throw all this
surveying gear into a backpack. But it started to make sense after
a while. Everything was literally at your fingertips, not at the bottom of your pack, and available as you walked, as you followed
line and searched for rock corners and bearing trees. The radio
was right there, handy as a six-shooter; the flagging in its case next
to the government-issue notebook and the paperback you'd read
when you had to wait for the rest of the crew to catch up; the file
buried deep in the skinny chaining-pin holster. It kept the sweat-
soaked back of your shirt accessible to the cooling possibilities of
evaporation; it kept your center of gravity low to offset the heft of
the Gurley on its tripod slung over your shoulder, providing balance in exchange for weight.

The year before, one summer temporary had insisted on carrying his gear in a backpack. The older surveyors joked with him
about this departure from the norm, but behind his back, over
beers at the end of the day, they discussed with surprising seriousness the implications. Needless to say, he was not rehired for a
second summer: when a tool was needed, we waited around while
he pawed through his pack like a housewife searching for keys in
her purse, and although I'm sure the survey was never slowed to
any significant degree by this behavior, it was clear he wasn't with
the program, not acting like a *surveyor.* Now, we were all in that position, having to remove our belts and wrap them around the tops
of pack frames designed to carry our new electronic equipment,

looking like backpackers, like *tourists.* What was next? Fly-fishing hats from L. L. Bean?

The advantages of this new equipment were difficult to deny: clearer optics, tighter angles, more sure distances, no more busted chains. The disadvantages we were to discover over the next several weeks. For one thing, we had a lot more stuff to carry. A chain weighed maybe ten pounds, and once you got the hang of it, you could coil it in a neat package and drape it around your neck. That first-generation distance meter weighed forty pounds, not including ten pounds of battery pack that needed charging every night, plus the massive garish yellow-and-orange tripod necessary to support all those electronic bells and whistles. This tripod didn't fit the grooves in your shoulder worn by years of balancing the Gurley; it actually had a leather handle, requiring you to carry it like a piece of luggage. The theodolite itself wasn't a lot heavier than a transit, but it was a lot fussier, and we found ourselves tiptoeing around all this fragile new equipment, worrying suddenly about breaking something very expensive to fix.

Which is exactly what Larry and I did. Only a few days after we'd been given responsibility for all this new technology—our first week in the brave new world of electronic surveying—we dropped it from the helicopter. Luckily, we dropped the least expensive component, the battery pack, but we dropped it good, and it wasn't cheap, a couple of hundred dollars worth of NiCad cells and electronic circuits. Larry and I had simply lost track of the battery as we loaded our gear onto the helicopter at the end of a particularly long workday. We'd had an equipment drill down that was practically part of the surveyors' racial memory, an inventory that had proven equally useful in loading mules *and* helicopters: transit, tripod, chain, ax. Lath, shovel, digging bar, utility belt. Government surveyors had been accounting for the presence of these specific tools for centuries, and there simply wasn't room in this equation for all this new inventory, and in the deafening roar of the helicopter—we packed equipment into shallow mesh baskets mounted only inches from the heat and whine of turbochargers and gearboxes—either Larry or I left the battery on the relatively flat surface of the helicopter's step, where it rode safely until we were a few chains (a couple of hundred feet) above the ground, when it was nudged to its death on the rocks below by the helicopter's banking turn.

."Whoops," I thought I heard Larry say over the roar of the climbing helicopter, just as I saw something flash past the corner of my
eye.

"What was that?" I shouted into his ear.

"I'd guess that was the battery," Larry yelled back. "Looks like
we forgot about it." I was much relieved and a little surprised to
hear him say "we"—Larry could easily have blamed me for not se-
curing the battery; what else, after all, are flunkies for?—but perhaps
sensing what a big pain in the ass all this newfangled equipment
would turn out to be, he seemed to take a kind of Luddite pride in
accepting responsibility himself.

Besides having to safeguard all that expensive new equipment,
we found ourselves redefining our roles, revising specific jobs
within a hierarchy as old as the profession. A survey crew was also
an apprenticeship program, and a training sequence had been usefully established regarding what had to be learned first before moving on to what was more difficult. You started as flagman, as I did,
and you learned about line. You learned your not especially difficult but still necessary skills: how to swing an ax in an arc that
didn't include your leg, for example, or how to dig a hole with two
chaining pins held together a certain way when you didn't have a
shovel. And you learned what you needed to know about the entire enterprise, a personal grasp of the surveying gestalt that eventually made you a part of the team.

After a summer or two of flagging, you advanced upward in the
hierarchy to learn the more subtle skills of chaining. In doing so,
you added expertise in measurement—*distance*—to round out your
now almost intuitive understanding of line—*bearing.* Eventually,
you became the instrument operator, the person who turned the
angles, directed the flagman for line and the chainman for distance, and as crew chief you assumed some managerial and logis-
tical responsibilities—gassing up the truck, making sure it was
loaded with the pipe, lath, and other supplies and equipment necessary for the day's work, supervising the crew when the party
chief remained in camp to complete calculations or sleep off a
hangover. It worked. Like many social arrangements that have
evolved over many years, this sequence paralleled precisely the
learning curve peculiar to land surveying.

The new technology turned all this on its head. Suddenly, the flagman—me—found himself also to be the front chainman. All that was required of the front chainman now was to carry the reflector, which the flagman could now easily do—no danger here of snagging the chain—and besides, Tim, the crew member formerly known as the front chainman, was now needed elsewhere, toward the *rear,* to help carry all those backpacks. This would have worked all right if I'd served my apprenticeship as front chain, and learned *distance* the way I'd learned *line.* I suddenly had to estimate distances without ever having learned in my bones just what eighty chains looks like in varying landscapes, to have paced the hundreds of miles necessary to gain the feeling, the intuitive, in-your-bones understanding, of how long a single mile actually *is.* I suddenly had a lot more responsibility than I wanted or was prepared for. I was scrambling up the learning curve to occupy a position I wasn't sure could be occupied, kind of like that sandstone fin in the township just north of Vernal.

And although he would never have admitted it, I could see that Larry was a little disoriented too. Like the other party chiefs/rear chainmen, he'd been for years presiding over an orderly invasion, an advance in formation against the forces of unsurveyed terrain. From the rear he'd directed a sequence of flag planting, distance measuring, and angle calculating. Now, much of the action had switched from the rear to the front, yet he needed to stay with the equipment, the source of information for his calculations. He needed to be at all fronts at once, all the while carrying some heavy baggage. No wonder we'd thrown the battery overboard, killing the monster by depriving it of its power.

But of course the monster could not be killed. In the first place, there was a spare battery, which appeared the next morning, its gray concealed beneath a new, hastily applied paint job, a lurid and difficult-to-miss shade of orange. More to the point, we'd killed the wrong component. The most important change had to do with the smallest, most apparently innocuous technological innovation: the programmable pocket calculator.

We were still a couple of summers away from that particular tragedy, but we could see the future, and it was one in which surveyors would find themselves increasingly lost in the universe at the same time they understood with increasing accuracy just where they stood on earth. Calculators hit me at exactly the wrong time, at exactly the wrong point in my apprenticeship. Sometimes

I think that if the microchip had been invented a decade later, I'd be a surveyor today, able to have made the switch from primitive to modern methods from a more secure place. I'd have known where I stood well enough to survive the dislocation that accompanies any revolution, technological or cultural, which, of course, sounds like the story of my life.

But that summer, I was still slowly learning the calculations that converted an observation of Polaris into a specific bearing, a point of location on earth, a precise direction in which to run line. It was a long, involved calculation, more difficult than I'd ever been given in my high school trig class, but the logic of it was clear. The math was hard, but I could see where all the variables fit: the long equation, with well-marked blanks for the insertion of the variables of local time converted to Greenwich time for the purpose of reading the ephemeris; the relevant angles, vertical and horizontal; the time between shots. All these pieces of necessary information were grounded in sequence in their specified places, and the equation actually spanned *on a piece of paper* the distance between Polaris and that one exact point in the southern Utah desert. In looking at this equation, which I'd copied out in pencil on a clean piece of typing paper—sideways, so I could take in the whole linear logic of the numbers and functions—I could actually see the relation each number bore to all the others, and I could see (perhaps only metaphorically, but what more true way is there to see?) where it all fit. The numbers accounted for the turning of the earth, the orbit we took around the sun, the arm of the Milky Way we clung to as it swung us around. At one end of the equation was a star a thousand light-years away. At the other end was me.

This is how a star shot was accomplished on the Hewlett Packard HP-65, the programmable calculator we were issued a couple of years later. You pushed the appropriate button, entered the correct code, and called up the equation. You never saw the actual calculating; you never even heard wheels turning, gears meshing, or watched lights flashing as computers did in 1950s science fiction movies. What you did is this: you entered numbers. The calculator would call for the variables in a specific order, and you'd punch them in. After you'd provided all these numbers, the calculator would give you your bearing. That was it. It was that simple, and it was that confusing.

Gone was the context, gone the long mathematical equation that showed the link, the connection, the logic. Gone was a complex but comprehensible sentence, the grammar of which might lead me toward a possible answer to that all-important question: where the hell *am* I? Gone was the scripture of numerology Jim Williams and I had analyzed in conversations verging on the exegetical. Instead of a flow from one necessary subset to the next, there was an impolite demand for information, and then an abrupt answer, a series of disconnected digits. As with the theodolite, the complete truth was withheld. What the calculator gave me was merely a number.

As I've said, this was difficult for me personally. Of course lot of things were difficult for me then, and so my response might be idiosyncratic, maybe even simpleminded or hopelessly neurotic, probably shortsighted, certainly exaggerated. *It's just surveying,* you might be thinking. But you'd be wrong.

Land surveyors occupy a crucial (if largely invisible) place right in the heart of the whole nature/culture conundrum because they do something *profound:* they inscribe a culture's ideas about landscape into the landscape itself. Because their practices reflect exactly their culture's beliefs about nature, the way surveyors view themselves in relation to the world has repercussions beyond the mere running of line and production of field notes. Think, for example, about how many of our Founding Fathers were surveyors (it's actually more difficult to think of more than a couple who *weren't*). At least two of them, George Washington and Thomas Jefferson, took their experiences as surveyors with them into the meetings in which the outlines of the new Republic were drawn; and half a century later, this gridded union of states was preserved through the efforts of another famous surveyor emeritus, Abraham Lincoln.

Not only have surveyors-become-leaders played an important role in pushing America's agenda across the continent; even Americans whose concerns were different from, perhaps in opposition to, the imperatives of the American experiment found themselves examining their relationship with nature through the optics of a transit. Even that famous anarchist Henry David Thoreau hired himself out as a land surveyor, when he had cash-flow

problems and was between books, and Thoreau was the lonely father of American environmentalism just as surely as Washington
and Jefferson were the proud parents of American imperialism.

It's bigger than American history. Think of the history of the
world in terms of the history of surveying. Before you do that,
think of the problems that have resulted from humans believing
they are the focal point of all existence. Think of the tragic circumstances that followed from the belief that the earth stood at
the center of the universe—ask Galileo; look up "Dark Ages" in the
encyclopedia. Think of the progress of the human race as a direct
result of our understanding ourselves in increasingly broader contexts—as inhabitants of continents we share with other cultures,
occupying a planet in a solar system that is one of many planetary
systems that contribute to the glowing band of the Milky Way running a luminescent bearing and distance above our heads. Think
of human history as an evolution from eyes-on-the-ground provin-
cialism to heads-up cosmic cosmopolitanism.

What finally results from all this thinking about context, from
our finally understanding our place in a boundless cosmos, is a
healthy combination of grandeur and humility. It helps for human
beings to have perspective. It's good to be reminded of the great
scheme of things, the vastness of the landscape—both topographical and cosmic—in which we locate our lives.

If surveyors haven't actually led the way toward discovering our
place in the universe, they've certainly done more than any platoon of physicists to bring those discoveries literally down to earth.
In examining the evolution of surveying practice, we can observe
the process by which humans have come to understand the *idea* of
place, and then to apply that understanding to locating a specific
place for ourselves in the landscape. The first surveyors drew their
bearings from the horizon, from natural and man-made landmarks—
although the builders of ziggurats and pyramids sometimes
worked hard to align their portion of Earth with the cosmos, both
personal and national property boundaries were pretty much measured against each other, and were anchored by natural features
and physical artifacts. The application of the magnetic compass to
the determination of bearing was a mighty leap forward, a truly
cosmopolitan grasp of the world, an acknowledgment that because
lines of magnetic influence transcended petty regional, even continental, concerns, it was necessary to acknowledge that nations

and cultures existed distant from your own. When the compass grew sights and became an instrument for surveying boundary lines, the magnetic pole became a constant for everyone, a point of worldwide agreement, a sense of connection with something far larger than yourself and your immediate neighborhood.

The application of solar observations to land surveying—made possible at first through the use of more accurate clocks and navigational instruments, and later by means of that remarkable piece of overcomplicated ingenuity, the Burt's Solar Compass—pushed the sense of connection further outward toward the point that defined the earth's place within our immediate neighborhood of planets. Surveys located fence lines within contexts far beyond even the earth's, and when land surveyors began shooting Polaris—the sun literally proving to be too close for the purposes of applying Enlightenment principles to the earth's landscapes—something profound happened: a line was drawn literally linking a star on the other side of our galaxy to a fence post bordering a hayfield on the outskirts of a small town in southern Utah. That's *context.*

The new instruments and methods that arrived through the seventies didn't just shift the paradigm—they *reversed* it. Among other things, the electronic calculator abstracted the equation that linked Polaris with the work of a survey, snatched it away from the surveyor and concealed it, made of the equation something electronic, no longer grammatical, no longer tactile. But something far worse was on the horizon, and I left the Cadastral Survey just in time to avoid witnessing the end of surveying as human beings had known it for millennia.

Running line by means of the Global Positioning System is the surveying equivalent of talking to yourself, never an indication of sound mental health. Indeed, the placement of artificial satellites that communicated with compass-sized receivers on the ground gave birth to something profound, and ominous, in the history of the world: it meant that one instrument was telling another instrument information regarding a human being's place on the earth. The history of the world had taken us from bearings derived from a rocky point twenty miles away; to the magnetic compass, which detected lines of magnetic influence that transcended the local to embrace the breadth of the earth itself; to the Burt's Solar Compass, that connection with our planet's own star, which established a universal context for the surveyor's work; and finally to the greatest reach of all, instruments and techniques that determined the angle connecting the line you ran with Polaris, the star you saw each night, its own position firmly located by its adjacent constellation, Ursa Major. This progress allowed surveyors to get outside ourselves and beyond our species; it reminded us daily of two profound facts: that there was something far greater than the work of the Cadastral Survey, and that our work fit in the great scheme of things, had a place in the universe that was calculable and concrete. But the GPS is a return to Dark Ages solipsism, a belief that truth can be found in chasing our own tails, using machines we've built to communicate with other machines we've built—leaving us in the undignified position of eavesdropper—and telling ourselves that's progress.

Trust me—a discussion of *Moby-Dick* will be useful here in helping us plumb the depths of this tragic step backward. Even though few of us have actually finished reading the book, most of us know the story. We know that Captain Ahab, party chief of the whaling ship *Pequod,* chased a giant white whale named Moby Dick, and in the process he went crazy, and as a result killed himself, and took his crew with him. We'll leave it to English professors to come to grips with what his insanity *means.* Of interest to surveyors, and the rest of us, is something slightly different: *how* he became insane.

The last days of the *Pequod* are punctuated by the destruction of instruments that link Ahab with the universe, and their replacement with instruments that do nothing more than reflect his madness, that deprive him of his sense of context, of connection with something bigger than himself. In chapter 118, crying, "Curse thee, thou vain toy," he throws his sextant—which for our purposes is a kind of transit gone to sea, a blue-water version of the Burt's Solar Compass—to the deck, explaining, "no longer will I guide my earthly way by thee . . . thus I trample on thee, thou paltry thing that feebly pointest on high; thus I split and destroy thee." In other words, he takes his first step toward madness by depriving himself (and his doomed ship) of the one instrument that locates him in the universe.

A few chapters later, in a regrettable action not unlike the separation of the compass from the transit that culminates in the Wild T-2 theodolite, Ahab cuts himself off from his last means of determining earthly direction: he builds his *own* compass, an instrument oriented not toward the earth's magnetic poles—as the compasses of his fellow human beings are oriented—but instead oriented according to the supernatural mumbo-jumbo of his personal harpoon, which was magnetized crazily during an electric storm. This time, Ahab is pretty straightforward about his intention to determine his own bearing independent of the lines of influence that run from magnetic pole to pole, yelling, "Look ye, for yourselves, if Ahab be not lord of the level lodestone!" Lest the reader fail to grasp just how *bad* this is, Ishmael, the book's narrator, adds, "In his fiery eyes of scorn and triumph, you then saw Ahab in all his fatal pride."

As if depriving his ship of solar and magnetic bearings were not enough, Ahab then destroys the ship's only means of determining distance. Having been told that the ship's log, a line attached to a piece of buoyant wood that, thrown overboard, measures the ship's rate of progress—the seagoing equivalent of the Gunter's chain—is defective, Ahab nevertheless throws it into a heavy sea; the line breaks, as he *knew* it would, depriving him of the measurement of distance just as surely as the crushing of the sextant deprives him of his bearing, leaving the *Pequod* in roughly the position of a survey crew gone bad, laboring with a broken transit and a busted chain, and lacking even the assistance of a dependable magnetic compass, running a crooked line under the direction of an angry and insane party chief, miles from its bunk trailers.

Ahab's madness was accelerated by his increasing isolation; already cut off from the human community, miles from his hearth, home and wife, in the final chapters he cuts himself off from everything that connected him with the earth and the cosmos and replaces these dependable instruments with a series of GPS instruments, satellites of his own devise that instead of telling him his true position in the universe, merely reflect back his own flawed perception.

Jim Williams read *Moby-Dick* long before I did, and he did his best to persuade me that it should be read, over and over again, and I know Williams wouldn't be offended by my connecting his illness with Ahab's. Like Ahab, Williams excised Greenwich Mean Time from that most important of equations, and replaced his wristwatch with his stopwatch, acting upon the delusion that chronology is *personal,* that time can be stopped and started at whim. He ceased locating himself in the landscape he could see through our transit, stopped consulting the topographical maps we could all read and agree upon, and replaced the earth's angles of convergence with the perfect but isolated angles found in a fold of paper, a map of the side of the moon none of us would ever see, and the eye of god that looked down from the apex of a pyramid, that most artificial of human constructs. All this added up to a fatal error, perhaps the most tragic mistake a human can make: Jim Williams believed that he could control time and space, the bearing and distance of reality, the two tangents that define history, that all-too-real landscape humans are fated to occupy.

I'm not saying that land surveyors are leading us into solipsistic doom. What I am saying is that, as always, surveying exists as a microcosm, a extension of broader cultural and perhaps universal values and concerns, and it means something—something profound—that surveyors today operate in a kind of virtual universe, a closed system of artificial satellites and equations they never actually see, looking through lenses that never rise above the horizon to connect themselves and their work with the stars.

After going through modern-methods disorientation for a week, our crew got a reprieve. There were only two electronic distance meters and three crews. Larry said, *Take it. We'll do fine.* We became the crew that happily continued to operate using what all of us now called "primitive methods," and I felt relieved, believing that it actually was possible to stop time, to slow the juggernaut of progress, to dodge the bullet of innovation and change. We would be doing an original survey—the same thing those lucky nineteenth-century surveyors did every working day of their lives—and we'd use their methods and their tools, ones that had adapted themselves organically to the task at hand, ones that actually mediated, I told myself, between nature and man.

Of course, our becoming the one crew using traditional tools and techniques was the result of something more complicated than our merely being reluctant to embrace the future. Nor was it that our dropping the battery from the helicopter proved that we couldn't be trusted with nice things. I think I remember there being an understanding that the other two townships had terrain more suited to the electronic equipment because there were more places to land a helicopter, and fewer opportunities to triangulate.

Also, Larry was the youngest and newest of the party chiefs, and even if he'd wanted the equipment—which I know for a fact that he didn't—he lacked the seniority that might have been the most important factor in parceling out the goodies.

On the other hand, it means something that the following summer, my third summer surveying for the BLM and working with Larry, we became once again the one crew in Utah employing primitive methods. We'd dodged the bullet one more time, and that summer gave me the enormous gift of learning to chain, and learning to run a transit according to the old rules, and with the old equipment.

I believe I became that summer the last surveyor in the United States to become fully trained in the use and maintenance of the Gunter's chain. I pulled the dooley stick—a sawed-off pickhandle connected by a six-inch leather thong to the eyelet soldered to the end of the tape—through the steep shale terrain through which threaded the White River, eighty miles south and east of Vernal, Utah, a few miles from the Colorado border, I have to admit the ugliest, grayest, most bleached-out country I'd seen anywhere. It was oil shale we were surveying now—remember oil shale? That promised salvation for America's energy woes, now an answer to a Trivial Pursuit question no one ever gets?—and my cheap-date conscience was eased a bit by the fact that I never really bonded with this gray, windswept landscape, its rugged features rendered bare and featureless in my memory.

What I was able to focus on that summer was distance. I learned—not without a great deal of hard criticism from Larry—ways to drape the chain gracefully from branches and over rocks that would allow a clear tug and a clean pull. I learned neither to leave too much droop in the chain as I pulled it taut, nor to yank the rear chainman off his feet. But most important, I learned distance. Spending the day walking exactly on line and measuring that line with dozens of legs of measurement, dozens of times repeating the sequence of drag, loosen, pull, and mark. *Eight chains!* Larry would shout, reading the final brass marker on the tape; *Cut two-tenths!* I'd shout back ritually, noting just how much more of the chain I'd pulled over the chaining pin when we'd stretched it taut. Doing that over and over again gave me a usefully intuitive sense of distance, in much the same way I'd learned to feel where line went more surely than I'd been able to reason it out. I could walk a given distance, know I'd come six chains, and the subsequent measurement would tell me I was right. I'd be able to look down a hillside and know it was seven chains to the bottom, even correcting for the vertical angle. I'd be able to lay out a base that was just short of eight chains in distance, without measuring it—bases needed to be as long as they could be measured in one pull, and I developed an ability to know just about where that base could best go. I wasn't the best chainman ever to pull a dooley stick, but I was pretty good, and I was the last.

The next summer, my fourth as a surveyor, we all had the new technology, and from then on, I'd go whole summers without even seeing a chain, let alone using one. As new summer temporaries and newly minted college-educated surveyors joined us as permanent employees, the idea of "chain" became merely a system of measurement, not an actual measuring tool. I noticed that these younger surveyors lived more completely and comfortably in the abstraction of numbers and readouts, a chain existing for them simply as a number a person arrived at by converting feet and inches into the archaic numerology of chains and links. Chains existed in infrared radiation and laser beams, invisible and ephemeral flashes of light measured by circuits, not human beings, and the only skill that was required involved knowing which button to push when.

For me, a chain will always be one-eighth of a very long steel band, evolved from corset stays and always threatening temperament, an actual physical connection across space that one sweated over and pulled against to know distance. During my last several summers as a surveyor, when distance was measured by means of pushing buttons and recording the numbers that popped up in glowing red readouts, I missed the touch of the chain, the feel of its friction along the ground, the threat of tangle, and the satisfaction of the pull.

CHAPTER FIVE

Friday Night in the Virgin Narrows

I spent that summer living a couple of lies, supported, as most lies are, by selective forgetting. I forgot as routinely as possible that although I was working for the Bureau of Land Management merely to complete the township survey mandated by public land-use legislation, I was actually serving the purposes of the resource extraction multinationals of the world and, closer to home, the power and light cartels of Arizona and California. When amnesia failed, I tried cheap rationalization. I tried to tell myself that a good rectangular survey was morally neutral: it could be used for good or for evil, for locating environmental impact reports as well as mineral leases. I kept this line of reasoning to myself. I knew just how laughable it would sound stated out loud to my colleagues, and I was getting enough crap for the length of my hair. I didn't want to subject the agonies of my conscience to public ridicule, especially this particular public.

The other lie I was living was this: that the Kaiparowits Plateau was too far from Salt Lake City to allow me to drive home each weekend, as I'd done the summer before from Vernal. When I'd explained this to Karen—that once we started the Kaiparowits job, I'd be spending weekends away—I thought I was telling her the truth about distance and possibility. Wahweap City was only a few miles away from the Arizona state line, the very foot of the very tall state of Utah, and it would be a long, long drive coming and going, and anyway, my rusted-out, oil-burning Fiat just wasn't dependable enough for all that driving. We'd made plans for her to travel south for a long weekend in July, and I promised I'd make it home every few weeks at least. And we'd write and talk on the phone. And I'd really miss her.

That only turned out to be a lie when I found myself alone each weekend in Wahweap City. Every other surveyor, every person I worked with, routinely drove the hours necessary each Friday night to reach homes as distant as mine. We began working an extra off-the-books hour Monday through Thursday so we could knock off work by midafternoon on Friday, which meant that, like my compatriots, I could have been in Salt Lake City in time for a late dinner and a movie, and Saturday would be ours, and Saturday night, and most of Sunday—I wouldn't have to leave Karen until late afternoon. I had my pick of rides, going and coming back in a variety of dependable cars, and Matt Shaw's girlfriend, who lived not far from Karen, saw him every weekend. My telling Karen that it was just too far wasn't the truth, and we both knew it.

The actual truth, only a small part of which I understood that summer, was at least as complicated as the lie. I stayed south because I wanted to spend my weekends, as well as workweeks, in the desert, which was partly about not wanting Karen the way I thought I should have, and partly about wanting some solitary time alone in the canyons. Because that is what I did, nearly every weekend: I'd wave good-bye to cars filled with surveyors heading north to wives and girlfriends, and I'd stuff my sleeping bag into my rucksack with trail mix, packets of dried soup, a box of macaroni and cheese, and a couple of canteens, and I'd commence hitchhiking down or up Highway 89, to trailheads or campgrounds or rivers in the lonely but beautiful country that surrounded the Kaiparowits Plateau.

The first weekend I'd found myself alone at the other end of the state, distant from the woman I was still pretty sure I loved, I hitchhiked to Zion National Park. I caught a ride up 89 to Carmel Junction with Matt, who was, like a *good* boyfriend, heading home for the weekend. Sticking out my thumb, I caught another ride over the summit into the park, trading hitchhiking stories with a stranger through the long tunnel and back into the fading canyon sunlight of late afternoon. It was almost dark by the time I'd managed a ride to the end of the canyon road, and in flagrant violation of federal law—I had neither permit nor stated destination, both required by the National Park Service—I waded up the Virgin River into the Narrows, less than a mile past the trailhead, at which point it started to rain. I was already soaked up to my knees, had no tent, and was not looking forward to a night wrapped in my Vietnam War–surplus poncho waiting for a flash flood to make my first solitary outing memorable. I began to get a little worried. Nobody knew where I was—I'd cavalierly told my surveying comrades that I'd go where I ended up—and the park service certainly didn't know where I was, or they'd have arrested me.

I lucked out. Looking around in the very last gleam of twilight, I made out the mouth of a shallow cave, a dark hole at the head of a high sandbar with a pretty good overhang, deep enough for me to stretch out, my feet pointing in, my head even with the cave's opening, just inside the rain dripping like a curtain from the overhang. I lit my Svea backpacking stove and boiled enough water for some soup, which I gulped down with the smashed remnants of some French bread I'd bought in Page a couple of days before. I pulled on my sleeping bag, bunched up my shorts and spare T-shirt into a pillow, and fell sound asleep.

I was awakened a few hours later by bats. I felt, more than saw or heard, them fluttering by my face, and although my fear of bats is no greater than anybody else's, visions of their landing on my head and getting tangled in the long hair Larry routinely joked about kept me deep in my sleeping bag until, unable to breathe the accumulation of carbon dioxide and hiking sweat old and recent, I stuck my head out and noticed that I couldn't hear falling rain. I wiggled my way out of the cave, stood, and still wearing the sleeping bag like a fish's tail, hopped a few yards beyond the overhang, looking up. Balanced unsteadily on the bank of drying sand, I saw stars framed between the narrow walls of Zion Canyon. I spread my poncho, stretched myself out on the sandbar, and stared past the canyon walls into the blackness of the moonless sky, the bright points of stars. There was a clarity to the sky that night I'd never seen before.

Whether this translated into more personal clarity is another story. All I knew was this: this was how I wanted to spend my weekends. This was where I needed to be, and this was whom I wanted to be with, as pathetic as that sounds. That night I began to understand a couple of things, the first being that I didn't exactly *miss* Karen. We'd been a couple for about a year and a half; we'd worked together on the McGovern campaign and then had fallen in love during the months after that horrible (if not unexpected) loss, when the old McGovern staffers, along with the campaign staff of a unexpectedly successful Democratic candidate for congress, one of whom was my roommate, got together for parties and beers, during which we itemized our hatred for Richard Nixon and gloated over the expanding revelations of Watergate. Karen was beautiful. She was tall and wore her black hair long and straight down her back, and she was quick and funny; she operated from a kind of reckless spontaneity that jostled my own more self-conscious deliberateness. As my friends were fond of pointing out to me, she was just about perfect, especially for me.

Karen hadn't backpacked very much until I met her, but she took it up happily, as if it filled some space in her life she hadn't known was vacant until I'd pointed it out. We'd spent more than a few nights like this one in the desert, making love on a gentle slope of sand under a huge dark sky, and I thought about her as I lay there alone camped in the Virgin Narrows, looking up at a more constricted wedge of dark, the memory magnifying my aloneness in a way that had a strange effect. It scared me to realize how much I liked being there by myself, not just not missing Karen but knowing that there was something deeply wrong in the way I felt about her, maybe about the way I felt about everybody, especially that summer—family, friends, coworkers, even the strangers I'd hitched rides from earlier that day. I understood then that I'd been relieved when everybody had left Wahweap for the weekend, not only content to not be going home to Karen, but also happy to find myself alone. I was prepared to make plans with somebody, especially if that somebody had a car, maybe even somebody from the missionary trailer, but as I watched the cars head north without me, I understood that this was better.

Why alone, and why in nature? I don't remember pondering this two-part question that summer, but the alone part would have been pretty easy to explain, at least superficially, and even factoring in my feelings about Karen. I'd grown up in the crowded tabernacle of Mormon life, sharing space with my family and my extended family and even my long-deceased ancestors, those pio-

neers whose trek to Utah had established a peculiar kind of closeness bred of isolation and mutual dependence, and whose polygamy had churned out family ties of overpopulated complexity.
The ward chapel I attended each Sunday, and several evenings
through the rest of the week, had seemed at least as close, crowded
with my Mormon neighbors and, it seemed, *their* ancestors as well.
In combinations ranging from Sunday-school class outings to
squads of paired missionaries, Mormons seemed to travel only in
packs. I've come to believe that Joseph Smith may well have been
both the first and *last* Mormon to seek god in nature through solitary prayer—not long after his early lonely walks into the woods
in search of truth and prophecy, he began inviting along friends
and associates to bear witness to increasingly crowded meetings
with visitors from the other world. It felt good, even luxurious, and
even a little *sinful,* to find myself alone.

And why nature? I didn't know *what* I was searching for in those
lonely weekend excursions. If it was enlightenment, I wasn't conscious of it, and in fact would have made fun of anybody who accused me of seeking out something as ostentatious, or ambitious,
or fuzzyheaded, as truth. On the other hand, I knew all too well
that my life was *lacking* something, and that if I had been able to
remedy that lack in the cheek-by-jowl Mormon crowds I'd grown
up in, or in the crowded sociability of the polygamist's bar, or the
tight fit of the bunk trailer, or even in Karen's warm bed late each
Friday night, that's where I would have been. Worse, I was at least
partly aware of the fact that these were things I was *fleeing,* that I
was putting some distance between me and anything more communal. It had taken some work to escape the comfy domesticity of
family and girlfriend in the first place, and I had to keep working
hard to escape each Friday afternoon being sucked northward in
the vortex of all those cars full of surveyors heading toward hearth
and home. I had some explaining to do, to Karen as well as to my
sometimes puzzled fellow surveyors, but I was never able to come
up with an explanation that made very much sense.

After all, I was getting plenty of nature all week long, and therefore regular weekends with Karen, in a city, would have provided
the kind of balance I might have understood to be healthy. I remember thinking that my weekends in the desert might have had
something to do with another kind of balance—work versus recre-
ation, straight lines and chainsaws versus soulful wandering and

meditation—but this was only partly true, or at least true only as far as logic or hindsight will take me.

The truth was that I *loved* surveying, even though I understood that if ever there was a love that dare not speak its name, this was the one. I'd spent the previous year—the school months that elapsed after my first summer as a surveyor—doing what I'd always done: hiking, backpacking, cross-country skiing, and voting as green as you could in those days, and alternately explaining or evading this basic contradiction in my life, an effort that culminated in a kind of intervention arranged by a group of my friends, a meeting during which I was forced to face the essential hypocrisy of my life and come to terms with my environmental incorrectness, a drunken all-night confrontation that culminated with a woman shouting at me: "How *dare* you draw lines on *nature!*"

"It's just a *job,*" I responded, exhausted, money for tuition and rent and auto repair, but even as I said the words, I knew I wasn't telling her the truth. The truth was that I enjoyed my work, was looking forward to taking it up again when school ended in the spring, and I didn't actually feel a pressing need that summer to balance my workweeks on the Kaiparowits Plateau with more gentle and less invasive weekends in other nearby natural landscapes I was under no obligation to organize or monument.

It's turned out that reading Emerson has helped a little, as sad and bookish as that might sound. Not that he helped much that summer—I knew his writings through a few short homilies excerpted from "Nature" and "Self-Reliance" in the American literature textbook I carried, mostly unread, through my junior year of high school, and like my students today, I'd found him mostly impenetrable, and when penetrated mostly self-righteous and pedantic. Like most of us, I learned my Emerson by reading Thoreau, which is to say I depended overly on Thoreau's own misreading of Emerson's essays, and suffered the consequences of Thoreau's not quite getting the point of their many conversations, through which I imagine Thoreau nodding off.

Nevertheless, *Walden* was probably the biggest influence on my budding understanding of how nature should be experienced, especially through the many ways Thoreau himself was incompletely translated by the various icons of sixties and seventies pop culture. Like everybody else in those days, I'd read "Civil Disobedience" as a scriptural guide for facing the imperatives of the Selective Service and the Vietnam War (I'm pretty sure I quoted at length from this essay in my many letters rejecting civil service offers of employment at military bases) and *Walden* as a yardstick against which I could measure my own lack of purity, not to mention lack of intelligence, given my inaction in the face of the obvious shortcomings of urban life. As a matter of fact, I sometimes think my generation's sequential reading of Thoreau had much to do with the back-to-nature impulse of the later sixties. "Civil Disobedience" having failed to halt the war in its tracks, it was time to try something else, say, escaping to the woods, and by the time I'd hitchhiked myself to Haight-Ashbury in 1970, the streets seemed depopulated, its denizens by then having retreated peacefully, I imagined, toward every available Walden Pond. All this—a little Emerson, a lot of *Walden,* some Wordsworth, as much Edward Abbey as I could get my hands on, way too much Richard Brautigan, and a progression of Sierra Club books with names like *On the Loose* and *The Place No One Knew,* Elliot Porter's elegy for Glen Canyon—encouraged me to experience nature firsthand, and brought me to the conclusion that this was the way to do it: self-reliantly, and far from the noisy distractions of cities.

I've since figured out that I misunderstood all of them, and like many other misunderstandings that have led me in one direction or another, I'm as grateful as I am embarrassed—not having a clue, or at least a rational clue, can still prompt you in a lot of useful directions, and I'm profoundly happy that I spent the summer of 1974 the way I did. Still, if I'd been paying attention, and actually read the whole long first version of "Nature," it might have helped me understand a few things, because Emerson actually was speaking to who I was that summer, a reader very much like his contemporaries, which is to say a person caught between two drastically different ways of understanding the world.

Emerson wrote for a generation raised on the assumptions of the Enlightenment, an audience even more convinced than most human beings of the physicality of the natural world—I mean, they might as well have been *surveyors*—and Emerson understood that if he wanted to lead his readers into transcendence, he had to first pay lip service to the actual rocks and trees and Walden Ponds of the physical world. The Buddha, in contrast, spoke to cultures and traditions less imbedded in the merely physical and more at home in the spiritual, and so they could pretty much skip over the material universe—a world of little relative importance, one that maybe didn't even exist in any useful or relevant way—and proceed straight to what was *important,* that being the spiritual and eternal. According to this tradition, you could approach truth anywhere: in a monastery cell, on a street corner begging for daily sustenance, even in your bedroom, contemplating a pebble on the floor, or the floor itself, for that matter, or simply the transcendent notion of *floorness.* If you really wanted to, it was okay to build a house on the shore of a lake and contemplate the cosmos there, but it was what was inside your head, inside your soul, that was important, not what you saw on your walks around the pond. Or, for that matter, hiking alone in the Zion Narrows.

Of Emerson's many students, Henry David Thoreau and I may well have been his slowest. Together we misunderstood spectacularly the prophetic conclusion to "Nature," in which Emerson finally tells us what, exactly, is *what,* exclaiming that "Nature is not fixed but fluid. Spirit alters, moulds, makes it. . . . to pure spirit it is fluid, it is volatile, it is obedient," then adding, perhaps to his later regret, "every spirit builds itself a house, and beyond its house a world, and beyond its world a heaven." I can imagine Emerson shaking his head sadly when he learned that Thoreau's response to all this visionary transcendence was to *build an actual house,* and on land owned with far too much Oedipal symbolism by Emerson himself. I can picture him probably not even bothering to point out to Henry that his language in that final chapter was *metaphorical,* if not downright visionary, and that if Thoreau been paying attention to even the essay's more accessible early sections, he would have understood that the quickest way to shortcircuit your most ambitious and transcendental goals was to tie yourself to actual real estate, even if it's owned by someone else— the Father of American Transcendentalism, say, or the National Park Service.

So it's not really Emerson's fault that the transcendental movement never actually moved more than a few miles beyond the *real* shore of the *actual* Walden Pond, the all-too-nontranscendental rocks, trees, and waters of New England, the region's flora and fauna serving finally as a kind of visual aid for the spiritually challenged. But I hadn't yet learned this from Emerson, and therefore still needed the crutch actual scenery provided, so by the time I began sticking out my thumb weekends that summer, (a) alone and (b) in nature were the ways to go, and that's how and where I went.

Why I couldn't find with Karen whatever it was I was looking for puzzled me, and I thought about her a lot that night, because being in love with her had not simply felt good—it had seemed to locate me, locate (I'm pretty sure) both of us, and I was missing that sense of solid ground. Each week of the summer before, I couldn't wait to drive home on Friday; as a fledgling surveyor, I was still getting lost on a daily basis, and the drive from Vernal to Salt Lake felt more than natural—Karen made my apartment (which I'd kept that summer and to which Karen decamped from her parents' house, where she was still living) feel like an actual home. I can still remember a good number of those weekends, and not just the hours and hours in bed, either—Friday night we'd eat at a new Mexican restaurant we'd discovered, go to a movie, or just watch late-night TV. We'd take long drives, go backpacking in the Wasatch, and, over one long weekend, in the Wind Rivers. She drove my commute to Vernal one weekend, which we spent in the motel I was living in through the workweek, and having her there reminded me of the uses to which motel rooms could be put beyond housing itinerant government employees. That first summer, spending the weekend alone was basically unthinkable as long as Karen was in the picture—I would have felt lost, and wouldn't have known what to do with myself.

So why was this summer different? Moving my stuff to Karen's apartment should have felt better than it did, for both of us. Over the past year, Karen had moved into her own apartment, and we loved the privacy it gave us—my apartment was not only crowded with roommates, it was also a kind of gathering place for friends who lived in campus dorms and other lost souls, so giving up my apartment for the summer had made sense. But I'd made sure that the guy who'd taken my room understood that I'd be back in September, and although Karen had made it clear that she wasn't ready for the big step of moving in together—having just escaped the crowded house she'd grown up in, she exulted in having her own place—she was clearly puzzled by my feeling homeless, by my acting as though my *real* home was that hot, crowded bunk trailer parked on that hardpanned lot in Wahweap City, which was to say I didn't feel at home anywhere.

I lay awake for a couple of hours that June night, hearing the muffled slap and squeak of bats flying in and out of the cave, listening to the slow suck of the Virgin River pulling itself between the narrow walls of Zion Canyon, and watching stars too clear to be sparkling, each burning with a cold intensity that scared me a little but mostly felt just right. That's what it added up to: just right. It was partly large-R Romanticism, a feeling of some possibly profound connection with that big black sky; and partly romantic with the small r, the sixties version of Byronic narcissism I'd grown up with. I'm pretty sure I knew even then that there was something sentimental and clichéd about my aloneness, my alienation, my spending a dark night of the soul for recreational purposes. But this was, I'm still certain, the real thing, one of the few times in my life I was exactly where I wanted to be, under circumstances I'd chosen myself. For better or worse and for whatever reasons, I found myself alone and almost content that night, camping illegally in the dark canyons of Zion.

CHAPTER SIX

Visitors

Focus is just about everything to the surveyor. Squinting into the transit's eyepiece and turning the knobs to center the crosshairs and magnify the details, you apprehend only a tiny framed circle of reality. It's like peering out of a tunnel, or the barrel of a gun: the rest of the world becomes peripheral and unimportant, fading into the dark that surrounds that bright round fragment of what you can see. Later, doing the calculations, you focus on the exact numbers: the degrees, minutes, and seconds of an angle; the miles, feet, and tenths of distance; the coordinates that define a precise point of intersection between the abstract and the concrete, between doing the math and running the line. Because a good survey is the result of an almost compulsive attention to detail, it's easy to forget the big picture: what it means, why it's done, how it fits in. It's easy to forget what all those bearings and distances, all those numbers, add up to.

For most surveyors, this isn't much of a problem. If you do your work well, the numbers slowly assume the shape of something tangible and familiar: a highway, a house, a white picket fence. But if you're a government surveyor, as I was, the problem of focus becomes more serious, because the particular lines we ran added up to something substantial. The current BLM *Manual of Surveying Instructions* told us only what we needed to know: the lines we measured and calculated added up to the thirty-six-square-mile grid called a township, and the lines that defined each township's boundary connected with other township boundaries to throw a precise net over the broad expanse of America. The *Manual* helped us understand that the field notes we sent in to the central office were translated into maps and documents that served a larger national purpose, but beyond that we didn't think about it too much. We seldom paused to consider the audacity and ambition of our work, the fact that our lines determined quite literally the shape of the landscape upon which the United States of America has been constructed. Surveyors worked entire summers without ever questioning the reasons for spending their days imposing Western civilization's most prized artifact—the straight line—upon the irregularity of natural landscape.

I began asking a few modest questions that second summer, probably because it was my first experience working on an original survey. The summer before, I had served as a soldier in an army of occupation, our resurveying intended merely to resupply and fortify a position already taken by surveyors a hundred years before. This summer, however, I was storming a fresh beach, a grunt enlisted in the most recent campaign advancing the five-hundred-year European invasion of the New World, using technologies and tactics that had recently—as I was to learn—been perfected in Vietnam.

We spent the day the helicopter arrived flying over the more rugged and less accessible portions of our township north of Nipple Bench, and that evening, over Warren Knowles's expensive beer, Matt and I pondered the twisted and chaotic expanse of southern Utah desert we'd been assigned, wondering out loud for the first time that summer just what the central office had in mind. We understood that the coal deposits and power plant sites were high on *somebody's* list, somebody *important,* and were the most obvious reasons why we'd been funded so lavishly for so isolated a survey, but we also knew that there was a bigger picture to be considered, and that night we talked a little about what that big picture might be.

Our discussion was prompted in part by the helicopter pilot, a slight man with thinning hair and muttonchop sideburns and a soft English accent named Alan, who turned out to be not at all like the other pilots I'd fly with over the next several years. I'd discover that most helicopter pilots working for the private companies contracted by the BLM had learned and practiced their craft only a few years earlier in Vietnam; they were invariably small, wiry men in their late twenties, and fucked-up in a variety of ways, not all of them the result of having spent a couple of years being shot at, and in return firing rockets into Vietnamese hamlets that might or might not have been sheltering the folks firing the shots. Alan was in his fifties, and was vastly calmer in temperament than the other pilots I'd encounter, and vastly more *interested* in things. Where other pilots generally napped while waiting beside their copters in the field, Alan always brought reading material, ranging from the day-old *New York Times* he managed to find somewhere— Alan was a quiet man of many secrets, one of which was the source of his *Times*—to a complete works of Shakespeare, which he'd peruse while sitting comfortably in the lawn chair that he folded and strapped to the helicopter's landing skids.

Alan was vastly experienced: in the course of his thirty years of flying, he'd accumulated tens of thousands of hours in helicopters of various sorts, often in exotic locales around the world. It took us weeks to weasel this information out of him, and the few other details about his life he'd allow—he'd go on and on about the plays of Mr. Shakespeare, or the theories of Dr. Comfort, whose book *The Joy of Sex* accompanied him into the field in lieu of the Bard's for most of one memorable week, but would say very little about his own experiences, which left him shrouded in myth and conjecture. We finally found out that although he'd been born in England, he was actually Canadian, and that he'd learned to fly in the only setting more dangerous than a helicopter zigzagging over a free-fire zone in Vietnam, which was a troop-filled glider over Normandy on D-Day. At least I *think* that's what he told us.

Alan was vague and indirect in his answers to personal questions, but he loved asking the big ones, and that's what he asked us that night in Warren's cafe: basically, *why*? Although he'd been flying people in helicopters all over the world for literally decades, including a variety of different kinds of surveyors—he told us he was taking a break from flying Geological Survey types in Alaska, enjoying the relatively mosquito-free air of the desert Southwest—we were his first "Cadastrals," and he expressed doubt, possibly feigned, about the need to survey lines that aren't actually necessary to map someplace, or build something, or fence in somebody.

"So we're just drawing straight lines, is that it? Square mile squares?"

Matt and I began filling him in about the power plant site on Nipple Bench, the coal deposits under Smoky Mountain, but Alan pointed out that these plans weren't really the point. He'd flown surveyors as they established mineral claims in the Yukon, thousand-mile-long oil pipelines in Saudi Arabia, and logging roads in Amazonia. He'd landed USGS surveyors on peaks all over the American West as they mapped and measured, and he *understood* all that. But he professed wonder, and confusion, and more than a little doubt regarding the obscure purposes of the Cadastral Survey.

I tried the approach I knew Jim Williams would have taken—the ambition, the metaphysical underpinnings, of Jefferson's grand scheme to rectangularize the breadth of America, but this didn't exactly answer the "why?" question either, which Alan kept asking, probably as a way of not telling us very much about his own history, or even his own opinion, other than shaking his head sadly and saying, not for the last time that summer, "Oh, you *Yanks.*"

Undeterred by Alan's condescension, we kept trying that night to find reasons beyond the power plant and mines, energy needs and public lands, rationales that might even transcend the Land Ordinance of 1785 and the Enlightenment's obsession with linearity, thinking hard about Alan's taunting question, thinking hard about the great scheme of things. But the next morning we began our work, began to focus on specific lines, on particular problems of mathematics or logistics, and we were only jogged into context with the arrival of visitors from the central office, the various men in white shirts and dark ties who had driven the length of Utah to keep us company for a few days and to remind us why we were there.

Our most frequent visitor that summer was Woody Sylvester, the man in charge of government surveys in the State of Utah who'd treated us to lunch in the Hotel Utah Skyroom on orientation day. Woody carried with him the anachronistic title of chief deputy U.S. surveyor the same way he wore his bushy white mustache and hand-tooled cowboy boots, as if it actually *meant* something to be in charge of surveying one of the few states in the union in which could be found unsurveyed terrain. There was something a little forced about his swagger, and yet something authentic, too. He was in the dark the way deskbound bosses are always in the dark, never quite knowing the details concerning what his workers actually *did,* yet his quick speech and medium-priced cigar somehow spoke beautifully to what we accomplished in the field and how it connected with what they made of it in the office, the ways in which our work contributed to the vast surveying project set in motion by the Land Ordinance of 1785, Thomas Jefferson's imposition of Enlightenment ideals on the previously unenlightened landscape of North America. Woody's job was to negotiate between the hard and dirty world of surveying in the field, the murky waters of the civil service, and the lingering imperatives of the American Experiment, and he did all this very well. He managed to get answers from Washington that nobody else could get, and he managed to keep his troops more or less in line as well.

We were more loosely supervised by another Sylvester, Woody's brother Craig, a man who'd worked even longer in the field than Woody but had somehow remained a *surveyor,* had stubbornly resisted being kicked upstairs into an office job. It would be difficult to imagine a greater contrast between the two: Craig had not the slightest whiff of the office about him, even though by the time I'd met him—the summer we'd inscribed into the Kaiparowits Plateau the mandates of the Land Ordinance of 1785—he was spending more time in his trailer doing calculations and writing field reports than trudging alongside us in the field.

Several days a week, however, Craig would travel among the crews, providing answers in a way that made no one feel stupid for asking the questions. Craig would chainsmoke his way through the various problems we brought him, shaking a cigarette an inch out of the pack and placing it directly between his lips, sucking the cigarette into ash without ever touching it until he dropped the butt on the ground and carefully rubbed it into the desert with the toe of his boot. He offered solutions to problems ranging from balky chainsaws to failed calculations, talking us through the procedures slowly and quietly, his directions softened with comforting phrases such as "I believe I'd . . ." or "You might try. . . ." The summer temporaries, me included, thought he was the smartest man in the universe.

It was difficult for us to understand how two brothers could be so different, but as is sometimes the case, the family history helps. According to Woody, the original Sylvesters had been sent to southern Utah in 1864 for a specific purpose: the family patriarch (himself a recent arrival in Salt Lake City from England) had been called by Brigham Young on a mission to lead a Danish settlement named Elsinore into a more fluent partnership with the other Utah colonies. The Danes had been baptized in their homeland by Mormon missionaries sent from Utah, brought to the New World in ships chartered by the church, and led in wagons and handcarts across the increasingly arid breadth of America to the Mormon Zion. After a brief rest in the relative comfort of Salt Lake City, the Danes were exiled to one of the blank spots that remained on Brigham Young's map, a hot, dry corner of the Sevier River Valley just off the wagon road that connected a string of Mormon out-posts stretching ambitiously all the way to California. There they were left to figure things out for themselves, to somehow translate the Prophet's vague mandates into the building of a community, to farm the desert according to the agricultural traditions of Scandinavia.

This was a joke nearly as cruel as Iosepa, a desert ghost town that had once been home to a mournful assortment of Pacific Islanders. Mormon missionaries had sailed to Hawaii, waded ashore with their valises in one hand and the *Book of Mormon* in the other, and while availing themselves of the hospitality for which the is-lands had become famous, patiently taught their hosts to cover their breasts and pray to the god Joseph Smith had encountered in a shadowy woodlot in upstate New York (Iosepa is Hawaiian for Joseph). Like the Danes, they had been brought to Zion and sent to colonize an unsettled corner of Utah Territory, in this case a west-desert depression named Skull Valley in recognition of the unburied Indian skeletons found there by Mormon cattlemen. The town of Iosepa was laid out on terrain so parched and godforsaken as to make Elsinore seem tropical, and a good number of the Islanders died within the first several years. Many of the survivors returned to Hawaii (the Mormons eventually fortified their empire in the Pacific by constructing a temple in Hawaii, providing the permission the Islanders needed to end their exile); more than a few remained in Skull Valley, becoming inmates of Iosepa's next incarnation as Zion's first leper colony, the cluster of frame build-ings providing the combination of shelter and isolation required for lepers to linger and die. This brief experiment left enduring scars in the slow-healing landscape of Skull Valley: you can easily read the outlines of what remains today, a still-drivable arrange-ment of streets laid out in a grid oriented to the cardinal points of the compass, the familiar crisscrossing of straight lines and right angles adored by Brigham Young with an intensity matched only by Thomas Jefferson.

Things turned out better for Elsinore. The central office acted with more wisdom in saving Brigham Young's Danish experiment—word of the Danes' sunburned, frostbitten, and culture-shocked condition had made it back to the central office before they'd actually started *dying*—and according to Woody's telling of the story, Young sent his personal representative, Woody and Craig's great-grandfather, to show them the way. It must have worked, because Elsinore is today a thriving and comfortably assimilated community, the central square presided over by a prosperous brick chapel, the perfectly square blocks lined with modest but neat houses.

You don't have to search century-old records to understand the reasons for Elsinore's success: you can see from their leader's descendants, Woody and Craig, just what the original Sylvester was made of, the tools he used to whip the Danes into shape, to make of Elsinore something not so melancholy, a place more productive, more *English,* as a first step toward becoming, finally, more *American.* You could easily guess that it was part bullshit and part competence. It was a lot of keeping in touch with the central office, and it was a lot of good common sense, short, clear answers to questions that bypass the obstacles of language and culture, the directions that tell you how to force together an empire from the most alien materials.

We respected Craig Sylvester, even revered him, but we loved Woody. It was difficult to carry on an actual conversation with Craig: you'd ask him a question, and he'd answer it. Woody wouldn't wait for a question—he'd flood you with information, with stories, with gab. Woody visited his crews three or four times that summer, and each time he arrived with the bright-eyed and nervous manner of a hyperactive child, smiling and smoking his huge cigars, eager to rise early with his boys, order steak and eggs in the polygamist's cafe, join us in the helicopter flying us to line.

The first morning of the summer's first visit, Woody took the window seat as Alan ferried me to the next ridge, leaving Larry happily Woodyless with only Matt and the Gurley for company. Woody wasn't trying to be annoying, and he understood that he'd already messed up the dynamic a little—a four-man crew was ideal, there being only two seats alongside Alan in the helicopter, and we'd had to leave Tim temporarily behind. But that morning Woody had, as usual, insisted on looking through the transit, checking his reading of the angle against Matt's, and offering unasked-for advice about the usual triangulate-versus-chain question—the decision to triangulate over the deep chasm that line traversed was obvious even to me—so I'm sure Larry was relieved when Woody offered to accompany me in the helicopter for the short hop to the next ridge on line.

As we circled around possible landing sites, Woody shouted stories of his previous helicopter experiences to Alan over the helicopter's whine and roar; then, once we'd landed and I began negotiating with Matt over the radio concerning where line went and where to place the flag so that it could also be seen from where Matt and Larry were measuring a base (Alan had flown off to fetch Tim from home base), Woody just kept talking: about other surveying jobs, problems on other townships, telling me what he told all the crews, which was that we were his favorite, the best of the best, the highest scores on civil service exams, the most energy and initiative. Once the lath had been lined in and we had nothing to do until the rest of the crew caught up, Woody and I found a shady place against a sheer sandstone wall, and Woody did what he enjoyed most, which was talk about the good old days when the BLM had been the General Land Office, his earliest years surveying on horseback during the thirties and forties. I liked listening to these stories—unlike Larry, I hadn't heard them all yet—and as a bonus, his cigar smoke kept partly at bay the hardworking gnats of the Kaiparowits Plateau.

We spent the rest of the morning running line to where the quarter corner needed to be set, then on to the section corner, where we spent an hour building a good-sized mound, to which Woody contributed a couple of medium-heavy rocks. Around two o'clock Woody said, as we knew he would, *Let's head in, boys,* and that's what we did. There was drinking to be done, and that was best begun early. Even I knew how the rest of the day would go: Woody would buy rounds in Warren Knowles's bar until five, then switch to scotch in his motel room, then we'd head back to Warren's cafe for dinner. Inevitably, after a meal of the meager steaks Warren's wives served up rare, and after the requisite number of scotch rocks, Woody would tell us stories about his wartime experiences, the years he'd spent surveying the suddenly strategic Tonga Islands, a jungle paradise he described to us deep in the South Pacific.

That evening Woody felt especially effusive, describing Tonga's jungles in even more breathless terms than usual, and the work the army had sent him there to do. "Jesus, it was green, and hot," Woody said. "And wet. Rained all the time. But the surveying was *great.*"

The surveying was great. Even today, I have only a vague idea what Woody meant by this. I suppose I grew up believing everything I read in our family's *World Book Encyclopedia,* which explained that Woody's wartime experiences were played out in an archipelago "sometimes called the *Friendly Islands* because of the happy and carefree ways of the people." I knew that over the years Mormon missionaries had baptized and imported significant numbers of Tongans, and that the Salt Lake City police department currently ranked Tongan gangs among its more serious inner-city problems, the most recent expression of the unease with which Pacific Islanders have occupied the Utah landscape.

But as Woody told his stories that evening, and later that summer when he inspected the troops once again, it never occurred to any of us to ask the kind of question Alan liked to ask: *why* survey Tonga? Perhaps we didn't ask because we were surveyors, and were up to our necks in unexamined assumptions about the reasons for our work. Perhaps we didn't ask because we wanted nothing practical or even plausible to detract from the dreamy vision of tropical island utopia he'd brought to life. Long after Woody had returned to the central office, we'd talk lovingly about his surveying Tonga, reconstructing the landscapes he'd painted in the smoky barroom air: a deep translucent jungle, thick green leaves and white flowers, dense canopies that filtered light like stained glass, a canvas painted by Henri Rousseau. We'd place in this paradise the young, rakish Woody he'd described in such detail so many times, his eyes shaded by a pith helmet and aviation sunglasses, sporting a thin black mustache and smoking a long, thick cigar, one arm around a brown-skinned, black-haired, and bare-breasted Gauganian girl, the other reaching for a new bottle of Cutty, another arm (we gave him all the arms he needed—this was an *icon* we were constructing) stretching gracefully to twist the knobs on the transit, turning the angles necessary to shoot the Southern Cross.

Woody spoke fondly of the Southern Cross, that constellation pointing the way to true south. I'd come to develop something akin to affection for Polaris, its near-perfect northness adding up to a point in the universe that defined truth and constancy, at least for surveyors, but the Southern Cross was something else, a cruci-form arrangement of intersecting lines that echoed the transit's crosshairs as Woody oriented himself, focused, and extended line straight through the jungle, all the while basking in the warmth of the Southern Hemisphere, always summer when it was winter in Utah. Cases of scotch, blue lagoons, half-naked unresisting women. The way Woody described it, surveying in the South Pacific was as easy and natural as fucking.

Reflection has a way of complicating even the most banal image: the hula girls' bare breasts, warehouses overflowing with cases of Cutty Sark, the Southern Cross. I've spent a lot of time thinking about Woody and his wartime experiences, and about my own years spent in the service of the Bureau of Land Manage-ment. Each fall, during the first weeks in September, when I tran-sitioned awkwardly from surveyor of the public lands to student of the world's literature, I'd think hard about what I'd been doing for those preceding three months: I'd go from pounding in surveying flags to kind of admiring those who, following Edward Abbey's rec-ommendation, yanked them from the ground. As I came slowly to understand just how Western, how European, is the laying out of grids—how connected this practice is to the displacement of native populations that favored circles over right angles, people who took comfort in cycles of growth and return and found little to recom-mend the cruel linearity of Judaeo-Christian thinking, the tri-umph of mathematics over flora and fauna—Woody's surveying of Tonga started seeming less like myth and more like history.

Missing from the fantasy we'd constructed was the fact that his work was somehow connected with a world war, with the storming of white-sand beaches, the mining of peaceful lagoons. I thought more and more about traditional cultures caught in the crosshairs, the indiscriminate shelling of enemy emplacements and native villages alike. I wondered about the role surveying played in the military, my curiosity prodded and complicated by other unexpected connections between the Pentagon and the Bureau of Land Management. For example, why was the best manual explaining the use of the instrument that replaced the Gurley transit, the Wild T-2 Theodolite, a U.S. Army publication, one volume in a series of instruction manuals that included a booklet describing for grunts fighting in Vietnam the operation of the Claymore M-18A1 Antipersonnel Mine? And it meant something, although I didn't know quite what, that with the notable exception of Alan, the helicopter pilots who flew us to our work in the field were sometimes only a few months distant from flying Hueys in Vietnam, short, tightly wound men who flew fast at treetop level, scanning the landscape through slitted suspicious eyes as if the trees and bushes concealed resistance, the unsurveyed landscape a threat to our lives.

It was another visitor from the central office, the Bureau of Land Management's safety officer, who provided some of the context for considering this problem, this shadow of connection. Roy Koerner was about Woody's age, with some of Woody's bluster but none of his good looks. Koerner looked like he'd spent a good part of his life boxing: his nose recorded a half dozen breakings, and his brows were thick and gray. Like Woody, Koerner had spent his war years in the Pacific—we'd learned this at the orientation meeting in early June, when Woody had introduced him to us without irony as the BLM's safety officer, and by the way a hell of a machine gunner in the Big Two.

Koerner enjoyed his occasional trips to the field nearly as much as Woody did, and the two often toured the front lines together, and he made his way south during Woody's second visit to Wahweap City. His ostensible mission was to supervise our safety efforts, and he spent a day flying across the Kaiparowits in order to spend a couple of hours with each crew. That afternoon we'd been running line through one of the few juniper thickets our township presented us with. Because we were swinging axes right and left and climbing trees with chainsaws to decapitate branches that blocked Matt's view, this was particularly dangerous work, but I don't remember Koerner giving us any advice or instruction, showing us any techniques, or even correcting us as we labored without hardhats and filed our axes in the direction of the blade. Instead, he described in gruesome detail accidents he'd witnessed: in his stories, limbs intercepted by poorly managed chainsaws were always too shredded to reattach, and heads impacted by rotor blades always in his tales exploded like melons. He also gave us practical advice concerning ways to sidestep those increasingly annoying post–Earth Day guidelines and rules. Koerner had only recently been transferred from a more public position directing fire operations in Utah, and I remember his telling us the best way to attack a fire in a wilderness area: you send in the 'dozers, build the roads you need and carve out wastelands of firebreaks, then say, what? That's a *wilderness* area?

That evening, after a so-so steak dinner in Warren's overpriced and underfurnished greasy spoon, Woody and Roy did a tag-team explication of the War in the Pacific. As they poured scotch into their water glasses from the bottle hidden on the seat between them, Woody told us the usual stories of his own years in the Tonga Islands, stories that made Michener seem by comparison a stolid realist, and I remember Koerner telling us about his first postwar job as a guard at Alcatraz, perhaps the only career move that would have allowed him to return to civilian life yet still wield a machine gun on a fortified island.

But Woody kept bringing us back to the War in the Pacific, telling stories that chronicled Koerner's successes as a machine gunner on islands not far from Tonga. Koerner would smile his thin level smile, teeth showing just a little, nod his head occasionally, provide technical details about the difference between the BAR that awaited the tribulations of the last days in the trunk of Warren Knowles's Lincoln and heavier machine guns of the water-cooled variety, but he left the body count to Woody. Koerner *fought his way across the Pacific Ocean,* Woody said, flicking his cigar ashes into the dim ether of the cafe as we considered this oddly biblical image, part GI Joe and part Horseman of the Apocalypse. Woody told us that Roy had stormed every important beach, was in the first wave every time.

"This man's probably killed more people than you're likely to meet in your whole life," Woody said, leaning across the table and gesturing dramatically with his cigar. "We'll never know how many—isn't that right Roy?—because Roy had more important things to do than keep track, but you fire that many bullets into that many jungles, into that many Japs—well, they add up."

Woody struggled to communicate to us just how many people our safety officer had killed. Koerner, not embarrassed by all this attention but wanting to get the facts straight, pointed out that on Iwo he'd led a crew of four, fired a machine gun that required men to feed the ammo belts and tend to the other complexities of this specific weapon, that his crew had helped carry all that equipment to where it had been needed. There was nothing modest or disingenuous in this, just a slow, careful specification of the facts as he remembered them, Koerner talking with the same measured clarity that Craig Sylvester employed in explaining the solution to a problem of surveying.

"Yes, but you aimed the weapon," Woody said quickly, "You lined up the crosshairs, and the *numbers*!" Woody waved his cigar around the room, taking in the Formica tables, the smudged mirror behind the bar, the room's dark corners.

"You could fill this room with the men Roy killed," Woody said, finally thinking—as the good surveyor he'd spent years becoming—spatially instead of merely numerically, translating numbers into acreage, surveying the boundaries of the story of death and devastation he was trying to tell. Spreading both arms as wide as the booth allowed, Woody repeated: "You could fill this *room* with the bodies, floor to ceiling, and they'd be spilling out the door." For a moment I could see all of them.

I grew up surrounded by images of World War II, absorbing the textures and colors through the focused reminiscences of the adults who presided over my childhood, the black-and-white movies that lit the afternoon channels with framed vignettes of romance and death, and later by way of those never-ending comparisons to Vietnam, the routine and finally irrelevant contrasting of a good war with a bad one. While most of these images are relatively clear and unambiguous—pictures of Pearl Harbor, the Normandy landings, even the mushroom cloud over Hiroshima still come to me with precise clarity—I had a hard time reconciling other images. I had difficulty balancing the nostalgia with the horror, the stories of romantic interludes with sexy French girls and the empty sleeves shortened with neat folds and a safety pin, the memories of heroic deeds and the continuing embarrassment of nightmares. I had trouble, in other words, reconciling the two stories I'd hear when the deputy U.S. surveyor and the BLM's safety officer visited us in the field, the two different faces of war—Woody's soft as a baby's, lucid blue eyes floating wide open above the white wisp of his mustache and the pale haze of his cigar smoke; and Koerner's craggy, broken face, sunburned and chainsmoked-dry, lined and flinty-eyed, a thin, level smile that remained disconcertingly cruel—as part of the same South Pacific story.

I was reminded of this problem one afternoon a few years ago, ten years after I'd given up surveying for good, the year I'd begun teaching a course that focused on the literature of nature and wilderness. To get a discussion going, I'd shown paired slides of contrasting landscapes: Thomas Cole's luminous Oxbow and William Jackson's stark Tetons, the rounded granite of Yosemite and the checkerboard regularity of Iowa. To these I'd added a juxtaposition from my own life: a recent slide of my family's Forest Service campsite in the Sierras, and a slide I'd taken years earlier of a survey line I'd helped cut the summer I'd worked on the Kaiparowits Plateau, a corridor of devastation we'd chainsawed across a tableland of thick junipers and piñon pines, a narrow, straight clearcut that I'm sure will be recognizable a half century from now. I explained that I'd been a government surveyor, and that this employment had given me another interesting perspective (I had become by this time fluent in the distancing syntax of academia) from which to view the relationship between human beings and the natural world we'd been investigating all semester.

After class was over, a quiet man about my age, a student who had said very little through the semester, waited to see me. A short, thin man, he'd made it clear in the few words he'd spoken during class discussions that he was *not* a literature major; he was completing a degree in math, needed this class for a general education requirement, and was working toward a teaching credential with which to tame the wilderness of the high school classroom, his weapon the dependable order of numbers, the discipline that results from struggling to find the correct answer to a given problem. He was woefully out of place in my class, resistant to even the most superficial or cynical approaches we'd taken in considering all those nature/culture complications. But now he was animated and smiling as he waited for the few remaining students to leave, finally finding something in me besides a difficult-to-defend admiration for the romances of James Fenimore Cooper and a lot of fuzzy ideas involving art and philosophy.

"I didn't know you'd been a surveyor," he said, as if I'd been holding back the evidence of my credibility he had been searching for all semester, information that might have given him the permission he'd needed to take the class seriously. I told him a little about the work I'd done for the BLM.

He told me that he'd been a surveyor too, in Vietnam, and he explained a little about his experiences there. It turned out that he'd used the same instruments I'd used, even the same olive-green Wild T-2 Theodolite, learning its use from the same army manual I'd been issued the summer Larry's crew had finally been forced to give up our worn-out transits and embrace the brave new world of inverted images and one-second accuracy.

I could easily picture this man laying out airfields, camps, access roads, the kind of surveying private surveyors do, surveying that lacks the historical context that surrounded the surveying of America's townships. Eager to define some contrasts—to put some distance between my experience and his, between me and this student that, frankly, I didn't like very much, a man whose humorless rigidity and complete lack of curiosity about cultures different from his own boded ill for his future students—I asked him if since Vietnam he'd done any land surveying, running straight lines that extended themselves according to the points of the compass, subdividing the landscape into precise rectangles.

I thought I understood where this was going. I'd been through this conversation a hundred times before and had developed the habit of delivering a preemptive (and usually unasked for) explanation of the difference between my work and the work of other surveyors. The surveyors most people see occupy construction sites, their transits set up amid the familiar clutter of highway construction or housebuilding, their crews attired in prissy fluorescent vests against the danger of passing automobiles or loaded forklifts. Government land surveyors—a breed rarer and more difficult to observe from the road—regarded this kind of surveying as fussy and inconsequential, necessary for something as mundane and domestic as laying out a house foundation but hardly in the same category as their work. To confine the breadth of one's survey to the boundaries of a building lot or the width of a highway amounted to massive underachieving, selling short the entire profession. We believed these surveyors lacked ambition.

So when I told people I'd worked summers as a surveyor, I immediately set out to correct their misconceptions. I was a *land* surveyor; more important, I'd worked for the federal government, for the Bureau of Land Management, the descendent of the original General Land Office, the only government bureau authorized to establish township boundaries. We measured our distances in miles, not feet or meters, and we spoke the antiquated vocabulary of chains and links, terms enshrined in legislation that dated to the eighteenth century. If the person I was talking to seemed interested, and if I was feeling less guilty than usual concerning the ramifications of the work I'd done each summer, I'd deliver the same lecture I was giving to this suddenly comradely student, a speech that had picked up steam in the years I'd been in graduate school and traded the vocational focus of the surveyor for the even more abstract and constricted focus of the scholar.

The speech—which had its origins in discussions Jim Williams and I had during those ominous two weeks we'd surveyed together, a version of which we'd tried out on the Canadian helicopter pilot that night in the polygamist's bar—went something like this: our lines ran for miles, and they connected everything earthly in a neat web of intersections and straight lines, lines that ran absolutely straight and at the same time, through the miracle of solid geometry, accommodated the curvature of the earth. We derived our bearings from observations of Polaris, and our distances were checked against those orderly lines of latitude and longitude that contain the planet, the north-south lines that run from pole to pole, the east-west lines that connect London with Tibet, Houston with Manila. Our work stretched from southern Utah to Polaris, from Washington, D.C., to prime meridians in every state, from the mathematical truth discovered in the Enlightenment to the section corner we'd mound with heavy rocks at that exact point our lines intersected. We weren't laying out fences over which neighbors might chat about the weather. Our kind of surveying was *ambitious,* I said, trying to define something far beyond what the military would have required of this flat-stomached, closed-minded, and in all things limited man.

But my student had nodded enthusiastically as I'd spoken, enjoying the discourse much more than most who made the mistake of asking me what I'd done summers through the seventies. "That's exactly the surveying I did in Vietnam," he said, smiling for the first time all semester. He described details I was all too familiar with, surveying straight lines that ran north and south, east and west, clearcutting vegetation to get a clear sight, laying out square-mile grids, marking intersections between straight lines with permanent monuments, even shooting Polaris to check the accuracy of his bearing, to connect the army's work in Southeast Asia with the lines that grid the globe, to account in his equations for the rotation of the earth, the movement of our solar system within the Milky Way.

I was puzzled. I wondered about something so Jeffersonian in a place so far from America, the reasons for following the directives of the Land Ordinance of 1785 all the way to a war on the other side of the world.

"I was with the artillery," he said. "We had to survey the place before we could shell it."

"Oh," I said, finally beginning to understand.

CHAPTER SEVEN

Bearing Objects

I learned about time, and about the way time flows through and beyond a person's life, from reading names and dates carved nearly a half century before into the soft white skin of a quaking aspen. I was seven years old. My family had pitched our tent in a Forest Service campsite situated where the pines and spruces of a steep mountainside gave way to the aspen groves that carpeted the gentler slopes of Snow Basin, a bowl-shaped valley high in the Wasatch Mountains of northern Utah, not far from where I grew up. Snow Basin was home in winter to a small ski resort, and when the snow melted, to campgrounds and picnic areas, and although I'd spent many winter days here, this was my first time visiting in the summer. I recognized the ridges and chutes of the surrounding mountains as the backdrop to my several years of ski school, but I was surprised to see that those groomed ski runs threading gracefully between stands of aspen and evergreens melted away each summer to reveal bulldozed scars of bare dirt and the jagged, eroded switchbacks of service roads.

I was distracted from my insight into the profound unnaturalness of a ski resort by the dates and initials that rose in deep black ridges against the pale skin of the aspens. As I walked from our campsite through the grove reading names and dates—and some more comprehensive messages like *D. G. and H. R. June 28*—I started keeping track, connecting the age of the inscription with the diameter of the tree and the depth of the black eruption that represented the tree's attempt to heal itself, a ridge of textured bark I could trace with my fingers. The most recent carvings, those from the late fifties, were easiest to read, still more green than black, still a little moist with the watery sap that oozed from beneath the tree's bark. The oldest inscriptions dated from the first decades of the century, years that had until then existed for me only in the pages of the *World Book Encyclopedia* I'd thumb through when housebound and bored, or the antique cars I'd recently taken an interest in. These scarred the bark of the largest trees, those rare aspens a foot or more in diameter.

I read out loud to myself the letters and numbers, and admired even as I struggled to make out the more elaborate and formal inscriptions of full names, some carved with flourishes that could be identified as actual handwriting preserved in neat swoops and stops, the names pushing their distinct personalities through the layered years of growth and healing, the figures asserting with surprising force and clarity the identities to which they bore witness. The lines and circles rose like welts above the almost translucent outer skin that curled and broke to the touch like papyrus, and through the slightly more substantial bark, the scars reinforcing themselves with layers of hard black wood, forcing their meaning into the present, it seemed, from deep within the inner rings, the younger life, of the tree.

To these almost unimaginably old inscriptions I added my own name and the date: *John Hales 1959.* I found a relatively unmarked tree, and as I carved circles and lines a quarter-inch wide and a half-inch deep (my older brother had explained that a mere slit disappears beneath the seamless healing of the aspen's flesh the same way the routine nicks and scrapes of my childhood melted into the fresh blank of new healthy skin), it dawned on me that other lives had existed before mine.

I suppose this shouldn't have been as overwhelming a discovery as it was. I had been introduced to historical figures in school, and I'd learned the names of family predecessors at home: the Mormon culture in which I was raised valued its ancestors, the family patriarchs of the last century who were responsible for preparing our way into eternity, guiding us into a hereafter that came across to me then as something vague and insubstantial compared to the sounds, colors, and textures of the world that overstimulated my senses every day. But as I examined one of the oldest inscriptions, one whose particular grace I wanted to replicate in my own carving, I had a sudden view of a *person,* perhaps a logger or sheepherder, wearing different clothing and living a different life than mine, but nevertheless assuming the same difficult posture as he pulled his knife through the soft white parchment of the aspen's skin, working to cut just so far and no farther, negotiating the difficult curves of the S and the 8, the awkward colliding linearity of the H. I imagined someone a century in the future pondering the message I was inscribing today. I imagined this person wondering who I had been, and what I had made of my life. At the very least, I understood that this person would know I had lived.

I'd taken quickly my first summer to the more menial of the tasks necessary to a government survey—as the newest member of the crew, I dug holes and pounded in flags where I was told—but I struggled to understand the context, unable to translate in either direction between the mathematics and the terrain, between the straight lines we were running and the crooked landscape over which we hiked. Because my conceptual disorientation sometimes led to embarrassing instances of real-world disorientation (as I said, more than a few times I'd turned up on a ridge a half mile distant from where I'd been sent), various crew members attempted to educate me. They drew diagrams in the dirt, reviewed high school geometry for me, and assigned an evening's worth of reading in the Bureau of Land Management's *Manual of Surveying Instructions,* but my disorientation continued. There were the numbers, which I understood well enough, and there was the specific piece of dirt, a precise point we'd mark with an iron pipe, blazed trees, and rock mounds. But how did they connect?

Larry finally took me aside and told me to imagine an invisible grid hovering in the air above the landscape we were surveying. Speaking slowly so as not to further confuse this overeducated college boy, he described a suspended ceiling of invisible panels, each one a mile square, defined by intersecting lines running straight from horizon to horizon, always north-south or east-west. Because the measurements we made across all that uneven ground added up to something other than a perfect mile, we recorded angles and plugged them into equations that corrected for the ups and downs of topography, the calculation finally yielding a figure that coincided with the numbers that defined the perfect grid suspended above our heads. When the calculations for east-west and north-south lines converged, when the numbers agreed upon a specific point in space, we'd translate those numbers into an exact bearing and distance, and then we'd measure our way to that spot. Then we'd mark it and move on to the next point where mathematics intersected landscape.

I continued to think about this image throughout that summer and into the next, surveying on the Kaiparowits Plateau, sometimes looking deeply into the blank blue of the southern Utah sky for traces of the grid Larry had described, and eventually surveying began to make sense. Observing the impossible distance that separated the perfect and transcendent order that hovered above from the chaotic fallen landscape anchored below had the ironic effect of allowing me to understand the possibility for connection, for contact. It even began to feel *personal:* I came to feel a little less confused concerning broader questions that similarly involved reconciling the distance between theory and practice, between meaning and experience. At rare moments that summer I could picture in the transparent atmosphere above my head a clear point of intersection between impossibly perfect lines from which dropped a kind of Platonic plumb bob that made an indentation I could almost see in the earth at my feet, an actual mark in the world I came to revere in ways far beyond what the job required.

A substantial part of the surveyor's workday is spent physically marking those points where the idealized grid intersects the actual landscape. The Ordinance of 1785 determined that surveyors laying out townships would place physical monuments marking each half mile—called a quarter corner—and each intersection between north-south and east-west lines, the section corner. The ordinance also required that these monuments be referenced by what the *Manual* calls "corner accessories": geometrical arrangements of rocks and sod, and figures inscribed into trees and rock faces. These markings and monuments are what make the survey legally unambiguous and economically useful. Land claims must begin somewhere, and a physical monument, a pile of rocks adjacent to a large vertical stone into which is carved $1/4$—the standard nineteenth-century indication of the quarter corner, the point from which a section is divided into four quarter sections—becomes in practice the starting point for fencing in a 160-acre homestead.

This act of inscription, however, adds up to something much more complicated than mere applied mathematics. Forcing together the ideal and the real—the continual occupation of government surveyors—is difficult, and not every human being has the mental balance such employment requires. One surveyor I met my first summer, a man in his mid-twenties who had completed a two-year degree in surveying and joined the BLM's Cadastral Survey with the intent of making it his life's work, would not survive his first year, something even I, with only a few months' experience, could predict. He worried too much. He focused too much on his calculations, spent too much time in the world of the ideal grid; he expected the work he did in the field to reflect precisely the mathematical equations he labored over in his motel room each night. He looked for the same kind of perfection in running line that he found in his equations: the phrase "acceptable limits of closure," written into every piece of surveying legislation since the time of the Sumerians, gave him no comfort. The other phrase we repeated constantly—"close enough for government work"—was in no way an excuse for sloppy practice (we were anything but sloppy, and we ran lines over and over again in order to discover the source of legally allowable but still troubling deviations), but a mantra we chanted to remind ourselves of the ultimate impossibility of bridging the gap between trigonometry and geography, between math and landscape, between the essence and the actual.

Of course, Ray's problem was bigger than surveying; he worried about the trim of his narrow mustache, the effectiveness of his flossing, the fidelity of his beautiful wife. The moment that great American exercise in redundancy—bed protectors for pickup trucks—hit the market, Ray had one installed in his Ford F-150. As the summer proceeded, unnaturally straight furrows lined his forehead, circles deepened under his eyes, and the morale of his crew plummeted. His surveys were neither less nor more accurate than those of his fellow party chiefs, always well within the legal limit for acceptable error, and yet he'd sleep only on weekends, driven to exhaustion by sex with his wife that was never quite climactic nor hygienic enough. The last any of us heard, he'd moved on to a very different kind of surveying, laying out foundations for industrial plants, work that involved theodolites and distances measured electronically in millimeters, not chains and links, but we all understood that he'd never get a good night's sleep until he changed his vocation completely.

The best surveyor was one who accepted error as a condition of the fallen world in which you did your work. You struggled against it, but accepted its inevitability. You understood that a survey was at least partly ephemeral, a process rather than a product. You understood better than any postmodern critic that a survey was basically a text, and as such bore a complex and undependable relation to reality.

But like any other producer of texts worth the effort, your effectiveness was directly related to your willingness to act upon the assumption that what you did *meant* something, had significance beyond the mere exercise of skill or the marking of a boundary. Like a poet or a sculptor, you believed deep within yourself that there were moments, there were actual places on earth, where text and reality intersected, and although you'd never use the word *sacred,* you'd celebrate those intersections with words and procedures that bordered on the religious. You'd want those moments, those spots of time and landscape, to endure.

As the Greeks well understood, for truth to have any meaning, it must be beautiful, and it must be eternal. Beauty I'm not so sure about, but as far as eternity is concerned, government surveyors have always been held to a high standard. The canonical *Manual of Surveying Instructions* reminded us "the law provides that the original corners established during the process of the survey shall forever remain fixed in position." Because forever is a long time, most of the work of the Cadastral Survey today involves the maintenance of corners established by the eighteenth- and nineteenth-century surveyors who had laid out the first township and section boundaries. Called a dependent resurvey, this responsibility requires surveyors to retrace the original lines, following in the footsteps of surveyors of the last century in order to locate their rock corners and replace them with brass-capped iron pipes and new corner accessories, ensuring the corner's perpetuity, at least another hundred years' worth.

During the decade I worked summers for the BLM, I participated in the retracing and rehabilitation of dozens of original surveys, an experience that taught me a great deal about the ultimate
ineffectuality of human action. I would estimate that we found
only about half of the original rock corners we searched for, and
no more than a few dozen looked the way they were supposed to
look. The manual guiding many of these nineteenth-century surveyors—the 1855 *Instructions to the Surveyors General of Public
Lands of the United States*—included beautifully engraved plates intended to illustrate the ways in which enduring monuments could
be constructed from "local materials." These plates portray giant
stone pillars, native rock hewn into obelisks and marked with chiseled divots inches deep, buried four feet in the ground and standing at least that far above, mounded in place by pyramids of stone
and earth and surrounded by arrays of shallow pits and rock walls,
the arrangements of stone and sod resembling nothing so much as
ancient temples, altars of carved rock and raised earth.

What we found when we retraced these lines, of course, was
something quite different. Between individual will and eternal
truth stands the problem of human weakness: laziness, incompetence, the still-observable consequences of awarding a job to the
contractor who submits the lowest bid. These early contract surveyors had a lot of unsurveyed landscape to cover, and they moved
fast; when their calculations revealed that they'd reached the point
where those ideal overhead lines intersected, they found the nearest rock, knocked a few chisel marks into it, half buried it, piled a
few rocks alongside, and moved on. Section corners were distinguished by chiseled hash marks representing the number of miles
to the north and west township boundaries; each quarter corner
was supposed to be marked with an actual "$1/4$," and the *Manual*
provides an example of stone-carving prowess worthy of a cathedral. In reality, a "$1/4$" still readable after a hundred years of erosion and abuse was rare enough for us to retrieve our cameras
from the truck in order to record the find for posterity. I learned
not to expect to easily find the marker I was looking for. Instead,
I'd look suspiciously at every rock larger than a football, trying to
determine whether it had been scarred by the random processes
of nature, or nicked by the halfhearted efforts of my nineteenth-
century counterpart, a teenager recruited for the summer from a

nearby settlement, a boy living in the moment, not looking toward eternity.

More often than carelessness or incompetence, however, the rock markers were done in by time and natural processes. It was sobering to see the way rocks could erode and crack in so few years; the marks even the most scrupulous surveyors carved in their monuments only served to provide purchase for ice and wind, a place from which cracks could be widened and deepened on their way to eventual sandy dissolution. The ancients understood that even the most beautiful urn would inevitably fade and collapse, made dull and brittle by the weight of time, and although the purely fictionalized lines recorded in notes and on plats and maps would survive a little longer, safe from the elements in file drawers in Washington, D.C., and in state and territorial capitals, the lines themselves could not long endure. The best surveyors understood the Sisyphean nature of their work and accepted the inevitability of error and erosion even as they fought against it.

Surveyors who were accustomed to spending summers rediscovering and remonumenting the work of predecessors long dead and buried (in graves referenced by only slightly more elaborate stone markers and corner accessories) understood something of what they were up against when taking on the rare original survey, as we did that summer on the Kaiparowits Plateau, and although we knew that our work wouldn't ultimately last forever on the ground, we still operated as though it would, that we'd be the first surveyors to actually fulfill the dictates of the *Manual* and leave marks and monuments that would "forever remain fixed in position." Our *Manual* instructed us that the best hedge against destruction was a combination of natural and artificial materials. Our most unnatural material was the iron pipe, a thick-walled, thirty-inch-long, two-and-a-half-inch-diameter tube galvanized to within an inch of its life, split into a Y at the bottom end to allow us to anchor it firmly in the ground, and topped with a thick cap of a brass alloy said to be impervious to corrosion. The cap was engraved with the warning that the might of the federal government enforced the security of this monument, and that a $250 fine would be levied against anyone who tampered with it. This threat was embossed around the perimeter of the cap; upon the blank spot in the center we inscribed the specific figures that defined the marker's position in time and space:

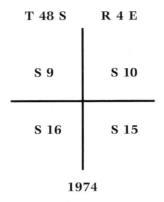

The summer before, a couple of weeks into my new job, after I'd watched and considered silently for hours (because Larry had put me on notice concerning stupid questions, I'd tried to ration the ones I actually gave voice to), I still hadn't guessed the secret behind the numbers Larry pounded into the brass caps we mounded upright every half mile.

So, with some trepidation, I asked: "Larry, what do those numbers actually *mean*?"

Apparently, *this* question *wasn't* stupid, so Larry described the arrangement of sections and the assignment of section numbers, from 1 to 36, according to an order spelled out in the *Manual,* and he explained that townships were numbered according to township numbers and range numbers. The first figures indicated the number of townships south or north of the primary east-west baseline, and the range figures indicated the number of townships east or west of the primary north-south baseline, which was called the prime meridian. A section was identified this way: S 22 T14S R6E. Translated according to the code, this specific square mile was understood to be section 22 of the township known as 14 South, Range 6 East, which meant the township was 22 townships south of the principle baseline and 6 townships east of the prime meridian.

So as not to cross the line into stupid questioning right away, I digested this information for a while. Doing the math in my head, multiplying the township numbers and range numbers by six, the number of miles that constituted each township boundary, I made a guess about where the baseline and meridians must intersect. I said it looked to me to be around Salt Lake City somewhere.

"Good," Larry said. "That's pretty close. You might surprise me and make a surveyor yet." I thought, maybe the state capitol building, but wisely kept this to myself, because Larry went on unprompted to reveal the correct answer: the two lines intersect in downtown Salt Lake City, at exactly the corner of South Temple and Main Streets, the southeast corner of Temple Square. I couldn't help it—I asked if there was some religious reason for that. Nope, Larry said. The surveying had to start somewhere, and that's where it did.

The next time I found myself in downtown Salt Lake City, I made a point of visiting the spot, partly out of curiosity, and partly because I understood the way my mind works. Some people can remain easy with an abstraction, or merely an idea, or just the knowledge that at a certain place, something happened, or something was made or destroyed there, or here someone died. Me, I have to see the place, take its physical measure, smell it, and touch it. My faith had been measurably boosted by visiting the Sacred Grove. Feeling the leafy soil give way under my feet at the exact spot where Joseph Smith had first conversed with visitors from the other world *affected* me; it started to become real then, and got me through the first few years of adolescence until more insistent doubts tugged at my sleeve and pointed me in another direction on earth. I didn't really expect to find a marker at the corner of South Temple and Main, but there it was, a beautiful four-foot-high obelisk planted at the exact corner of the high rock wall that enclosed Temple Square, sandstone the color of orange sherbet carved in glorious script *Great Salt Lake Base and Meridian* and enclosed in its own graceful little wrought iron fence.

I spent an hour that day wandering Temple Square and thinking, and I finally came to understand the Temple in a new way. This wasn't simply Mormondom's most sacred house of worship, the building I would never enter; the Temple was also an immense corner accessory, the world's largest mound of stone to the north, referencing with much dignity and skillful stonecraft the sandstone monolith marking the exact point from which all survey lines in Utah extend outward, the building's own placement determined by an observation of Polaris carved with such subtle care on the Temple's west facade in company with its Big-Dipper accessory. So this is where it all begins, I thought, and from then on, whenever I carved those numbers and letters into a bearing tree, dug a hole, or completed a calculation, I was able to picture in my mind this sandstone monument, connected to, yet located on the margins of, the gray wall that protected from outsiders the secrets of Temple Square.

Larry had let me mark a few corners that first summer, with predictably mixed results. After watching me pound out one exceptionally lousy brass cap with letters and numbers arranged with the kind of randomness that called to mind blocks spilled across the floor of an toddler's playroom, Larry ordered me thenceforth to first draw pencil lines on the copper-colored surface as a guide along which to incise the information in a more professional manner, and by the time we'd started running line on the Kaiparowits, he'd more or less turned over the marking of caps to me, everybody else regarding the duty as among the more tedious of the jobs involved in surveying. But I enjoyed the task, and flattered myself that I did it better than anybody else, mostly because I *liked* doing it and took special care. Using either the blunt end of an ax or, more conveniently and less dangerously, a small ball-peen hammer I began carrying in the chaining-pin holster that dangled from my war-surplus utility belt, I'd pound a steel die into the golden brown cap, cast from a brass/copper alloy soft enough to accept the mark but resistant to the slower forces of oxidation. After marking the cap, our instructions were to plant the split end of this unnatural object as deeply as possible, leaving eight inches protruding above the ground. If we couldn't bury it—as we often couldn't, much of Utah being solid rock naked of dirt or sand—our instructions were to build a mound of rocks sufficiently high and wide to buttress it just as firmly above the ground.

On those occasions when the precise point we established through doing the math and running the line occupied a steep hillside of exposed rock, we'd spend hours building a mound as tall as an oil barrel and half again as big around, starting several feet down the slope from the base of the pipe, necessitating a foundation four or five feet across, which we'd construct by carrying large rocks as far as we needed to, sometimes hundreds of yards. It is this lifting, hauling, and difficult masonry work that uses up a surveyor's back and contributes to the limp most older surveyors walk with. It also accounts for the experienced surveyor's sense of the way rocks work, the way natural irregularities in stones' surfaces can be made to mesh and interlock. Some fine stonemasonry can be found in the township our crew surveyed on the Kaiparowits Plateau, rock mounds that withstood the challenge of what we called the "Andy Test," a procedure named for Andy Nelson, a legendary surveyor of the generation before Larry's, a man who had whipped Larry and the other master surveyors into shape through the forties and fifties. The Andy Test required that the largest crew member balance himself on the four-inch diameter face of the brass cap and jump up and down, testing the iron pipe for looseness.

Only one mound that summer on the Kaiparowits was not evaluated according to Andy Nelson's procedures, and that was a pile of rocks surrounding a pipe perched so precariously at the edge of a cliff that to fail the test would mean not just building a new mound; it would probably mean the loss of the pipe itself, not to mention the surveyor administering the test, which would have been me. I was flattered that Larry believed enough training had been invested in me that I wasn't completely expendable. He was saving me, he said, for a greater purpose.

Soil deep enough to allow planting the pipe the necessary twenty-two inches didn't spare us from carrying rock: taking into account the fact that a mere eight inches of pipe might be easily overlooked, covered by vegetation or drifted over by sand, the *Manual* required that we stack rocks ("no fewer than five") into a pile "not less than 2 feet base and 1½ feet high." Echoing the language of the *Manual,* which employed words enshrined in surveying legislation dating back to the eighteenth century, we always referred to this as a "mound of stone." I wondered at first about the archaic formality of this phrase but soon found myself using the words, savoring the way they rolled off my tongue, language that anchored our work in the distant past and hence far into the future. I came to believe that a mound of stone carried a kind of dignity that gave it an edge against the elements, a stature that would allow its integrity to endure long after a mere pile of rocks would slump and disperse, scattered into the randomness of nature.

The other natural materials we made use of were more stationary: trees and rock faces. I'd learned from retracing earlier surveys which trees stood the test of time and which ones didn't. Quaking

aspen didn't. It was the rare aspen that survived into the distant future I'd imagined as a seven-year-old. The ease with which aspens could be inscribed was directly related to the short life span
of the species: the soft bark and the brittle, pithy wood beneath
contributed to a middle age unresistant to insects and vulnerable
to the weight of snow. We seldom found aspens that had been
marked more than twenty or thirty years before, and we used aspens
as bearing trees only when there were no other trees within range.

Juniper trees, however, were more durable than rock. A
hundred-year-old stone corner may disintegrate, being dead and
therefore subject to decay; a living tree, however, maintains its
structural integrity, and the ubiquitous desert juniper grows so
slowly and directs so little energy toward healing its wounds that
the letters and numbers a surveyor carves into the wood remain
legible long after the rock corner it bore witness to has returned to
dust. Conifers were another story—they grew quickly and put a
substantial amount of effort into closing the blaze made by the surveyor, woodflesh and bark creeping at an inch a decade to finally
enclose the cut, covering the blaze and the numbers with new pith
and bark, leaving a puckered line like an appendix scar facing the
corner.

The *Manual* regarded this healing process as serendipitous, nature's way of keeping the inscribed information safe until it was
needed, the annual layers providing a means of dating the inscription and proving its authenticity. Occasionally, if a lot depended on reestablishing a specific corner, Larry would perform
surgery. He'd reopen a healed blaze by trimming back the scar
tissue with careful swings of his ax, finally peeling the moist
membrane away from the dried and gray surface of the hundred-
year-old blaze, sometimes revealing the figures impressed backward in the newer skin of the scar tissue, a mirror image of the old
carvings. More often we'd forgo the surgery and accept clear evidence of healing as proof that the tree at hand was the one listed in
the original notes, and we'd sometimes reestablish corners based
on scars alone, more dependable than rock corners and mounds of
stone, which can be moved and scattered, either by unscrupulous
landowners or through the slow but insistent forces of nature.

Trees are rooted in the earth, however, and they stay put. Even
lightning strikes fail to move trees completely; trees can burn, rot

from within, be chopped down (sometimes by a soon-to-be-chagrined surveyor cutting line, retracing his way to the corner), and they can be cut and trimmed into posts—juniper makes a good fencepost for the same reason it makes a good bearing tree, and more than one Utah rancher's barbed wire fence is held up by a post still faithfully proclaiming the numbers associated with a distant section corner—but the stump remains many more years than you'd imagine, and a certain number of stumps the requisite distances from a center point gives the surveyor information substantial enough to reestablish a corner.

So we were careful in our original survey on the Kaiparowits Plateau to leave as many bearing trees as possible. The marking of bearing trees was generally the responsibility of the crew chief, but I eventually persuaded Larry that seeing as how I'd done okay marking the pipe, maybe I could be trusted with the trees, and I'd shown him that I could do a pretty legible job, even though it took me twice as long as my more experienced colleagues. He found another leather pouch to add to my utility belt containing a scribe, a screwdriver-like tool with a metal handle as thick as a flashlight supporting a sharp spike and, screwed to the side, a blade curved at the end into a tight "u."

I'd begin by trimming off the bark with careful axe work— aspens could be marked directly through a covering that seemed more like skin than bark, but other trees required blazing. In trimming the bark it was best to not cut into the wood itself, instead leaving exposed only the smooth, moist surface of the cambium, which provided a clean canvas for your work. You'd pull the u-shaped blade for straight lines, carving a deep, clean channel in the hard skin of the blaze. For curved segments of letters and numbers, you'd plant the spike and swing your cut around it like a compass, full circles for 0s, and linked half-circles for B's and S's. For example, a surveyor marking a section corner would carve these figures lengthwise along a foot-long blaze, indicating to the educated eye that in a northwesterly direction could be found a brass-capped iron pipe monumenting the intersecting boundaries of sections 9, 10, 15, and 16 of Township 48 South, Range 4 East:

T 48S R 4E S 16 BT

Bearing trees marked with this tool had small holes punched in the center of each curved line, the fulcrum around which the curved blade had pivoted.

When possible in referencing section corners, we'd leave four bearing trees, a tree in each section, all within a chain (sixty-six feet) of the brass cap, each blaze facing the corner. After the corner was marked and buried, the mound constructed, and the trees blazed, we would set up the transit over the brass cap, turn angles to determine the bearing to each tree, measure each distance, then record all these numbers—bearings, distances, the diameter and species of each tree, and the exact letters and numbers of each inscription—in the small yellow fieldbook:

> a juniper, 10 ins diam. bears N. 80 E., 134 1/2 links dist., mkd. T48S R4E S10 BT
> a pine, 12 ins diam., bears S. 44 1/2 E., 71 lks. dist., mkd. T48S R4E S15 BT
> a juniper, 14 ins diam., bears S. 31 W., 31 lks. dist., mkd. T48S R4E S16 BT
> a juniper, 8 ins diam., bears N. 39 1/4 W., 67 lks. dist., mkd. T48S R4E S9 BT

I'd record this information we'd punched into the soft alloy of the brass cap into Larry's yellow fieldbook, and sometimes we'd augment this record with a special notebook provided by the BLM for taking a pencil rubbing of the embossed surface, requiring me to kneel and patiently rub gray smears with the side of Larry's pencil lead until the figures I'd inscribed appeared as ghostly blanks amid the gray, serving as a primitive Xerox copy for the archives.

All these figures would be translated into more formal notes the party chiefs spent each winter typing up, a prose narrative of the summer's work that would eventually be submitted to the state office, where the story would be copied, filed, and eventually transformed into plats, the numbers now sprawled across the flat paper expanse of a map, a gridded apotheosis of landscape rising from another kind of negotiation between numbers and terrain, the ideal grid that gave up numbers easily, the fallen world we'd wrenched them from.

Sometimes we'd leave our inscriptions in stone, which was the other means mandated by the *Manual* to bear witness to the monuments we erected. There were bearing trees, and there were bearing objects, which were marks chiseled in the surfaces of rocks too large to be moved, either boulders bigger than Volkswagens (our generally agreed-upon unit of measurement) or rock faces, the revealed surfaces of the granite and sandstone mountains we surveyed across, vertical or horizontal expanses of exposed rock within a chain of the corner.

We seldom found bearing objects in our resurveys; they had not been mandated in earlier *Manual*s along with bearing trees or mounds of stones or pits. And we tended to take the often considerable time necessary to make these inscriptions only when the corner was an especially important one, or when the mound we'd built was in a precarious spot. If the corner was doomed to imminent destruction—if the corner fell on the steep dirt bank of a wash, or amid the loose talus of a constantly moving slide; or if that sacred point of intersection between the real and the ideal occurred in midair, beyond the edge of the cliff, but before the intersection hit the bottom—then we'd place a witness corner, a monument on line that featured the usual numbers plus an arrow pointing to the spot the inscription actually monumented, and the inscribed letters WC. But if we were just a little worried, if there was reason to believe the pipe would be there for a long while, but not exactly *"forever* fixed in position," we'd find a rock face, a surface as sheltered from erosion as possible, and carve these figures:

BO
X

The X was the spot we'd measure to, and turn the angle toward, as we would the surface of the blaze of a bearing tree.

Sometimes the rock would give itself easily to our inscription. I remember a couple of reference points I carved into the Kaiparowits using only the sharpened tip of a chaining pin, roughly the diameter and hardness of a tenpenny nail: I'd drag it back and forth along the B and O and X until I'd worn a channel in the sandstone a half-inch deep. But I began carrying in a pouch on my ever-heavier belt a small chisel, sharpened to carve letters four inches long, an X as big as my fist, into the more resistant limestones and granites our lines sometimes traversed.

≋

As I think about what all this means, it starts sounding like desecration, slicing utilitarian numbers into the skin of mother earth, defacing some of the most beautiful landscapes in the world. As I slowly added bearing-object experience—if not necessarily expertise—to my surveying repertoire that summer, I sometimes thought of those aspen trees in Snow Basin and, more painfully, my own pre–Earth Day contribution to canyon-wall art, of the day only a few years earlier when I'd carved my own petroglyphic initials into a sandstone wall in an offshoot of Glen Canyon twenty miles upstream from the dam, the result of both the native irresponsibility of fifteen-year-olds and an abject surrender to the powerful mojo of the river's side canyons, which had suggested Glen Canyon's name, defined its uniqueness, and determined its personality, first for John Wesley Powell and later for those few thousand hikers and rafters who followed him down the canyon before the reservoir made it both convenient and diminished. In following these branchings you entered the *glens,* the twisting slits in sandstone, the impossible mix of gloom and incandescence, of red bare rock and the green surprise of maidenhair fern growing from a dripping wall. Even today in the altered landscape of Lake Powell, side canyons continue to draw tourists in speedboats, who forsake waterskiing long enough to sightsee slowly up the dozens of dead-end canyons, still dramatic—dark, echoing, narrow—in the reduced splendor of their drowning.

That's mostly what I remember of my trip on the reservoir in 1967, only a few years after they'd stopped the drain and flooded the canyons. My father had driven our rented boat into several of these picturesquely named canyons—Cathedral, Hidden Passage, Dungeon Canyon—and when we had motored slowly up each narrowing channel as far as we dared, we'd shut off the outboard and gazed upward into the narrow crack of blue sky, listening to our muted voices amplified above the slapping of the boat's wake against the walls, the Navajo sandstone not yet stained with the whitish bathtub ring that has since become Lake Powell's purest legacy. There was something a little unnerving in those twisting caverns, a sense of our smallness in looking up, and near-blindness in looking down, looking hard into the opaque murk of lake water hundreds of feet below our keel, trying (and failing) to make out the shrouded ghosts of Glen Canyon's glens.

Bridge Canyon offered something even more dramatic than the others: Rainbow Bridge. Today, an arm of Lake Powell reaches all the way to this world-famous natural bridge, and when at capacity even laps against its base, but that summer the reservoir was still filling, and so we were required to do some hiking to reach the bridge, where I experienced one of those rare moments in tourism that results when the experience matches the hype. Rainbow Bridge wasn't just huge; I had *expected* huge, having read somewhere that you could fit the state capitol building under its span. It might have been the grace of the arc, or maybe the colors, that homey blush of cream and orange that I would be drawn to so strongly when I floated the Colorado on one of my weekends away from the Kaiparowits; or maybe it was the feel, the texture, of the stone itself, warmed by the noonday sun, the gritty sensation of crystals abrading my palm as I passed my hand over the sandstone of the bridge's abutments.

Still, I don't remember what specifically led to my committing something I understand today to be an especially obnoxious kind of vandalism. It was one of those compulsions I could do little but obey, even though I was overwrought as I did it with something more powerful than mixed feelings. It was like the time when I was six or seven, about the time I'd carved my name into the aspen at Snow Basin, when bored or possessed, I made some marks with a dark blue ballpoint pen on the bottom sheet of my bed, curious to see whether I could mark a point that would be visible only to me. Without thinking, I started connecting the points with inked lines, then expanded on the lines, drawing finally a scene, a hillside and flowers and—for reasons I still don't understand—a cross. (I was a Mormon boy, and crosses had no place in Mormon iconography. Crosses were for Catholics. We were told in Sunday school that Jesus may well have been crucified on a "T" arrangement of wood.) But I drew and drew and then suddenly realized that I'd covered with indelible ink a considerable expanse of bedsheet. I didn't bother attempting to disguise or blot out what I'd done; I went crying to my mother, confessed, told her the truth— which was simply that I'd done it and I had no idea why, an explanation so straightforward yet unhelpful that my mother was puzzled into inaction, unable to decide on a punishment or a even a warning concerning future behavior.

I'd noticed that countless visitors had carved their own names into the very base of Rainbow Bridge, and I understood that they shouldn't have done it—the word *desecration* may not have occurred to me, but I believed that they'd crossed a line. Nevertheless, this was 1967, and although I understood something about the wrongness of marking up a national monument, I wasn't any more enlightened than anyone else about where that line exists between making a mark and committing an offense. I was, after all, a Utah boy, destined within a year to blast away at his first legal deer, and I'd grown up in one of those towns along the Wasatch Front that routinely whitewashed house-sized letters on the steep hillsides above our neighborhoods representing the local high school. My family took great pride in the fact that my grandfather, a physics professor at Brigham Young University, had helped survey the huge cement Y on the mountainside above the campus, a mark that can be seen from fifty miles away still looming importantly over Provo. My friends and I routinely carved our names, and the names of girlfriends we were lucky enough to have, or optimistic or deluded enough to *think* we had, into just about any tree unlucky enough to be in our path.

And the fact is that I *loved* Glen Canyon Dam. I'd been overwhelmed during our tour through the dam itself, which we'd taken the day before, and there seemed to be no downside to what Lake Powell made possible: waterskiing one minute, motoring through the side canyons the next, hours of oohing and aahing over the convenient scenery. I appreciated having to hike less than a mile to reach Rainbow Bridge, instead of those seventeen hazardous miles from the prereservoir trailhead on the flanks of Navajo Mountain, or the weeklong raft trips that had brought a small number of tourists to the bridge before 1957. And, as I said, I'd been smitten by the dam itself. Traversing the many stairways and galleries within, you could still smell the curing cement, feel the rumble of water flowing through the penstocks, and then measure the impossible distance between the river-level observation deck where we stood and the graceful stretch of the Highway 89 bridge a thousand feet above, a distance that felt *important,* huge and otherworldly in much the same way Rainbow Bridge would strike me the following day. It would not have occurred to me then that the natural bridge and the Bureau of Reclamation dam might represent opposite forces or perspectives, conflicting ways one might define power and significance.

But I was still torn, somehow, between what seemed wrong—the dates and initials carved into Rainbow Bridge itself—and the carving I'd done without much thought all my life into a variety of natural surfaces. So I did what I've always done when troubled by the possibility of guilt and shame: I slinked away, and indulged my compulsion secretly. I found a sandstone face a hundred feet distant, facing the bridge but out of view of the tourists milling around its base, and carved *JRH* with my beat-up pocket knife into the soft Navajo sandstone, and felt triumphant at the same moment I felt guilty. Although I was worried that in addition to defacing a natural wonder, I'd maybe even broken a law, I couldn't help admiring the job I'd done, taking pride in the evenness of the letters, my ability to carve just so far and no farther, to leave clean endings to the straight letters in my name, to carve the half-circle of the J and R and stop exactly where the curve intersected the line.

Like most experiences of sin in my life, it was less an admission of failure than it was a statement of defiance, perhaps even of power. I knew I would keep my guilt to myself at the same time I knew I could find these figures when I came back as an old man, leading my grandchildren up the trail; this thought filled me a with a sense of the eternal, and at the same time a deep sense of groundedness. The sand shifted beneath my feet on a daily basis in those days, at that age when I was beginning to understand just how complex and incomprehensible the world actually was, and the knowledge that I'd made a mark that would last beyond the confusion of the moment seemed at least equal to the shame of having done it. What I'd carved into that side canyon felt permanent, undeniable, maybe even true.

Years later, while researching the history of Lake Powell in order to advocate for its draining more comprehensively, I found some help in untangling all these feelings—the mixture of disconnection and connection that seems to sum up my several early experiences with Glen Canyon—in the words of no less a postmodern theorist than Lady Bird Johnson, words she'd uttered close enough in time and space to that complicated day at Rainbow Bridge that I might have heard them still echoing between the walls of Bridge

Canyon, if only I'd been listening. The first lady had been dispatched from Washington to speak at the dam's dedication in late summer of 1966, her husband having been otherwise occupied escalating the war in Vietnam I would eventually demonstrate against so diligently, and Lady Bird's environmentalist credentials having been established by means of her heroic attempts to decommission all those unsightly billboards promoting commerce alongside the nation's rapidly expanding interstates.

The record shows that Mrs. Johnson began her speech predictably by praising the "dreamers and doers who brought this project, live-born, into its rocky cradle," and adding a few more compliments regarding the project and the men who'd inseminated it. But then Lady Bird's speech took an odd turn, abandoning childbirth metaphors for richer ones having mostly to do with vandalism: "I'm sure you all have seen, as I have, those disfigurements of rock or tree where someone with a huge ego and a tiny mind has splashed with paint or gouged with a knife to let the world know that Kilroy or John Doe was here." Mrs. Johnson paused, allowing her audience time enough perhaps to wonder just where she was going with all this talk of knife-gouging and paint-splashing and big egos. How many in her audience glanced involuntarily in the direction of Floyd Dominey, the unapologetic owner of the biggest ego around, sitting behind her on the dais? But then she continued, "As I look around at this incredibly beautiful and creative work, it occurs to me that this is a new kind of writing on the walls, a kind that says proudly and beautifully 'Man was here.'"

She may have sensed lingering disquietude among the assembled concerning the implications of the connection she'd explored between that not-quite-cuddly offspring of Floyd Dominey's huge ego, Glen Canyon Dam sitting below in its rocky cradle, and the less ambitious offspring of other huge egos such as Kilroy's or John Doe's—or John *Hales's*, she might have added—because Mrs. Johnson went on to reassure the crowd, making clear whose side she was on with regard to the big-ego question: "I am *proud* that man is here."

So Lady Bird Johnson got it, in a way. So did Jim Williams, which was another reason for me to worry about the joy I felt as a surveyor in gouging letters and numbers into rocks and trees. If anybody had plumbed the metaphysical depths of the bearing objects phenomenon, it was Williams. Earlier that summer, after we'd finally tracked him down and persuaded him to return with us to the real world, we'd left behind what must have been the most elaborate collection of corner accessories ever assembled by a surveyor in the combined histories of the General Land Office *and* the Bureau of Land Management, an arrangement of rocks, pits, sand, and wood, and even *water*—all bearing witness to the monument of Williams's own location in time and space, an intersection between the real and the transcendent he'd calculated, established, and referenced according to a *Manual of Surveying Instructions* only he'd been issued.

All this—the guilty personal history, the Earth Day paradigm shift, the example of Jim Williams—should have given me pause that summer. After all, I'd grown a little more enlightened in the years leading up to my employment as a surveyor, eventually coming to feel a degree of uneasiness remembering the hour I'd spent carving my name and the year in that quaking aspen tree, when a child camping with my family in the mountains above my home. And I didn't need Lady Bird Johnson to tell me that the blazing and gouging I did for the Cadastral Survey was something even more problematical, at the same time less personal and more political, the carving of section numbers somehow representing the whole troubling assumption that defined surveying, our scratching lines into the landscape, imposing ideas of linearity and order on nature as if it lacked character, had no internal integrity of its own. "What have we done to the earth?" Jim Morrison asked rhetorically in a song I listened to over and over again my senior year of high school, 1970, the year of the first Earth Day. His answer, which involves stabbing and biting and ripping and tying up with fences and dragging the earth down into some dark place sounded bad to me then, and it *still* sounds bad to me, looking at the whole thing from my present perspective, having since read Muir and Thoreau and taught a course in nature writing. But ambivalent I remained, as I am about much of what I did while in the employ of the Cadastral Survey.

I recognized a similar ambivalence a few years later on a field trip to the San Rafael Swell with a geology class I took during the school months that elapsed between my seasons as a surveyor. Our professor, a man who had literally written the book on Utah geology, had brought us to this rugged corner of southeastern Utah partly because the formations to be found there were representative of many of the geological processes we were being lectured on, and partly because the Swell was his old stomping grounds. He'd grown up a half century before in a tiny settlement huddled on the edge of this boundary where the Wasatch Mountains met the Colorado Plateau, and as a boy he had ridden his horse into these canyons to round up lost cattle, to let off steam, and to experience the particular joy he felt in finding fossils and arrowheads.

Our caravan of student cars and school vans stopped at a blind arch formation, a concavity in a sandstone wall that forms a gigantic alcove, the kind of natural architecture that resembles nothing so much as an arched wall in a Gothic cathedral, space filled with colorful murals that preserved Christian theology in fresco, the blending of paint and plaster, message and medium, that offered medieval artists and architects the illusion of permanence and hence the possibility of the sacred. The sandstone wall we pondered that day with our teacher was covered with a variety of small and large pictographs, graceful shapes and figures painted into the sandstone wall by the ancient people who had made their lives in this dry and tortured landscape. Right in the middle of all that ancient art, amid the human figures with long spears, the delicate running animals, the more abstract arrangements of concentric circles and intersecting lines, was a modern addition, a row of large black letters that spelled out the first initial and last name of our own geology professor.

He didn't explain right away why he'd brought us to this particularly self-incriminating blending of art and geology. He described the formation, explaining the way sandstone, formed millions of years ago under the pressure of a mile of rock overlay, peels off in arcs when exposure relieves the pressure, forming the familiar arches of southern Utah. If this process takes place in a thin blade of sandstone, the result is an arch; if it's combined with the erosive power of flowing water, if the blade interrupts the occasional flood in a streambed, the result is a natural bridge—like Rainbow Bridge, he said, making my conscience flinch a little at the example.

He then explained the day he'd encountered this wall for the first time, when he was a teenager riding his horse with his friends through the Swell. He had come to love this wall of Indian writing,

he said, and had been moved to add his own name. He said this
without exactly apologizing. I expected at least that; what I was
sure was coming was a morality tale, a story of a lifetime of guilt
and remorse, a vivid illustration of the venerable truism that you
live with the consequences of your misdeeds, that a moment of
carelessness or irresponsibility can lead to a burden of shame you
carry your whole life.

That's what I expected, but that isn't what he said, exactly. He
said of *course* I shouldn't have done it; I was young and stupid.

But he also said something I will never forget: "We believed we
belonged here, the same way these people did. We believed it was
appropriate to add our names to the wall. They'd made their mark;
we made ours," he said, and then he became our white-haired professor again, explaining the way the chemical properties of axle
grease in cooperation with the absorptive properties of sandstone
meant that his marks would occupy this wall for centuries, bearing witness to a precise moment of intersection between cultures,
a point in time and space where history collapses, where the per-
ishable breath of the individual connects for a moment with the
timelessness of landscape.

I keep pondering that statement: *We believed we belonged here.* Of
course, the difference between graffiti and art is a subtle one, having to do partly with who decides what art is, and partly with how
long the graffiti has been there. The sense of who belongs in what
landscape—and the appropriate way to celebrate that belonging—
is another tough one to figure out, and to carve one's identity into
a specific piece of earth is at the same time an expression of con-
nectedness and an admission of failure, of disorientation, a desperate attempt to pin down a feeling of connection so rare as to not
last beyond the moment.

I grew up, like my geology professor, a Mormon boy, distrusting
my body and the wildness I prayed hard to tame, and at the same
moment loving it, loving the uncontrollable joy buzzing in my
nerves, in my skin, in the wind that disturbed the air around me.
I grew up in a landscape with which my culture had cultivated a
spiritual relationship, and had also *cultivated,* wrenched from it the
raw materials from which the New Jerusalem would be built, leaving as evidence of its existence concrete-arch dams, clear-cut hillsides, and the world's largest open-pit copper mine. Beneath the

groomed surface of reverence for the Utah landscape we sang about each Sunday in church—"Our mountain home so dear / where crystal waters clear / flow ever free"—were the bulldozed gashes that served up Snow Basin's recreational possibilities.

Mormons believed they belonged in these mountains and deserts as surely as the Israelites belonged in the Land of Canaan, a gift from god that begs the question of the previous birthright, the belongingness of the people—Canaanites then, and Paiutes more recently—who had occupied the same land for centuries before, land similarly bequeathed by another deity, their own connection ritualized and documented with carved and pigmented figures on rock walls throughout the west. The landscape was both mother and father to the first Mormon settlers, a land that nurtured and also scourged my ancestors when they required scourging, which, considering the harshness of the Utah landscape, must have been pretty often. We belonged here; otherwise god wouldn't have made it so *difficult*.

How do you act on this feeling of connection—that you don't just reside here; that perhaps you've been placed here for a purpose? That beyond the specific theology that ties your culture to a particular place, your personal and individual occupation of the landscape, your own place in the world, might be an expression of something cosmic and universal?

All I know is that summer I found an unexpected and strangely familiar satisfaction in the process of inscribing numbers into the brass cap of an iron pipe, stacking rocks into a mound of stone, carving figures into the soft skin of a tree and the hard varnished surface of a sandstone face. I'd put my cheek close to the pale, smooth surface of the blaze and inhale the scent of fresh pitch as I pulled lines and circles into a phrase that spoke to a future I could never quite imagine beyond the fact of the mounded rocks, the inscribed stone, the opened bark. After turning the angles to each tree and stone, measuring distances, and combining it all into a neat mathematical web described in the prose of my fieldbook, tracing the brass cap inscriptions as if they contained some kind of truth to be preserved and pondered, I'd look with satisfaction at the job I'd done, the mark I'd made, the intersection with that ideal ethereal grid I'd found and made tangible.

At such moments eternity seems possible. You find a point of contact between the dirt at your feet and a truth that hovers beyond, a transcendent fact not exactly visible but as real as the breath you exhale. You identify that point, that moment of connection, and you mark it. You carve an X, or paint your name, or you rearrange the natural scattering of stones into something geometric and human. You carve figures into the living flesh of a tree, and for a moment you believe that life on earth—your *own* life— has meaning.

CHAPTER EIGHT

Family Men

Larry's family joined him for a couple of weeks in July. They rented a motel room across the state line in Page, Arizona, and each day after work, instead of settling in his trailer to complete the day's calculations, Larry would climb into his Blazer and drive to Page to spend the night with his family. Although I'd known, of course, that he was married and had kids—like the other married or otherwise attached surveyors that summer *other* than me, Larry had driven home to his family each weekend—this was a side of him I hadn't seen up close, the domestic, *normal* side: in addition to being a skilled if sometimes cranky party chief, he was a husband and father, a family man.

Observing Larry's nightly commute to his family in Page reminded me of how strange, even perverse, was the all-male parody of family life that populated the survey trailers in Wahweap City, a social organization that rivaled the Jesuits in its undiluted maleness. The Cadastral Survey had defined itself that way since its inception—you can search the archives in vain for any mention of female participation (beyond the occasional camp cook) in the two hundred years government surveyors had been dividing America into neat squares. Things were set to change, although we didn't know it yet: women would be added to the ranks of surveyors the following summer, at the nonnegotiable order of Department of Interior higher-ups, but that summer, our isolation from any family life other than the strange version provided by Warren

150

Knowles, his many wives, and their countless anonymous off-spring made it a little easier for me to forget that not everyone lived lives as screwed-up and solitary as mine.

The Daniels family had planned to visit various scenic attractions in northern Arizona the same weekend I'd planned to float the Colorado below Glen Canyon Dam, and because my drop-off spot was on their way, Larry offered me a ride. His beautiful wife, Suzette, and their two incredibly blond-haired children crowded themselves into the tiny backseat of Larry's Blazer so I could sit in front with my bulky packframe, and the family talk that moved back and forth over my shoulder—Larry telling his kids to stop deliberately annoying each other, then asking Suzette what she'd packed in the cooler; Suzette reminding him to stop for gas—disoriented me a little, so different was it from the surveyor talk I'd gotten used to while Larry drove his crew, his *other* family, to work.

We turned off on an unmarked road that intersected Highway 89 near the visitor center, a quarter-mile dirt path that wandered between sand dunes and over slickrock, and underneath the crackling array of high-voltage lines that angled upward from the powerhouse at the base of the dam to a fenced acre of transformers and relays on the canyon rim. The road ended near the edge of the canyon, where we all got out, walked together to the cliff's edge, and looked straight down at the river eight hundred feet below, Suzette holding her kids back from the edge with the same straight-armed crossing-guard gesture I remember my mother using to keep my little sister and me from flying through the windshield whenever she slammed on the brakes.

"Are you sure you want to do this?" Larry asked, concerned on a Saturday for my well-being in a way he had never been Monday through Friday running line. He invited me to join them on their trip through Monument Valley, an invitation as moving as it was unexpected, but the Blazer was crowded with family already, and I was looking forward to two days alone on the river. I explained that this was the easiest stretch on the entire river, less than fifteen miles, no rapids to speak of. Trying to be reassuring—Larry actually seemed a little worried, and Suzette clearly was—I added that the river only ran one direction, so I wouldn't be getting lost.

"Ah, John," Larry said, shaking his head more in sadness than in sarcasm. "If anybody could get lost on this river, I believe *you* could." As they drove off, the two Daniels children, their eyes somber, waved slowly at me through the Blazer's dusty back window.

As Larry's family disappeared behind the fenced village of transformers, I considered the river below me. I could see a nicely graded road on the other side of the canyon that emerged from a tunnel at river level, a road that allowed Bureau of Reclamation trucks to drive directly to the powerhouse, but I'd been told at the visitor's center that this route was off limits to civilians. I remember arguing that my employment in the Bureau of Land Management (a partner in Department-of-Interior crime with Reclamation) accorded me some kind of professional courtesy, but even this appeal failed to open the tunnel's doors to me, and so I'd been left with the only alternative, a vague trail that began at the head of a steep rubble-filled crack, which (I'd been told) eventually broke through the vertical canyon walls to a beach on the river. This trail wasn't especially difficult at first, even with my pack heavy with a raft constructed of rubberized canvas, the same thick material they'd used to build World War II pontoon bridges—as tiny as the raft was, it probably weighed forty pounds—but then the cleft ended in midair, leaving several hundred feet of steep, smooth sandstone between me and the narrow beach below.

I had two choices: find my own way down the sandstone face, doing some scary cheek-against-the-cliff downclimbing, or trust a frayed rope that looked like it could have been set in place by the Powell expedition. The *first* one. I remembered something more experienced climbers had told me—trust only your own ropes, the pitons you'd hammered in yourself—and I might even have had some mixed feelings about the rope's presence, as if using it might be a form of cheating, or somehow connected with what I did through the workweek that summer, so I climbed down the sloping sandstone face until I ran out of places to put my hands and feet and had to admit I was stuck.

I thought for a moment about one-armed John Wesley Powell trapped on a canyon ledge during his own voyage down the Colorado, rescued by members of his crew who'd lowered a knotted shirt and pulled him to safety. Although I had two good arms, I was without companions, so it was fortunate that I was able to climb out of my difficulty by myself. I went sheepishly to the rope, decided it wasn't so bad after all, even comforting in a human-presence kind of way, and let myself down nervously, dropping heavily the last several feet where the rope had rotted into frayed strands.

A brightly colored three-dimensional map of Lake Powell and its surrounding landscape occupies center stage in the Glen Canyon Dam Visitor Center. Bigger than a grand piano, lit by a circle of spotlights, and hovering at the level of your belt buckle, the map focuses your attention like the altar in a dark Gothic cathedral, rendering the visitor center's other offerings—postcards on racks, a slide show in a small theater to the left, restrooms down the hall, and information offered over a map-cluttered counter by uniformed employees of the National Park Service—peripheral and unimportant. Positioned to match the orientation of the actual landscape outside, the map makes you think of Chinese boxes, infinitely alternating, ever-smaller landscapes-within-visitor-centers-within-landscapes. It makes you consider the power of representation, the power of abstraction.

By mid-July I'd visited the visitor center four or five times; we stopped there sometimes on our drives into Page in search of dinners served up by someone other than a polygamous wife and bars that offered up something stronger than 3.2 beer, and each time I found myself lingering over the giant map, matching its topographical details with the actual landscape I was getting to know pretty well that summer: Nipple Butte, of course, and Wahweap Creek, and Rainbow Bridge occupying the tiny side canyon I'd defaced not that many years before. The map also previewed for me landscapes I hadn't seen, or had only observed secondhand through the flattened perspective of a USGS map. Imagining the real landscape by tracing its likeness sometimes made me think of the imperfect way the West was first understood by easterners, by General Land Office draftsmen and bureaucrats, by politicians and land speculators, as they strained to visualize the thirty-six-square-mile landscapes rendered by survey notes sent east by the hundreds each fall, the harvest of survey crews filling in the blanks, running their precise lines over the yet-unknown landscapes of the West.

It was on this visitor center map I recognized for the first time the relationship between the Straight Cliffs of the Kaiparowits Plateau and the perfect bubble of Navajo Mountain, the way together they constituted a gigantic exclamation mark, their forested blue-green heights separated by the pale orange wasteland carved by the Colorado River and its thousand tributaries. And it was on this map I began to understand the truth about Lake Powell, the unalterable finality of the way it erased forever the tangled glens and canyons that lay beneath the opaque blue paint spread flat from one end of the map to the other. Sometimes, when the National Park Service was looking the other way, I'd lean over the guardrail and trace with my finger the reservoir's ice-flat arms and channels, my nerve endings confirming the utter flatness of the reservoir, the simple two dimensions of pure *surface,* amid all the contorted orange topography that emerged from its shoreline.

I found myself obsessing on that dramatic point in the long complex sentence that is Lake Powell, where its blue waters are punctuated by the tiny gray plug of Glen Canyon Dam. You have to look closely on the visitor center's 3-D map to see it isn't a waterfall, the Colorado River spilling over a shelf of hard gray rock, but around a corner to the right, twenty feet away, you can view the real thing through the floor-to-ceiling windows of the center's overlook, and you can see that it is no waterfall. Exactly the opposite: from the overlook you see water above, and then somehow water far below, with an oversized cement-gray statement of disconnection between the two bodies of water, one paralyzed into a flat unreflective stillness, the other a boiling rapid that appears below from no source you can really see.

I eventually began paying attention to the map's topography below the dam, my eye drawn to what the shrine seemed to indicate was peripheral, lacking such amenities as marinas and campgrounds: a sheer twisting channel slicing through the orange plaster, a short deep cleft that represented what remained of Glen Canyon. It looked a little mysterious, and somehow possible.

I unrolled the raft on a damp rocky beach that had been under water only a few hours earlier. I'd consulted the tables in the visitor center to learn what I could about the vastly unnatural level of the river, which fluctuated in response to the need for lights and air-conditioning in the urban sprawls of Phoenix and Tucson, factors that determine the amount and time of release of Lake Powell water through the roaring turbines, the noise a combination of Niagara Falls and a thousand diesel trucks, a sound simultaneously whining and rumbling, noise so distracting I could hardly concentrate on inflating the raft with my small hand pump. But the raft eventually blossomed into something that seemed much lighter than it had been rolled up and carried on my back, and I took off my sneakers and waded alongside the raft into the cold clear water, water sucked from pipes near the bottom of the reservoir where it had been insulated from the warmth of the desert sun, cleared of the mud and sand that had colored the river in the tones of the desert until being slowed and stopped and rinsed clean behind the dam.

Relieved to finally be on the river, I climbed carefully into the raft and floated away from shore with a loose freedom that contrasted comfortingly with the limited choices of my climb down. After a few turns of the river between the vertical canyon walls, the roar of all that power and industry faded into silence, replaced by the sounds of the breeze and of the deep pull of the river, an almost imperceptible bass note I felt more than heard as the water eased itself beneath the thin blue membrane of the raft's floor.

I don't remember seeing more than a few people on the river that first day, leaving me to consider alone what remained of Glen Canyon, the final ten-mile segment the Bureau of Reclamation hadn't quite been able to squeeze behind their dam. The "glens" John Wesley Powell described had been sculpted by the abrasive action of water—the Colorado and its countless tributaries—cutting through a thick blanket of Navajo sandstone, the turned-to-rock remnant of an ancient desert, homogenous sand particles blown by Jurassic windstorms into drifts and dunes miles high. This fossil desert was sandwiched between rock layers with very different geological histories, origins that explain the contrasting landscapes that stand like bookends at each end of Glen Canyon. The limestones, shales, siltstones, and more layered sandstones of these formations—upstream, the Carmel, Entrada, and Morrison; downstream, the Kayenta, Chinle, and Moenkopi—were set down in shallow lakes and inland seas, aggregations of thin, muddy layers sealed flat by gravity, each layer made distinct by the different rocks and minerals eroded from distant mountains, and this variation in grit, in the size and color and hardness of the tiny rock particles, when exposed finally by two hundred million years of erosion, results in the familiar steps and plateaus of the southwestern desert, the wedding-cake formation of vertical cliffs that terminate in ramps that give way to more vertical cliffs and steeper ramps, colorfully alternating layers of materials and matrices that erode at different rates to produce the stepped buttes of Monument Valley, the banded staircases of the Grand Canyon, the alternating round and vertical surfaces that shaped the soft and hard contours of Nipple Butte.

With its vertical walls rising unstepped and unrelieved from river to sky, Glen Canyon was unlike any other section of the Colorado: in his photographic elegy to the canyon *The Place No One Knew,* Elliot Porter calls the canyon "a unique natural museum exhibiting examples of erosion found nowhere else in the world," and the fact that the doors to this very museum have been cemented shut since 1957 lies at the heart of much contemporary anger concerning Glen Canyon Dam. Instead of the stepped, gravity-flattened layers and horizontal textures that determine the shape of most desert landscape, you can see in the walled faces of Navajo sandstone the exact outlines of ancient sand dunes, a graceful layering that took place *against* the pull of gravity, a piling of blown sand upon blown sand. You see fractures that run straight for miles, cracks caused by the slow, heavy settling of the earth's crust eons after the particles had been cemented together, become concrete, transformed from a pile of shifting particles light enough to be blown hundreds of miles by the briefest of winds into a blank mass of red-orange stone, gritty as sandpaper, heavy and brittle as cinder block, the walls of a canyon that widen little if at all as they rise from the river to the canyon's rim a thousand feet straight up.

Although the narrow walls kept out any but midday sunshine, floating in a raft along the bottom of what was left of Glen Canyon left me feeling more enfolded than enclosed. The flat sandstone faces tended to reorient the light of the sun, the walls working less like curtains than lenses, shades, and mirrors to bathe the canyon floor with a soft amber light, an unusually warm, almost sentimental color, a quality of illumination lacking the hard edges of direct desert sunshine.

Because I'm plenty angry now, I wonder why I didn't feel more anger then, why I didn't focus more specifically on what was lost and invisible beneath Lake Powell's blank surface by taking in what was unfolding along the undrowned canyon walls above my head. Maybe it was that sedating soft-edged light, or the uncharacteristic gentleness of this stretch of the otherwise mighty Colorado, but I'd go hours not quite thinking of the buried expanse of similar but vastly more inspiring glens, deeper canyons, more exaggerated narrowness of sky above, views now sealed beneath the waters of Lake Powell, so taken was I by what I *could* see. Still, a difficult-to-describe sadness, more regret than either sorrow or anger, settled somewhere inside as I wondered about what was lost in the building of the dam I'd first seen as a child when it was rising from its huge concrete base, not yet backing up the Colorado, not yet flooding the canyons upstream.

Perhaps because I've never really been ahead of my time—I wasn't old enough to get much of a clue about the Vietnam War until the Nixon years, for example—I think I'd pretty much embraced the view canonized during the sixties that Lake Powell was a done deal, its defeated canyon a martyr whose bloody shirt could be waved during the pitched battles to come against future dams, but pretty much a lost cause the movement had best move beyond. That very summer, however, in a rented house in Moab, Utah, a hundred miles upstream, Edward Abbey was putting the final touches on the manuscript that would become *The Monkey Wrench Gang,* a book that gave many of us our first glimmer of possibility, of hope for a restored Glen Canyon—or, as Abbey more specifically recommends, a blown-to-bits Glen Canyon Dam—but we were still more than two decades away from anti-dam organizations and activist websites with names like "drainit.org."

And, of course, I was a surveyor, and my feelings were at least as complicated as my situation, weekends such as this one notwithstanding. Even then, I knew the connection between land surveying and environmental devastation, and I'd done some thinking about the John Wesley Powell connection. At various times I'd staked out various positions in the continuing argument over whether Powell would have endorsed or hated the reservoir that bore his name, but I understood that history had pretty much implicated me and my surveying predecessors in this crime against the river and its canyon. Expedition photographers recorded black-and-white images of Powell observing vertical canyon walls through an instrument that looks a lot like the Gurley transit my survey crew employed, a device that directed and organized the first white man's first glance at these canyons, that found numerical equivalents for the natural lines etched

into these sandstone surfaces, that took the canyon's measurements for the inevitable reservoir, the inevitable mark of the
Enlightenment on natural landscape transformed into something
located and calculated, useful and safe. Although this was only my
second summer as a surveyor, and only a few years had elapsed
since the first Earth Day, and although I was even younger in
many ways than my twenty-two years, I understood pretty well
that this is how it begins: a man looks carefully through the focused eyepiece of a transit, measures angles and distances to find
his bearing, his exact mathematical place amid the apparent chaos
of nature. It ends with a body of water—placed against nature and
logic, of a breadth and extent that can be fully apprehended only
from outer space—bearing that man's name.

If that particular irony—or, more to the point, my complicity—
wasn't lost on me, neither was the beauty. From time to time I
pulled my camera from its sandwich baggie long enough to take a
few photos, several of which I continue to show my students in
trying to bait them into taking seriously the questions that arise
when engineering meets nature. A couple of times I stripped and
slid carefully overboard, sidestroking in the water alongside the
raft, feeling chilled enough when the sun was overhead and shining directly into the canyon, but as the river turned, and the sun's
shadow fell over me, I suddenly felt the actual temperature of water
locked away from the sun at the bottom of the reservoir, water perhaps a decade old, as old as the dam itself, released only minutes
earlier into the slow thawing warmth of sunlight, water shut up in
the profoundly unnatural deep freeze of Lake Powell until it could
be used for the good of man. Then I pulled myself into the raft,
taking care to let in as little water as possible, and shivered as the
water dried on my skin.

I remember that afternoon passing quietly against pale orange
walls of Navajo sandstone, stained in dark streaks of desert varnish
and broken by blind concave arches and hanging canyons, shadowed overhangs and ledges. I should say *most* of the afternoon
passed quietly—my peace was interrupted for a minute or two by
the shattering clatter of helicopter blades, as Alan the English
(and/or Canadian) pilot hovered for a moment over my raft, paying me a visit. When I'd told him my plans for the weekend, he
said he'd check on me, but I hadn't believed him at the time, and
in fact had forgotten that he'd be flying southward for reasons of

his own, which he characteristically didn't explain. Alan routinely disconnected the Hobbs meter—the clock wired into the helicopter to keep track of billable flying hours—on weekends in order to do some of his own, more recreational flying, a practice officially frowned upon by the BLM, and forbidden by the helicopter contractor, but overlooked in Alan's case because he was otherwise such an exceptionally sober and dependable pilot.

Sober and dependable, and competent beyond comparison to any other pilot I'd fly with during the years to come, but his skill led us to several specific kinds of recklessness that were forbidden by both BLM rules and common sense. For example, Alan allowed us to do low-hover landings. A safe by-the-rules helicopter landing required that both skids be firmly grounded and the engine idling or shut down before we clambered out of the chopper's doorway, but when there wasn't ground sufficiently clear of brush or level enough to set down safely, Alan would sometimes hover a foot or two above ground while one of us stepped onto the helicopter's landing skid, and eased himself, chainsaw in hand, onto solid ground, then cut trees and arranged rocks, clearing and flattening an area large and level enough to allow a more stable (and legal) landing.

This kind of military-inspired maneuver was incredibly dangerous; we were flying a small helicopter, the bubble-cockpitted Bell 47 made famous in the M*A*S*H television series, and the removal of the weight of one surveyor, however skillfully and smoothly accomplished, left the helicopter unbalanced and bobbing way too close to rocks and trees as Alan compensated for the shift; this type of landing *should* have been forbidden, if only for the simple reason that few pilots were up to the challenge. But Alan knew that taking this risk saved us hours, sometimes even days, of hiking to line that ran distant from any certifiably safe landing zone, and he understood as few helicopter pilots did that line was *important,* even if he continued in our more philosophical after-hours discussions to question exactly why. If landing a surveyor for the purpose of building a more secure LZ was not quite as significant in the great scheme of things as landing Tommies behind enemy lines on D-Day, he still believed it was worth the risk, and with Alan it actually felt kind of safe, if heart-poundingly adventurous.

Alan would insist on maintaining eye contact with me as I took that long first step, and although I'd glance quickly at my boot as it searched nervously beneath the wavering landing skid for the ground, I'd mostly look at Alan, who would nod at precisely the moment he was ready for me to unload. As I stepped off the skid, he'd lean the stick in my direction to compensate, twist the throttle, and pull the collective, roaring immediately up and away in a cloud of stinging sand and noise.

I was always a little scared when it came my turn to practice this maneuver, but I trusted Alan, even if I didn't really understand him much of the time, and I knew he wouldn't get me killed, and not just because getting me killed during a full-hover dismount would probably get him killed as well. And so that Saturday I didn't resent the way his flying between the walls of Glen Canyon left me deafened and jostled in my raft, and reminded of the world I'd left behind that weekend. At first it sounded a little like the power plant I'd put an hour behind me, but then I made out the clap of the rotors and realized that Alan had made good on his promise, flying down the canyon less than fifty feet above the river, squeezing between canyon walls that seemed at that moment particularly narrow.

Alan paused to hover directly over my head, the chattering blades turning the water to chop and threatening to blow away the T-shirt I'd draped over the raft's edge to dry. He leaned his head and shoulder outside the bubble's doorless opening, his long thin hair a brown waving halo around his balding head, his tan safari shirt and white ascot clean and pressed as always, and gave me the quick not-quite-military salute he customarily did in the field when he'd flown in my direction and then circled as he evaluated the landing spot I'd identified hopefully as being up to his inconsistently high standards for safety and easy departure. I understood then that he really *was* checking up on me, making eye contact before zooming off downstream, tracking through the canyon's turns as if they were long swooping esses at LeMans, providing those less conflicted nature-lovers who might have been floating the Colorado that afternoon with a story they could tell back home of a lovely summer day rudely interrupted by noise and reckless menace, a vision of war and mechanical violence erasing for a moment the beauty of the brief fragile fragment of Glen Canyon that remains.

≈

A few hours later, around the time the sun's shadow had climbed to the top of the eastern wall, a little more wind had kicked up, and for the first time all day I had to paddle to keep the raft in the current, finally pulling myself toward the sheltered inside wall of a wide curve, feeling chilled and resenting a little the need to work so hard on my day off, when I'd counted on drifting passively with the current. As I made my way around the bend I could feel the wind starting to help me a little, and just ahead, where the canyon and the river widened and the current slowed, I noticed a spit of sand, a beach lit from the west with the very last rays of the afternoon sun, an unexpected gift of direct sunlight just when I'd accepted that it was gone for good.

That's where I made camp. I pulled the raft onto the sandbar, high enough I hoped to avoid its being swept away by the unnatural rise of the river, the Bureau of Reclamation's offering to the streetlights and tanning parlors of the urban Southwest. I fired up my tiny backpacking stove, a procedure that resembled too closely the lighting of a Molotov cocktail, boiled some water, made macaroni and cheese, my favorite backcountry dinner, and read a few pages in the novel I'd brought along—as I recall, F. Scott Fitzgerald's *This Side of Paradise;* I was trying that summer to finish reading the books I'd only pretended to read in my lit classes the semester before—until the last light faded to dark. I wiggled into my army-surplus mummy bag and fell asleep watching stars proceed across the narrow slice of black sky.

As I fell asleep, I thought about Karen, as I always did on nights like this one, and I began to feel a little lonely. Some of the best nights we'd had together were like this, miles from anybody else, wrapped in each other under a warm desert night, stars that seemed close enough to touch. I missed Karen that night, but I understood that it wasn't exactly the kind of loneliness you feel when you're away from somebody you love. This loneliness was something else, something I'm still not able to explain. Maybe I was getting tired of the solitary weekend story I'd written for myself. Maybe it was watching the surveyors leave each Friday, eagerly heading home for the weekend. I joked about biology, about their driving upstream to spawn, but I understood that there was something going on I couldn't help but envy—they *missed* their women and their families, missed even the company of friends who occupied a world different from the community forced upon us by this summer's surveying assignment.

Maybe it had something to do with being dropped off by Larry's family that morning, the disorientation I'd experienced as Larry conversed so domestically with his wife and kids. Why *hadn't* I taken Larry up on his offer to join them for the weekend? Whatever campground we'd have settled in tonight would have been a lot noisier and more crowded than this quiet sandbar, the stars washed out by the harsh light of Coleman lanterns and overlarge campfires, but I'd be among families, adopted for the weekend by Larry and Suzette, jostling good-naturedly with my provisional siblings. Or beyond loneliness, maybe it was just that familiar feeling of being lost. Larry's joke about my losing my way on the river might have been truer than he'd known, because that's pretty much how I felt.

I awoke as the canyon night eased into morning, curled up warm in my sleeping bag watching the dark slowly lighten to reveal the canyon walls that blocked the view upstream and down, the shadowed rock faces softened by a mist that rose from river water calm as glass, a view more like a high mountain lake than the great Colorado, then got dressed and packed, pausing only to boil water for coffee and instant oatmeal. I was on the river by six o'clock, thinking for the first time about getting to Lee's Ferry with enough daylight left to hitchhike back to the survey trailers before dark.

I'd been floating only a few minutes when I spotted a man in a canoe paddling upstream slowly against the dark eastern wall. He waved, I waved, he pulled his canoe toward me, and we floated side by side as he told me about some petroglyphs he knew about, downstream a mile or so, he said, some of the only ones left in Glen Canyon (he didn't have to mention the fact that literally thousands of petroglyphs had been buried, along with other ruins and artifacts, beneath the rising waters of the reservoir). He described in precise detail the next few turns in the river, the brief beach at the foot of a varnished cliff, the trail I'd have to walk. He was a man in his fifties, bearded, wearing a faded Stetson, making his way slowly, almost lazily, up the river. I told him thanks, and he paddled off.

His directions were easy to follow. I beached the raft on the narrow belt of sand he'd told me about and followed along the base of the wall he'd described, walking a narrow path between mesquite bushes and the bright green grasses that grew against the sandstone wall, and there they were, the petroglyphs, only a foot or two above the sand, chipped into the desert varnish that darkened a flat screen of sandstone the size of an elementary-school blackboard.

I could make out a stick figure of a man holding something long and delicate, standing next to what might be a dog, an animal whose arched spine echoed the arch of the man's legs where they met his backbone. These small figures seemed to be examining the wall's central work, a complex intersection of three curving shapes, an arrangement of circles and lines that suggested nothing so much as pure movement, simple but intense. A circle or sphere, squared slightly on one side, was the center from which curved two sweeping arms spiraling outward, as if spun away by the rotation of the central sphere. My first thought was of two whales, attached by their open jaws to the central circle, chasing each other's tails, but with slightly pointed fins rising from their backs more sharklike than whalelike; beyond that I was stumped.

I'm not sure why I worked so hard to make sense of that shape, that combination of circles and lines chipped carefully through the shiny brown varnish to reveal its design in the rough beige of a petrified sand dune. But I looked for a long time, reaching out once to measure the petroglyph against the spread of my fingers, thinking of whales, of a whale chased by a shark, or the other way around, a blur of pure motion, and then finally I saw the universe. I understood that I was looking at a galaxy, a rendering of the Milky Way, the curved arms extended gracefully as a dancer's as the collection of dust and glowing nebulae and stars—including the star around which the earth revolved—held together at the center by the communal pull of gravity at the same time they were being scattered into tapering pinwheels of centrifugal motion, still connected by birth and history to the center, yet flung apart in lonely accelerating distances measurable only in light-years. I understood then the connection with the human figure and the dog, viewing the universe they had intuited, examining their place amid all that motion, the spot occupied by their own portion of the galaxy, their own glowing arm, their own sun and planet, their home.

Of course that's not what it was. Even then I understood my presumption and my arrogance, knew that it was impossible to transcend time and culture and language to decipher what had been inscribed here. And of course I was obsessed that summer with finding my own place in the universe, slowly learning the procedures and mathematical formulas that would allow me to connect my own marked rock with a distant star. Maybe it was nothing more than a Rorschach test, but it felt *right,* and years later—years corrupted by scholarly cynicism and too much reading in critical theory—it *still* feels right. Here, at this spot, near the bottom of the canyon their people had revered long before the Sierra Club would publish coffee-table books documenting what was too late to save, through the simple act of chiseling his marks into the dark varnish of Navajo sandstone, this artist had connected the river with the stars, and perhaps with something beyond.

I spent about an hour there, sitting cross-legged on the sand and examining what by national park standards was a fairly modest example of petroglyphic art. There are walls the breadth of the Sistine Chapel, covered with herds of graceful animals, whole communities of human figures, the work of dozens of great artists over hundreds, perhaps thousands, of years. I knew that some of those walls were now deep beneath the waters of Lake Powell, and even the figures I'd seen near Nipple Butte were more elaborate, the human characters more richly suggestive. But there was something compelling, something as familiar as it was puzzling, about the slightly squared circle, the arms alternately leading and following each other in a dizzying whirl, the impossible combination of cosmic motion and complete groundedness suggested by that one small arrangement of lines and circles.

I was anxious after talking to the man in the canoe and seeing the petroglyphs—something unexpected and unlooked for—to spend some time exploring Water Holes Canyon, the only side canyon that remained unflooded in the whole stretch of Glen Canyon, the last distinctive feature before Glen Canyon itself peters out. As the river cuts its way through the lowest reaches of the Navajo formation, the flat vertical walls of orange sandstone give way to staircased layers of more conventional rock, bands of muddy sediment turned to stone of varying hardness, steps and ramps that widened the sky into something more familiar, more like the sky I was working under Monday through Friday that summer on the Kaiparowits.

But Water Holes Canyon contained the kind of scenery I'd read about, seen pictures of, and had even hoped survived, and because I'd thought through some of the significance of adding my own petroglyphic response to the crowded walls of Bridge Canyon, I knew I'd behave better this time. I worried a little about *finding* the canyon—I'd brought no map, but I had examined carefully that huge plaster representation that fills the spotlighted sanctuary of the Glen Canyon Dam Visitor Center, and I'd memorized the location of the only side canyon that remained, neither submerged upstream behind the dam, nor hanging and inaccessible in the ten miles of canyon that remained below. I remembered the problem Edward Abbey described in *Desert Solitaire* as he floated the canyon just before construction began; he'd had no map either, and found himself always on the wrong side of the river when a side canyon suddenly presented itself, so I hugged the east shore, where I believed it would turn up, and was happy when it appeared about where I'd expected it.

Tying the raft securely to some tamarisk—I didn't trust completely my memory of the Bureau of Reclamation's intentions for the river level—I stuffed my lunch and a small canteen in my rucksack and hiked my way up the sandy bottom of the canyon, and found nothing that I'd hoped for. I don't know whether it was me, or the canyon, or the time of day. My expectations weren't unreasonably high—I didn't expect it to measure up to what I'd seen in Elliot Porter's mournful book, and I remember this canyon displaying all the features that defined the side-canyon experience, if scaled down: the reddish walls of Navajo sandstone that twisted, grew alternately broad and spookily narrow, the dry bed curving against arched walls and fractured redrock faces, even the occasional seep, green plants testifying to the existence of the tiny pools that gather beneath rock fractured in just the right way.

But that day it all seemed diminished, washed out in the direct desert light of high noon. I walked slowly, stopping often to look up, to give the canyon a chance. I ate my apple-and-trail-mix lunch at a seep, finding a spot of shade against a gracefully arching sandstone wall, and focused, trying for the kind of full attention I'd felt at the petroglyph, but all I could manage here was a kind of distraction, a sense of disconnection far out of proportion to the task at hand, a simple hike up a side canyon, measuring my experience not in perceptions, but disappointments. The water I cupped in my palms was lukewarm; the walls less high than I'd imagined, the sandy floor merely flat, unrelieved by the graceful scalloped riffles Porter had so lovingly photographed. By the time I reached the last feature of Glen Canyon's offshoots—the dead end, the dry hanging waterfall that marked the canyon's abrupt elevation to a higher level—I was relieved that I'd hiked as far as I could, ready to return to the cool of the river, a little spooked.

The scene reminded me too much of a story I'd written in high school about a hermit, a man who had lodged himself in a lonely cabin up a side canyon of the Colorado, for reasons never quite made clear in the narrative. I didn't know then whether I wanted to be Edgar Allan Poe or Ernest Hemingway—the two choices that seemed available to me in my eleventh-grade creative writing course—but I knew I loved the southern Utah landscape, and only a couple of weeks before writing the story, I'd actually met a man who lived alone in a cabin in the desert. My older brother had drawn a rare late-season license to hunt deer in the Dolores Triangle, a pie slice of canyon country defined by the Dolores River's confluence with the Colorado, an expanse of landscape that includes cottonwood groves, high sandstone towers, and some rugged stepped cliffs amid which my brother succeeded in bagging a deer. We'd forded the Dolores in our jeep and had just set up camp when a smiling, wiry man walked by. He introduced himself—his name was Rusty Jarboe—and talked with us for a while, then invited us to his cabin about a half mile away for dinner.

I'm not sure why Rusty made this effort. He didn't seem particularly lonely, and we were hopelessly *city*, from our white-sidewalled jeep to my brother's gleaming Model 70 Winchester, but we happily accepted his invitation, and walked with Rusty up the road to where he lived, a small log cabin partitioned by a wall of rough-hewn planks. Rusty occupied the small room on one side of the wall, and furs hung like heavy fruit in the dark unheated space on the other side. I remember only a few details of what we learned about his life—he'd named his mule Old Aches and Pains; he played the guitar; he typed gruesome cowboy stories on a rusted portable typewriter; and he fed himself and earned a little money by hunting and trapping—I'd noticed the whittled carcass of a poached deer hanging inside the fur room. Halfway through our two hours as his guest, he suddenly said *sshhh. Listen.* I listened, hearing only the sound of the Dolores River sucking away outside. *It's a coon,* Rusty said, picking up his .22 from the corner of the room, handing me a flashlight, and motioning us quietly outside. He pointed to a branch in a cottonwood tree overhanging his cabin, whispered *shine the light,* and there it was, eyes glowing like lit matches. Rusty told me to aim the flashlight—not on the coon, which he could see just fine, but on the front sight of his rifle—and he quickly shot the raccoon dead, and then skinned it before our eyes with an efficiency that was a little scary.

Needless to say, I'd never met anyone like him before, and I soon made him fodder for literature, began writing a story about a man who led a solitary life in the desert, in a cabin hidden at the dead end of a narrow canyon a mile or two from the Colorado, a man who fought existential despair through each long winter so he could fight existential despair through the long hot summer too.

In this story, which made its way into the high school's literary magazine to become my first publication, the man kills himself, or is killed *by* himself (I understood then a subtle difference that I fail to grasp in reading the story today), or is killed by a stranger who may be a symbolic representation of himself. Or maybe he was *just a stranger!* It was very psychological, very Gothic, very *Poe,* now that I think about it, depending more on setting and mood than logic or characterization or plot or even plausibility in making whatever point it had to make.

But the story ended this way: a solitary rafter with problems of his own leaves his raft in order to explore a side canyon and stumbles upon the man's gruesomely desiccated remains. In the story, there's heat, and the blinding (if overwrought) light of a stark noonday sun, and—I hoped—the discovery of something significant. Looking back, I understand that the story was mostly effect, the writing intended to be merely creepy, nothing I took seriously enough to be touched by, mostly because it was written from a place distant from who I really was in high school, or at least who I thought I was.

Nevertheless, the actual place I'd hiked to, this last side canyon near the end of Glen Canyon, felt wrong. For all I know, the place is delightful, an unhurried narrative of rock and sand, of water and greenery, potholes and arches. Someone reading this might have walked the canyon and found only beauty and consolation, something saved from the catastrophe of Lake Powell, the lone survivor of a biblical tragedy preserved against all odds so that at least one short chapter of the story might be told, but as reasonable and hopeful as this perspective might be, that's not what I remember. Perhaps a part of me didn't *want* anything to survive. I wanted to find beauty, sure, and I wanted to find myself in Elliot Porter's photographs, but I think that summer I was just beginning to understand that we live in a fallen world. Glen Canyon was gone, and what remains can only be a faint, distorted echo, a pale impersonation, the runt of the litter of side canyons. I was, after all, a land surveyor, complicit in the canyon's death in ways I still find difficult to admit, and perhaps that day I couldn't let myself entirely off the hook. If only for a moment, I had to look at myself alone in this final canyon under the harsh light of day, and face the consequences.

What do I see when I look at myself thirty years later? I find a person less confused and more committed to environmental causes—the "decommissioning" of Glen Canyon Dam, of course, and the shoring up of legislative fences between Texas oil interests and the Arctic National Wildlife Refuge, for example—and yet somehow less complicated in his view of the relationship between humans and the environment. I'm both more dedicated to the protection of nature, and less aware of my place in it.

I'm capable today of clear thinking, even intellectual consistency, the kind of comprehensive arrangement of thought Lady Bird Johnson demonstrably lacked that day she gave her speech at Glen Canyon Dam, in which she explained her view that the dam was simply a giant "Kilroy Was Here" of which we could all be proud. I can summarize my feelings about man's place in the natural world this way: human beings inevitably mark the landscape they occupy. This is not only inevitable; this is as it should be. On the other hand, we don't have to leave marks everywhere—not only do few unmarked surfaces remain, we've marked up some places that should have gotten a pass, and might be candidates for *un*marking. Glen Canyon is an excellent example of a unique landscape that had been stupidly and unnecessarily destroyed. Therefore, I'm opposed to Glen Canyon Dam, and in favor of the restoration of Glen Canyon.

This far-from-revolutionary way of thinking makes a kind of sequential sense, but I'm sad to admit that it stops somewhere short of the truth, which is rarely sequential and, indeed, more often contradictory than syllogistic. Truth generally hovers some distance above clear logic and persuasive argument, and the difference between the need to save the whales and the story Herman Melville tells in *Moby-Dick* is the difference between a bumper sticker and six hundred pages of literature that, interestingly enough, neglects to take an unambiguous stand one way or the other regarding the need to save the whales. It's also the difference between simple clarity, which threatens to misrepresent the complexity of human perception, and incoherence, which can sometimes be defined not simply as the confusion I felt that summer, but as recognition of the incredible difficulty of explaining, let alone reconciling, a set of profound and yet seemingly incompatible truths.

How do we get to know the place no one knew? Is it even *possible?* Today I'm a lot more pessimistic in pondering this question, more aware of the ultimate impossibility of knowing absence. I suppose this is why I believe that the only way to really get to know Glen Canyon is to bring it back by means of decommission and restoration. Or even that *other* way, involving monkey wrenchers and C-4–laden houseboats. Back in 1974, I knew something more obscure and complicated—for one thing, I believed that I might experience the ten miles that remain without really hating the dam, which is to say I understood on some level the validity or power of the whole array of marks, the undeniable presence of the dam, the reservoir, the petroglyphs, and all those other hieroglyphics climbing the canyon walls.

Glen Canyon ended soon after its final offshoot. As the river cut its way through the lowest reaches of the Navajo formation, the flat vertical walls of orange sandstone gave way to staircased layers of more conventional rock, bands of lake sediment turned to stone of varying hardness, steps and ramps that widened the sky into something more familiar, more like the sky I worked under Monday through Friday, and after a final hour of shadeless floating and rowing, I arrived at Lee's Ferry. I pulled my raft up the boat launching ramp—Lee's Ferry is the point of departure for float trips through the Grand Canyon—and then wandered around for a few minutes, looking over the preserved corrals and orchards of John D. Lee's last home, the place he'd been exiled to as a way to escape more severe punishment for the part he'd played in 1857 in the infamous Mountain Meadows massacre. Lee's Ferry had been his Siberia, an outpost inhospitable, isolated, and grim, lacking the soothing glens, the reassuring colors of orange sandstone and brown varnish of the river upstream, or the quiet shady depths of Marble Canyon a few miles farther down the river.

Lee built his ferry where the aptly named Paria River cut its way south through the cliffs to add its seasonal brown water to the sum of the Colorado, the Paria's floodplain leveling the landscape sufficiently to provide a few dozen acres of something almost farmable, as well as the only possible route for a road down through the cliffs to the river for a hundred miles in either direction. Lee began operating the ferry in early 1872, floating Mormon settlers and Indian traders across the Colorado on their way to places perhaps more remote but probably less depressing. He was finally captured by federal authorities while visiting one of the several wives he'd left behind in Utah, tried and convicted, and then taken back to Mountain Meadows, where he was executed by a firing squad for the crime he'd been running from for twenty years, the well-planned murder of a hundred and twenty unarmed men, women, and children, a wagon train of families making their way to California.

The National Park Service has worked unevenly to interpret the way Lee's Ferry served as home for John D. Lee's own family. He'd brought with him into exile his seventeenth wife, Emma Batchelor Lee, who named the spot Lonely Dell, and the self-guided tour walked me past remnants of her house and garden, the signs explaining the way the family's daily life had taken on the appearance of domestic normalcy.

Emma's life here was isolated and lonely. Even though her husband had been excommunicated from the church and made a scapegoat, singled out from among the dozens of his brothers in the priesthood who had also participated in the massacre (even Brigham Young, who had years earlier formalized their close relationship by legally adopting him, turned his back), the church preferred to avoid the publicity that would result from his arrest, and the ever-useful Lee was quietly assigned various projects necessary for the southward expansion of the Mormon empire: building and maintaining roads, keeping track of Mormon cattle, and making peace with the local Indians. He was often absent from Lonely Dell, sometimes for months at a time, leaving Emma to operate the ferry, tend the gardens and orchards, and raise their young family, which continued to increase in number despite stern reminders by visiting Mormon elders that church law required her to stop sharing her bed with a man laboring under the disgrace of excommunication.

Emma gave birth to her last two children at Lonely Dell, both of them girls, and John D. was away both times. A visiting sister-wife helped with the birth of the first girl, whom Emma named Frances Dell in honor of their new home, but she was completely on her own for the second. Her husband could have been anywhere: at a distant spring constructing a way station for Mormons migrating to settlements in Arizona, or miles away surveying a new route for the difficult wagon road that ran south from the ferry. Perhaps he was supervising a crew of men called away from their own families, blasting and hauling rocks to straighten a particularly dangerous stretch of road known to those who traveled it as Lee's Backbone.

Wherever he was, Emma was alone when her time came. She sent the children outside to play and gave birth as quietly as possible so as not to frighten them. She named this girl Victoria Elizabeth: Victoria for the reigning queen of England, and Elizabeth in honor of her own mother, Elizabeth Batchelor, whom she'd not seen for more than fifteen years, and whose letters seldom managed to make their long way from England to Lonely Dell. If it had not been for Emma's teenage encounter with Mormon missionaries, she might have remained in England, might have become a husband's only wife, borne children, and lived out her life near her family in rural Sussex. It's not difficult to picture Emma distancing herself from the pain of labor by imagining the lush green landscape in which she had spent her own childhood.

Following her husband's execution, and after a few more lonely years operating the ferry, Emma and her children finally left their isolated home on the Colorado. She followed southward the wagon road her husband had worked so hard to shore up and straighten, finding work as a housekeeper and midwife in a succession of grim Mormon outposts in northern Arizona, moving her family to Snowflake, then to Hardy's Station, Brigham City, and finally

Winslow, where, less than fifteen years after her lonely birth, her youngest daughter, Victoria Elizabeth, committed suicide by drinking laudanum, perhaps finding her own necessary release from Lonely Dell.

I managed to hitchhike back to Wahweap City with only two rides. A woman driving a white pickup hauled me from Lee's Ferry up the access road to its junction with Highway 89, where she turned south to Flagstaff. In her late twenties, dark-haired and tanned beyond what I had believed was physiologically possible, she was employed by a company that rafted tourists through the twists and rapids of the Grand Canyon. She was working support— cooking, office chores, hauling rafts back and forth on trailers— hoping that she'd eventually have the opportunity to guide her own float trips down the river.

"I know this river about as well as anybody," she said in a voice that wasn't at all defensive, and I believed her. I asked her if there were many women guiding float trips. She looked at me as if I were a little crazy and said no. She told me she was at least as good on the river as anybody she worked for, but the whole enterprise was pretty much a guy thing, and it was really hard to break in.

I sympathized—I really did. It seemed unfair to me that someone so well qualified, not to mention so devoted and so *tan,* should be kept from doing the work she loved. But my sympathy didn't lead me in what seems now an obvious direction, toward consideration of the fact that I was hitchhiking back to a world even more completely male than the less profound world of float trips and tourism, back to a world of straight lines and hard angles more hostile not simply to the employment of women, but perhaps to something profoundly and definably female.

This insight would creep up on me with embarrassing slowness over the intervening years. As I look back at my life in the aftermath of the sixties, in particular the years between Watergate and Reagan, the years I alternated winters of graduate school with summers of land surveying, nothing strikes me so strongly as my inconsistencies and my blind spots. I thought I knew at least a few certain things concerning who I was and what it was I believed, and I defined myself politically by the many ways in which I was different from the southern-Utah party chiefs I surveyed for. They were Coors; I was pot. I was a cosmopolitan leftist; they were rural reactionaries.

The one thing we agreed on was the straight line. We argued about the various uses to which natural landscape should be put, but we all worked efficiently and hard to run those necessary lines. Although I was all for civil rights, and argued passionately that the BLM needed to get its shit together hiring minorities—over beers I routinely pointed out that there was something profoundly wrong with the fact that there were no surveyors of color on any of the survey crews the BLM fielded each summer—I don't remember staking out a position on the obviously related problem that there were no *women* surveyors *either.*

In view of the fact that I argued for women's rights in many other fields of opportunity and employment, it's tempting to explain this silence in terms of the gender implications of linearity, the essential maleness of our mission, the inscription of the straight line upon natural landscape. There are other explanations, of course: it's undoubtedly the case that in spite of my long hair and leftist views, I was still a *guy,* just one more old boy in an old-boy's network protecting its ranks, insulating its comfort zone. It's also true that I was in many ways simply an asshole, my sensibilities ranging from the stupid to the insulting in any number of areas, including the area of relationships with women, in which I wasn't doing so well, especially that summer. Nevertheless, I've come to believe that my unexamined resistance to hiring women surveyors had a lot to do with the specific work we did, the inscription of survey lines into the swells and folds of nature. On some level, I believe I understood that because linearity was a profoundly male concept, it naturally followed that running line was something *men* did.

My education regarding the complex relationship between gender and land surveying would commence the following summer, when women were finally hired to assist in completing the mission of the Cadastral Survey, several years (it's worth noting) after women had been added to BLM fire crews and FBI SWAT teams, the delay perhaps serving to underscore the fundamental maleness of the straight line. Two women were hired that next year, and as it turned out, both women were assigned to Larry's crew, the crew to which I'd also be returning, probably for the same reason

Larry was assigned the hardest-used surveying instruments and the trucks with the most mileage: because he was the youngest party chief, the newest full-time surveyor, the low man on the Cadastral totem pole. Or, as Larry explained to anybody who asked: they'd already assigned him somebody who *looked* like a girl (a nod in my direction); they might as well give him the real thing.

The change was both dramatic and inconsequential. Of course we stopped using pubic-hair units of measure for smaller-than-hundredths increments, even the vestigial CH and RCH acronym shorthand, with little damage to the lining-in process—overnight it was "a *tiny* bit west, okay, now a *teeny*-tiny bit west," and we adapted easily, understanding exactly how far to tap the flag west. Also, we men became more circumspect in the directions we'd piss after the long bladder-stretching rides to the job. It helped that the women who'd been recruited were just about perfect for such role-breaking responsibilities. Perhaps in an effort to make the experiment more scientific, the two women assigned to our crew were of two very different types, one dark and short and rangy and light on her feet, the other red-haired and pale, tall and really strong, a serious ax-swinger. They learned the ropes a lot quicker than I had (to be fair, I *had* set the bar pretty low). Bonnie—who by the way didn't mind being called a flagman; alternatives like flagperson or flagger or flagwoman were tried and dropped without much discussion—encountered none of the trouble I'd had in knowing where exactly to pound in the lath, and they were her well-placed flags I spent that next summer dragging the chain toward, and she and red-haired Gloria turned out to be excellent surveyors. And of course our lines continued to run straight and true, unbent by either monthly spells of moodiness or gender-induced incompetence, crew-demoralizing sexual tension, or annoying feminist critiques regarding the phallocentric implications of linearity, not counting the ones *I* began offering.

If anything changed, I think, it was the community surveying in the field inevitably creates. No longer defined by undiluted maleness, long summers in the company of surveyors began to feel kind of normal, and I'd like to think that after women joined the ranks, we men acted a little less often like jerks. That next summer, I know at least that *I* felt a little less exiled; life in the field felt more like home, possibly because for the only time in my experience as a surveyor, in addition to working with actual women, we lived in actual *homes*. After we'd finished the oil-shale job, we were assigned a Forest Service boundary near Bowman, Utah, and because Larry lived in Bowman and was looking forward to spending a rare month of his surveying career at home with his wife and kids, he got the assignment, and because Bowman lacked anything remotely resembling a motel, Larry rented rooms for us in neighborhood homes.

So I found myself sleeping in the basement bedroom of a house owned by the widow of Bowman's lone, late dentist, snug in the twin bed previously occupied decades earlier by their now-middle-aged son, under a beige chenille bedspread and between walls of knotty pine. Stan, Larry's new crew chief and instrument operator, occupied the other twin bed. Bonnie and Gloria shared a spare bedroom in another Bowman household down the street. The women had kitchen privileges, and those nights when we didn't drive the hour it took to get to a town with a cafe, we'd cook dinners in an actual kitchen, and eat them in a breakfast nook decorated with homemade wall hangings. Larry had us over to his house pretty often, where we'd join the Daniels family around a table to partake of one of Suzette's home-cooked meals or in the backyard to consume various cuts of meat Larry had grilled on his outdoor barbeque.

Most nights after dinner, the four of us would walk to Bowman's sole commercial establishment, a combination bar-and-barbershop that I'm pretty sure lacked a name; or maybe it had a name, but lacked an identifying sign. It felt sometimes like we were double-dating, two couples buying each other beers, arguing good-naturedly and listening to songs on the only jukebox I've ever encountered that really *did* have only country-western songs (not even *Sinatra*, or the Beatles) and most of those songs at least a decade old: much Ernest Tubb, and Loretta Lynn, one Faron Young song, some early Johnny Cash. Around ten we'd wander out onto Bowman's main drag, our good-byes lacking only the goodnight kiss to seem exactly like romantic partings, walk to our respective houses, and bed down in someone's childhood bedroom. Some nights as Stan and I crept quietly in the kitchen door we would be greeted by the dentist's widow, who'd been staying up late watching TV in her pink bathrobe and wearing slippers I'm pretty sure were fuzzy and the same color as her bathrobe, her hair in curlers, her face showing the same expression of worry and vague disapproval my own mother wore when I'd come home late. It added up to something both uncomfortable—this was, after all, the domesticity I'd been fleeing on any number of levels ranging from the political to the metaphorical—and okay.

I don't know if it was the result of surveying with women, or hanging out with them evenings, or the barbecues at Larry's house, or living in an actual *home,* but I eventually got used to it, even kind of liked it, and gave in a little to the attractions of regular life. So much so that late one night I finally agreed to let the bartender, whose day job consisted of barbering the short-haired heads of Bowman's male population, walk me into the barber shop you'd pass through to get to the barroom, where he shaved off the beard I'd been growing for a couple of years, leaving a moustache punctuated with those downward extensions you'd see in those days only on the jowls of rural rednecks. I think I took this step partly as a gesture intended to hold off the haircut that my better-groomed fellow bar patrons had been threatening good-naturedly for a couple of weeks (the mixture of small town, long hair, a handy barber's chair, and alcohol was feeling increasingly ominous), partly because both Bonnie and Gloria agreed it might be a good change for me, and partly because I was ready to fit in, to feel a little more at home in the place where I lived.

Fifteen minutes after the float-trip woman let me off at the junction with Highway 89, I was picked up by a truck driver, a guy about my age driving a faded blue semi pulling a trailer that looked beat-up and undersized, vaguely rounded in the streamlined style of the fifties, a trailer twenty-five years old and looking it. He gave me a cigarette, asked about my work, and told me about his. He couldn't believe his luck: barely twenty, a high school dropout, practically an *orphan,* he said, and here he was, making payments on his own truck, in full legal ownership of his own trailer. He waxed lyrical about the life of the gypsy trucker.

"I'm my own boss," he told me, relishing the fact that he was completely on his own and beholden to nobody, enjoying—I'm pretty sure these were his exact words—"the freedom of the open road."

We exchanged hitchhiking stories. He said he always picked people up if they looked okay because he'd spent half his life hitching, usually alone, usually from one shitty job somewhere to another shitty job somewhere else, until his lucky break, the trucker who had picked him up and helped him out, given him a job, and taught him a skill. I told him I'd just been let off by a woman who guided float trips down the Colorado. "She's a raftsman," I said, giving her the promotion I thought she deserved, if only in my telling her story. He said he'd been at a party a couple of weeks before in Flagstaff thrown by a bunch of raftsmen, said sure, there'd been plenty of gash around.

His truck was slow pulling its load up the steep dugway below Page, and it was after sundown by the time he dropped me off at Wahweap City, where the bunk trailers were dark and empty, the crews still on the road, men driving south toward work, away from their families, from love.

CHAPTER NINE

The View from Navajo Mountain

Navajo Mountain loomed over our surveying that summer. Only when we followed line deep into a canyon, or walked shadowed behind the broadened shoulders of a butte, were we deprived of our sight of the only real mountain for miles. Although not directly useful to our surveying—Matt couldn't use Navajo Mountain as a foresight, its being intersected by neither our north-south nor our east-west lines—it served to locate me in the same way the familiar peaks of the Wasatch Front helped me orient myself while hiking in the foothills above the neighborhood I'd grown up in, and I found myself a becoming a little obsessed with the mountain.

Navajo Mountain seemed like a geological visitor borrowed from some other part of the world. In contrast to the more angular landscape over which it presided, the mountain was made of circles and looked the same from every direction, a round bump, a big steep swell, a half grapefruit flat side down. I'd learned from that not-overly-apologetic-despoiler-of-petroglyphs geology teacher that there had been some controversy among geologists concerning whether or not Navajo Mountain was a laccolith, but the process I'd been tested on that semester fit exactly the way it looked: like a blister, an unlanced boil. A laccolith is the mountainous result of an igneous intrusion, an artery of molten magma frustrated in its attempt to become a volcano, a rush of lava pushed forcefully from the depths of the earth on its way to achieving a dramatic species-destroying explosion only to be blocked by a heavy blanket of reinforced crust, an unusually well-integrated layer of the earth's surface uncompromised by those faults and weaknesses that more routinely provide a route upward toward ultimate release. Instead, all that aggressive lava slows and puddles anticlimactically beneath the layers of rock above, forming the igneous version of a blood blister, a toadstool-shaped swelling that pushes the layers upward thousands of feet, a bulge that rises slowly like an enormous sun on the horizon, finally cooling and then accommodating, centuries of erosion eventually knitting it into the terrain.

This roundness, this ripe curve on the otherwise broken horizon, contrasted so completely with the angularity of the steps and ramps, and the flatness of the plateaus and the sheer verticality of the Navajo sandstone into which the stark walls of Glen Canyon had been cut, that the mountain stood for me throughout that summer and finally into the next spring as something like home, a kind of beacon, round and friendly, a subtle intrusion of igneous matter that pushed brittle rock into a gradual and gentle swelling, unbroken and motherly above the contortions of canyon and uplift that define the Colorado Plateau. Because Navajo Mountain could be recognized so easily from every direction, I could tell pretty much where I was on the Kaiparowits Plateau that summer—and, the next spring, when hiking with my students in the Escalante wilderness. This was, after all, some of the most rugged terrain on the planet, and to be able to locate yourself within even twenty miles is the most valuable gift a lost person can be given, especially someone as lost as I felt that summer.

That's what Navajo Mountain came to mean to me. I was to learn that it meant something at once very similar and very different to the Navajo, for whom the mountain was named by American military cartographers (the Navajo name for the mountain is *Naatsis'aan,* or "Head of the Earth Woman") and from whose reservation it rises; and to the Hopi, who remind us that their reverence for the mountain they call *Tokonave* precedes the Navajo's by at least a thousand years; and I'm still not sure how I feel about having climbed it that summer.

I was, after all, complicit in a survey that would provide the grid upon which mining claims would be staked, and from which one of the West's largest power plants would rise, a lab assistant setting up the apparatus necessary for continuing the failed experiment

that was the Enlightenment, the imposition of impossibly linear
and unnatural order upon the otherness of natural landscape,
working under rules that nearly everyone in America had long
since rejected, rules that the indigenous inhabitants of the landscape surrounding Naatsis'aan/Tokonave had never accepted in the
first place. Long after the doctrines of romanticism and the aes-
thetics of the Hudson River School had determined more gentle,
and possibly more wise, approaches to apprehending the natural
world—and millennia after the ancestors of both the Navajo and
the Hopi had figured out their own ways of articulating their connection with the landscape in which they made their lives—the
Cadastral Survey continued its mission to implement instructions
first formulated in 1785, the very climax of the Age of Reason in
America. And now I was about to climb the mountain I sort of understood to be sacred to the Navajo and Hopi people, the local
remnant of the populace those very ideas of order and exploitation
had driven to this presumably useless corner of U.S. real estate.

In his 1929 account of a series of well-funded expeditions into
the area surrounding Navajo Mountain, carried out by an unlikely
assortment of eastern museum archivists, Navajo guides, wealthy
amateurs, and local Mormon patriarchs, John Bernheimer—a self-
identified "cliff dweller" of Manhattan—casually mentions just before describing his group's own ascent of Navajo Mountain that
"the Indians do not ascend the mountain. They believe their War
God lives there and it is to this belief that the beautiful trees owe
their existence." Reading this reminded me instantly of Henry
David Thoreau, who if we are to believe his narrative in *The Maine
Woods* acknowledges the fact that the local Indians do not climb
Mount Ktaadn either, this as he ponders the implication of his own
climb to the summit. He writes, "The tops of mountains are among
the unfinished parts of the globe, whither it is a slight insult to the
gods to climb and pry into their secrets. . . . Only daring and inso-
lent men, perchance, go there. Simple races, as savages, do not
climb mountains,—their tops are sacred and mysterious tracts
never visited by them. Pomola is always angry with those who
climb to the summit of Ktaadn."

Even though Thoreau makes the usual condescending comparison—the brave insolence of the European versus the childlike
simplicity (not to mention the lack of ambition) of the natives—

he's gone where Indians won't, and has actually *learned* something as a result of his encounter on the bare summit of Ktaadn with what he can't quite call "Mother Earth," with aridity and cold and essential matter, the very lack of which defines that more famous and more congenial Thoreauvian landscape, Walden Pond. "I stand in awe of my body, this matter to which I am bound has become so strange to me," Thoreau writes, considering in uncharacteristically personal and sensual (and even ungrammatical) words the implications of the view from Ktaadn. "Talk of mysteries!—Think of our life in nature,—daily to be shown matter, to come in contact with it,—rocks, trees, wind on our cheeks! the *solid* earth! the *actual* world! the *common sense! Contact! Contact! Who* are we? *where* are we?"

It's the problem of *contact* that gets me in this passage, the way Thoreau locates us at some point where nature, spirit, and human flesh meet and negotiate, choose up sides, and leave me in that usual spot, on the outside wondering where I stand, whose side I'm on, what exactly alienation means to someone occupying the summit of a mountain. Like Thoreau, I grew up loving the woods and mountains, and even the less hospitable desert landscapes of southern Utah. I also feared that other face of nature, the chaos of landscape not yet made useful, the disorder of sexual urges not yet brought under control, the randomness of disease and disfigurement not quite comprehensible, let alone curable. Only nature could be held responsible for the central focus of my family's story, my oldest brother's life tragically altered by the polio virus that attacked him when he was eight years old, introducing a tragic narrative of neuromuscular assaults that whittled away his body throughout the forty years that remained of his life. In spite of my childhood spent visiting national parks, picnicking and hiking in the mountains just a block up the street, singing songs in church about "our mountain home," I suppose I grew up believing that Glen Canyon Dam and the Salk vaccine (which arrived a year too late to help my brother) were expressions of the same necessary goal: the control of the chaos that lurks beneath even the most tranquil and innocent surfaces of the natural world.

Thoreau on Mount Ktaadn says something right out loud that he pussyfoots around through all the other pages he churned out during his life. As condescending and conventional—and more than a little disingenuous—is his attempt to say Indians *belong* here, and

I *don't,* it is also an admission that he's missed something important thus far in his explication of nature as he's found it. He says, I can neither understand nor explain this, yet I'm here, having climbed this mountain; Indians probably understand *exactly* what this means, which is why they aren't here climbing it *or* explaining it.

We love these stories about forbidden landscapes—the sublime wastelands in which we struggle to survive recreationally, as well as more conventional Edens to which we long to return—nearly as much as we love the *conquest,* doing whatever it takes to actually occupy these landscapes: by means of pain and exertion, ropes and pitons, trekking paths and dirt roads, even a man-made lake that ultimately functions as little more than a hundred-mile-long parking lot for houseboats. It's an incredibly complex problem, speaking directly to the completely different ways one knows, one interprets, or one accepts the *impossibility* of knowing and interpreting, and what all this has to do with a human need for connection that is as desperate as it is universal.

Like Thoreau, I wanted contact. I wanted contact with something bigger than myself, and I wanted that contact to *help.* And like Thoreau, I believed that finding out *where* I was might possibly be the first step toward learning *who* I was. More ambitious contacts—god, truth, even love—had once seemed possible for me, but that summer I'd been reduced to more literally down-to-earth solutions, and I'd looked toward Navajo Mountain as a point of reference, a location bigger and, I hoped, more profound than the numbers I'd pounded into brass caps and inscribed on trees, which told me merely where I stood in relation to the state of Utah, the way in which I connected with known lines of latitude and longitude; useful to an unanticipated degree, but still limited. Navajo Mountain located me in another way, a broader context, perhaps even a different dimension. It was by no means anything like the Indian way of locating oneself, I knew that. My needing to know was not related to the way fear of the War God is somehow connected with the vegetation that colored Navajo Mountain a deep blue-green on even the sunniest days. It was simply this: all summer I'd been looking at the summit of the mountain from the carved breaks of the Kaiparowits Plateau; I believed that if I could reverse the view, trace my own movements from the summit, I might gain a better idea of where I was, how I fit, who I was becoming. I'd covered thirty-six square miles of the plateau link by link, so I knew what it looked like up close. What I needed was *contact,* but at this point in my life, I was willing to settle for context.

I don't know what worship is. I never really understood it during all those Sundays in the Mormon chapel down the street from my house, and I sure don't understand that obscure point where respectful attention, aesthetic appreciation, even low-grade obsession cross the line into worship. But I've spent my life focusing on specific landscapes that seem to say something to me beyond what most other landscapes say, a few mountains and at least one river, and a waterfall that I hiked to a dozen times each summer while growing up in the foothills of the Wasatch Front. Navajo Mountain was something like that. It told me roughly where I stood; it presented only slightly changing faces to me as I spent weekdays that summer surveying, weekends hiking and floating the landscape over which it presided. I have to confess here to a failure of imagination: by the middle of my second month on the Kaiparowits, making my way to the summit of Navajo Mountain was the only thing I could think to do.

The weekend I'd decided to climb Navajo Mountain was a little complicated. For one thing, I had company. There had been surveyors staying over weekends before, of course, but our inclinations and destinations were usually so divergent that I'd managed to get away by myself each time, sometimes catching rides (as I had with Larry and his family), other times hitching. And I'd spent a couple of weekends with Karen. I'd finally made a quick trip to Salt Lake City, mostly running errands and seeing friends, and late in July, Karen drove south for a weekend. Karen arrived in Wahweap City Friday afternoon as the surveyors were packing their cars for the drive north, and there was a lot of good-natured kidding about the uncharacteristic weekend in store for me; Karen hadn't met most of the men I worked with, and as I introduced them, I could see they were smitten, and even more confused concerning my reasons for staying behind each Friday.

We camped two nights in Zion, lazily visiting the easy sights, and took one long day hike, following a series of uphill switchbacks that led us onto Zion Canyon's west rim, and on the way down we left the trail long enough to hike the narrow rib that led to a cliff-edged viewpoint called Angel's Landing. This route reminded me a little too much of the day I'd failed to get a flag in along that treacherous blade of sandstone near Vernal the summer before, but with Karen's encouragement and a rusty cable bolted in place decades earlier by the National Park Service, we managed to avoid falling to our deaths, and enjoyed a view that wasn't determined by the need to stand in that one precise spot that marked line—we could wander where we wanted, and sit in one place for as long as we felt like sitting there.

I remember it as a nice couple of days, in spite of the weekend crowds and park rules and regulations, and there were moments when I understood that taking in a view with someone you loved had real advantages over pondering it alone. But I also felt I was *missing* something, even if I wasn't sure exactly what it was. Salt Lake hadn't felt much like home, and as much as I loved being with Karen, loved her company and good humor and familiar touch, I kept thinking vaguely that it wasn't the same as it had been the summer before, when we'd spent every weekend together, at home with Karen in my apartment, other weekends camping under clear high-mountain skies. During the Salt Lake City weekend, I'd missed the desert a lot more than I thought I would; it felt a little like I'd abandoned an important project, one that somehow included both surveying and lone weekend hiking, and taking a break in the city left me feeling a little distracted.

During the weekend that Karen had come south, although I was reminded of the comforts of love and companionship and remembered the loneliness I'd felt floating down Glen Canyon, I somehow missed being alone, something Karen picked up on. I remember that she asked me a couple of times whether I was okay. I *was* okay, I told her, and although that was more or less the truth, I didn't tell her that okay was something different than what I'd felt with her before, and I was a little scared that things might be changing, had maybe even changed already. It had been a good weekend for us, doing many of the things together we'd done before, carrying our sleeping bags away from the lights of the Zion campground to a quieter and darker place by the Virgin River, downstream a few miles from the lonely cave I'd occupied alone a month earlier. Late Sunday afternoon, when I'd waved good-bye as she drove north toward home, I'd felt honestly sad, but also a little relieved, and I'd spent the next couple of weekends on my own.

That Friday before the weekend I'd planned to hike to the top of

Navajo Mountain, however, after watching the crews pack their cars and head north, I found myself talking with Richard Hoskins, a crew chief on one of the other crews, about our overlapping plans. Richard's plan for the weekend involved hiking to Rainbow Bridge—not from the Lake Powell side, riding the ferry from the Wahweap Marina and then walking the short path from the dock in Bridge Canyon (the way I'd reached it with my family a few years before), but the pre-Lake Powell way, the long hike from the trailhead at the southwest edge of Navajo Mountain. Like me, Richard was a person accustomed to spending time alone. One of the peyote-eaters from the summer before who had so unexpectedly challenged Tim's understanding of truth and community, Richard was quiet, and smart as hell. He was a little eccentric, although firmly anchored far above the depths of eccentricity into which Williams had so recently plunged. He was somehow an engineering student who a few years before I met him had spent several months wandering through the Amazon jungle in search of something he wasn't finding in places closer to home, that rare engineering major who took a lot of classes in the philosophy department.

He'd had his own discussions with Warren Knowles far into the night, but Richard was able somehow to keep it all relatively neat and objective, even after Warren had grabbed the revolver he'd kept not quite hidden under the cash register and aimed it directly at Richard's head in order to make some obscure theological or metaphysical point. I'd spent too many years as a Mormon to be able simply to listen to Warren's pronouncements without responding from someplace deep inside, someplace *personal,* and I envied Richard's ability to weigh all assertions equally on some kind of scale that was an integral part of his personality calibrated as much in his engineering classes as in the philosophy courses he'd taken at the U.

Our discussion about weekend plans was a little cagey, however, partly because I was pretty sure he was looking forward to his *own* solitary weekend as well. I told him I was intending to hitch to the base of Navajo Mountain and hike to the top. He told me he'd be driving his beat-up but entirely dependable Volkswagen that direction in order to hike to Rainbow Bridge. We both knew that my hitchhiking through an Indian reservation would be more difficult than the hitching I'd done so far that summer, and I allowed as

how I'd appreciate a ride if he was going that way, which it turned
out he was: the Rainbow Bridge trailhead was located at the burned
ruins of a 1920s–era lodge, pretty close to the starting point for
what seemed to be the most plausible route up the mountain, a
ridgeline our lousy BLM map seemed to indicate ran gradually, if
steeply, up the south side.

We left the trailers at sunrise and spent a long Saturday morning driving the maze of dirt roads that crisscross the Navajo Indian
reservation east of Page, a process that involved many miles of
gravel roads, then, when those inevitably petered out, trying to
guess which curving dirt road turned eventually toward the mountain and which was actually a mile-long driveway that dead-ended
at someone's home, which consisted usually of a hogan, a square
cinderblock Bureau of Indian Affairs house, a slumped corral, and
a pickup truck. Roads ran everywhere, and even though Navajo
Mountain filled the Volkswagen's narrow windshield, it took a
dozen false starts to bring us to the undeniable flank of the mountain, a road that ended at a spring and its usual companions in this
part of the world, a corrugated steel tank and a mossy watering
trough. By then, it was midafternoon; we'd been driving nearly a
full day, Richard's ancient Volkswagen was down to half a tank—
and that was after filling up expensively at the trading post near
the end of the paved road—and the clock made the decision for us.
It was simply too late for Richard to find his way to his own trailhead, and I was so grateful by then that he'd driven me there (I'd
had an all-too-clear vision of the hitchhiking nightmare I would be
in the middle of still if I'd followed my original plan) I suggested
that we do the Navajo Mountain hike together.

I hadn't been able to find out whether there was an actual trail
or not; the map showed a dirt road that ran from the east nearly
all the way to the summit, but we'd heard that it was locked at the
base, and it looked like a lot more miles of hiking than we had time
for. We weren't worried about finding our way—we knew we had
the right mountain, this being the only one around for at least fifty
miles in any direction, and the only direction we could go was up.
We figured we'd probably hit the road that traverses in from the
east at some point, and we both liked the idea of just heading uphill. We were surveyors, after all; we followed line, not a trail.

It actually *did* feel like surveying—neither easy, nor difficult
enough to take much mountaineering pride in; no trail, but plenty

of long bare ridges, a few gentle rock faces, a steep rounded slope that allowed us to follow a more or less straight line uphill. We had below us, of course, great scenery; to the south—the only direction we could see for the first couple of hours—the maze of roads we'd been lost in that twisted through rolling desert and scattered sandstone bluffs, and beyond that the wrinkled spread of the plateau country between us and Black Mesa. Eventually we'd hiked high enough to see to the east an assortment of pillar and post formations that marked what we finally decided was Monument Valley.

Toward late afternoon, after the sun had declined enough to quit beating into our backs, things leveled out a little, and ponderosa pines took over, offering shade at the exact moment we didn't need it anymore. Knowing the hardest of the hiking was behind us, we looked for a place to camp. More to the point, we looked for water, which we didn't find; during the last minutes of fading sunset light, we began hauling windfall for a fire, and started dinner, my macaroni and cheese boiled in rationed water, augmented with the can of tuna fish Richard had packed, and fortified with flattened French bread. The acreage around our campsite was flat and wooded; it didn't feel like the desert anymore, and it felt like anything but the summit of a mountain, more like the forested swell of a pine ocean. I remember that we were able to build a pretty big fire, and that the ground was soft with pine needles, a luxurious change from the sand and slickrock of the desert I'd been sleeping on during weekends all summer. I fell asleep curled around the glow and warmth of the fire, at a safe distance but still close enough to feel the comfort and light through a night that turned out to be downright cold.

We were awakened just before sunrise by fleeting shapes moving briskly through our campsite. Actually, Richard woke first, then nudged me—*horses,* he whispered—and sure enough we were surrounded by horses, maybe a dozen of them, colorless in the predawn darkness, but large and wild and ghostly, quiet and moving steadily east. It was one of those experiences you have to share with another person in order to understand that it really happened—they were gone as soon as they'd arrived, spooked into running when they realized their route was blocked by interlopers, too fast for me to really comprehend their strange presence before they were gone, sounds of hoofs hitting dirt fading as they disappeared into the night-shaded trees, one more something moving past me that summer too quickly for me to grasp a useful idea of what it could possibly mean.

An hour later, after a cold breakfast of bread and frugally portioned water, we walked only a few hundred yards through the woods before intersecting the dirt road, which we followed to a clearing occupied by a once-bright-yellow semitrailer that apparently contained equipment for broadcasting from a nearby steel-braced antenna tower. NAVAJO NATION was stenciled on the trailer alongside a jagged black image of a lightning bolt. I began to feel—unjustifiably—that I was a little off the hook on the charge of desecration.

We couldn't see a thing. We were pretty sure we were standing on the summit, but there was no summit view, nothing but ponderosa as far as we could see. Richard suggested that we follow a vague trail in what we thought was the direction of the Kaiparowits, whence I'd spent the summer anticipating this moment. A half mile of gradual downhill walking brought us to the abrupt conclusion of the forest, and the beginning of a long bare-rock drop carved by the mountain's erosion into the Colorado drainage that opened all of Glen Canyon and its hundreds of side canyons to view. Suddenly Navajo Mountain didn't feel like a blister at all, but a big mountain with the requisite mountainous face.

The Kaiparowits Plateau spread itself out like a long seminar table to the northwest. Looking to the west, where the flatness fell away into exposed pale orange rock, we could barely make out what might have been Wahweap Canyon, and Nipple Bench appeared as one of many flat stairsteps climbing upward from the Paria River, Nipple Butte itself lost in the faint haze that colored the morning, courtesy of the Mohave Power Generating Station upwind to the south, powered by coal mined from Black Mesa, the coal delivered by a long electric railway that Ed Abbey was targeting for explosive derailment that very summer as he applied the final touches to *The Monkey Wrench Gang.* The plateau terminated much more abruptly to the east in the sheer walls of Fifty-mile Mountain, falling steeply to erode itself into the drainages that fed the Escalante River, which we recognized as a deep cleft, its fingers reaching into the stark cliffs of the Kaiparowits, and in the other direction, toward the Henry Mountains barely visible to the north, a range uplifted like the mountain we stood on by igneous intrusions, but with more violence, resulting in steeper sides and more aggressively pointed summits.

Between us and all that familiar geography was the divide of Lake Powell, a river widened unnaturally from the expanding mudflats many miles distant to the right to the huge concrete plug just out of sight to the left, the southwest corner of the view we'd perched ourselves over, framed and limited by trees that grew right to the very edge of our overlook. As I did every time I climbed a peak above a familiar landscape, I tried to find where I'd actually been, this time intending, I suppose with mixed emotions, to find traces of all my hard work.

I was tempted at that moment to believe our surveying efforts were puny, that Jefferson's dream of a gridded landscape was impossible, certainly no match for the enormity of the landscape below my feet. I began thinking about how meaningless is the grid, the *line,* when applied to this empty, mostly bare-rock up- and down-lifted landscape. I knew that the lines we surveyed over slickrock left no visible trace; aside from the rock mounds we'd build around the iron pipes that served as markers, our lines were ephemeral, belonging only to that abstract grid that hovered invisibly above our heads, and the only slightly more physical lines drawn on plats filed in BLM offices in Salt Lake City and Washington, D.C.

It was true, on the other hand, that the lines we surveyed through the juniper forests we could see upholstering the flat expanse of the plateau looked on the ground like actual inscriptions, deep, narrow cuts into the flesh of the earth. In order to see clearly to the next flag, and in order to drag the chain along flat terrain impossible to triangulate through, we'd cut line, trim branches when we could, and chop or chainsaw through the thick trunks of piñon and cedar when they were determined to be on line—on the ground, looking back at the work we'd done filled our heads with a sense, perhaps inflated, perhaps not, of the damage we could do in marking the lines in the actual landscape, in blazing linearity across the surface of the planet. I'd felt awful about this destruction my first summer, which I referred to self-righteously as "clearcutting," and I'd worked hard to trim the very minimum necessary, an approach that not only slowed me down and made me work harder—this selective trimming meant a dozen cuts when a quick slice of the main branch would do—it routinely annoyed Matt, the transit operator, who had to keep bringing me back to trim more branches. As I returned to surveying each summer after that, I joined the others in mocking those who, like me as a beginner, regretted all that destruction, and who disdained the smoky chainsaws we used to cut our way home to the next flag, or the next corner. I'd come to think of myself as a surveyor, and my job required doing what needed to be done to complete the survey I'd been assigned. Occasionally, I'd worry about this adjustment and accommodation, and ask the obvious question of myself: if I'd actually consented to being sent to Vietnam, how quickly would I have adjusted to the necessity of the napalm strike? Embraced the necessary logic of the free-fire zone?

It's possible that the surveyors who made their Jeffersonian way across the Midwest may not have understood the degree to which their own efforts would shape the landscape: the vast plains might have struck them the way the view of the Kaiparowits struck me that day, as too overwhelming, too *big,* to be affected in any significant way by the feeble lines they ran, the modest stone mounds and chiseled rocks they left behind. The intervening two hundred years, of course, have proven the ultimate domination of their straight lines. Anyone who has flown across the American heartland can see clearly from 40,000 feet exactly how the natural inclinations of streams and timberline give way to the Enlightenment logic of right angles and straight lines, of landscapes oriented according to the cardinal directions of the compass. Iowa is a landscape of precise squares; the Enlightenment grid exists unconditionally on the ground, imbedded in the roads and highways, windrows and fencelines, in fields plowed according to the imperatives of the Ordinance of 1785.

But from the top of Navajo Mountain, one gets a sense that in this particular landscape—even in the juniper and piñon forests we could see carpeting the flatter, greener, and more vulnerable heights of the plateau—the survey itself is a flea bite on the skin of mother earth. The idea of line as put into practice by Bureau of Land Management surveyors bore no fruit visible from the summit of Navajo Mountain.

The idea of line as implemented by Bureau of Reclamation surveyors and engineers, however, told another story. Their line was easy to see, and traces of that line would probably last beyond the range of human history. The line of the grid speaks to one kind of human presence; the line of water raised high by human will and made level by gravity, the line that imprints itself as the high watermark of an artificial lake, speaks to another kind of human presence, one that dominated the landscape below our feet.

You could trace that line as surely as you could walk a lined corridor chainsawed by a crew of government surveyors across a wooded plateau. In the same way that those apparently straight lines of latitude and longitude eventually conformed to the ultimately spherical nature of the planet, the shoreline of Lake Powell followed the curve of the earth, marking a specific number of feet above sea level in a landscape a thousand miles from the sea, a line that cut across washes and canyons and deep clefts carved by the Colorado River over the course of a million years. Like a survey, which is marked by mounds of stone and blazed junipers, it contains elements of the natural—sea level is, after all, that line drawn by nature on shorelines around the world—but in this land of dry arroyos and dozens of miles between streams or seeps, all this water is profoundly strange, odd in the way its deep blue flattens itself against a riotous landscape the color of sand and rock, odd in the white V's of houseboats and speedboats visible from here even when the boats themselves are dots too tiny to make an impression on our eyes.

Like the section lines we surveyed Monday through Friday, the line of water level that defines Lake Powell is a boundary. Simply put, it is a line between what you can see, and what you can't. The flat expanse of too-blue water runs from boundary line to boundary line, from one sandstone shore of Glen Canyon to the other, making of itself a shroud that conceals from view those glens visited by the explorer for whom the lake is named, the first white man to actually visit those places, who it turns out was also the first man to bring instruments to measure them, and to locate them on the expanding and increasingly lined and gridded map of the United States.

My view of all this landscape was already nostalgic, in some ways even mournful. I couldn't help comparing what I was seeing that day with what I would see from this viewpoint ten years in the future. I suppose my perspective was similar to the one an onlooker might have felt standing on Navajo Mountain only fifteen years earlier, during the last years of the fifties, understanding that the floodgates of the dam would soon be shut, and the view deep into Glen Canyon's narrow channel, the slot canyons that emerge from the base of the mountain, even the many buttes and promontories that didn't quite rise beyond 3,700 feet above sea level, the anticipated level of the reservoir—all these features would be smudged into absence by the relentless gray eraser that is Glen Canyon Dam.

"You think we'd see the power plant from here?" I asked Richard. "Ten years from now?"

Richard knew exactly which power plant I meant. "I think so," he said slowly. "It's some distance away, but that thing's gonna be *huge.*"

"Think they'll actually build it?"

He thought a minute. "Yep. They seem pretty determined."

"That's what I was thinking," I said. I was thinking that future views from the summit of Navajo Mountain would include a power plant complex the size and extent of several dozen Manhattan blocks, that on a day like this one, when I couldn't quite make out Nipple Butte, I would sure as hell be able to spot the giant cubes, the twenty-story-high stacks, the strobes flashing warnings to airplanes day and night, the scrubbed but still murky plume of smoke funneling from the stacks and the cumulus-white fog steaming from the condensers.

I don't remember talking about moral qualms that day, even though Richard would have been the most logical person to have that conversation with, now that Jim Williams had been trundled off to the psych ward. As a person who enjoyed philosophy as well as engineering classes, and whose nature was essentially curious and thoughtful, Richard would have been the ideal person against which to test my wavering moral resolve, and we'd discussed personal and institutional culpability a number of times that summer. But I don't think we had that conversation that particular day, and as I remember the details of that summer, it's the conversations I didn't have that I wonder about the most.

It might have been a pretty interesting discussion, because the day before Richard and I had driven past exhibit A: the Navajo Generating Station, from which it was easy to interpolate the impact the new power plant would have upon the landscape we observed casually from the edge of Navajo Mountain (so casual was our manner, Richard may actually have been chewing on a long stalk of desert grass, the end dangling from his mouth, as was his habit). We'd talked a little about the otherworldliness of the Navajo Generating Station as we drove past it just outside Page, mostly because it was impossible to ignore, hulking as it does just off the highway leading into the Navajo reservation.

Indeed, the Navajo Generating Station ranked alongside Navajo Mountain as the most reliable point of reference for my movements through the summer. From Nipple Bench, you couldn't quite see Lake Powell, even though it's less than thirty miles away, and the biggest man-made artifact for maybe a thousand miles in any direction. But you *could* see the power plant that was rising not far from its shoreline, still two years from generating its first megawatt, partly because it was *huge,* and partly because it was of a shape alien to a landscape even as varied as this one.

Even though I understood that the Navajo Generating Station must be pretty big if I could see it from thirty miles away, my occasional drive in its direction never failed to force my head through vastly unnatural contortions. "That's one big mother," Richard had said as we drove past the plant, and as usual he was right. From miles away, the upper stories and otherworldly smokestacks loom large, and you'd guess it was a few blocks, maybe a quarter mile away. But driving in its direction the half dozen miles from Page is a humbling exercise in pushing the limits of human perspective and comprehension, a failure to come to terms with scale. Each mile closer you think you're there—it's big enough. Another mile, and you think you'll plow into it any second; by the time you leave the highway and head up the access road to the parking lot at its base, you've begun to readjust your sense of what's possible in terms of design and construction, in terms of human will and ambition. Standing at its base and looking straight up at the ramparts of the Navajo Generating Station prompted the same thrill, the same sense of disbelief and awe I had felt that night so many years ago when from my father's arms I viewed the beginnings of Glen Canyon Dam, then taking the first step toward achieving its goal of drowning a hundred miles of canyon. I begin to understand: it's no *wonder* I can see this thing from fifty miles away.

But it's not just size. There are plenty of rock formations in the neighborhood of Page that measure higher and wider than the power plant, but I couldn't quite make them out from Nipple Bench, just like I couldn't quite see Nipple Butte from the top of Navajo Mountain. Power plants this size—the Navajo Generating Station near Page and the unnamed one set to be constructed on the Kaiparowits Plateau—stand out the same way those square-mile sections in Iowa stand out when you see them from above: because the eye is drawn to the starkness, the impossible linearity, the unnaturalness of straight lines and right angles. A modern coal-fired power plant is the biggest cube you can imagine, a complicated assemblage of girders and pipes and spaces and walkways when seen up close, but from even a short distance away those details fade into flat monolithic planes of dark, dull metal, and it might as well be the obelisk that drives all the obscure action in *2001: A Space Odyssey,* and for the same reason, too.

In working toward this point years later in a graduate seminar I was teaching, I made this pronouncement: straight lines do not exist in nature. One student went home and made a list of straight lines that, with all due respect, do *too* exist in nature, a list that included (for example) radiating threads of spider webs and the shear base of a cumulonimbus cloud. I stood by my guns, at one point retreating to a desperate and cowardly defense that depended mumblingly on the theory of a curved universe promoted by modern astrophysicists. Standing much more credibly by her guns, she mailed her list to *Harper's,* which published it as a poem, accompanied by a brief story of her misguided professor and the arrogance of making such academic pronouncements. But I'm still standing by my guns, however publicly I've been shamed and refuted. Maybe lines, squares, and cubes exist in nature too—I've seen crystals under the microscope that come pretty close—but I still believe a cube the size of a mountain, standing in contrast to the less faithfully squared buttes and the less perfectly vertical walls of what's left of Glen Canyon below the dam, are processed unambiguously by the human brain's nature/not-nature sorter as these shapes are comprehended, even (or especially) from a distance. Navajo Mountain looks like it *belongs* there, however starkly its dark color and half-grapefruit shape contrast with the brighter and more angular landscapes that surround it. In contrast, I was sure on that day in 1974 that the power plant I'd see from this point ten years hence wouldn't look like anything carved by erosion, or pushed skyward by internal fire, or even placed by god—

not counting the cube that sits at the center of Islam's most holy site. Even Frank Lloyd Wright couldn't disguise or integrate something this big, something this purposeful, something this *square.*

And the accessories that would rub up against this assortment of lines and squares would not partake of the Kaiparowits's wildness either: even the most modern underground coal mine requires service structures commensurate to the size of the mine itself, and all that noncoal overburden would have to be dumped somewhere. Plans in place that summer included above-ground conveyor belts the width of two-lane highways and slurry tubes the size of subway tunnels running above ground to transport coal from distant mines to the hungry mouth of the furnace. An even longer pipeline would be constructed to carry Lake Powell water to feed the boilers, another stark, if necessarily segmented, straight line. All these accoutrements would require all-weather roads, bridges, and embankments to surmount or bury the countless washes and canyons; warehouses, dormitories, water tanks and reservoirs; and the spider legs of high-voltage power lines running straight in various directions from the webs and grids of transformer farms. And all this would be accented by a smudge of unnaturally hued cloud even the most advanced and hygienic scrubber will fail to scrub into invisibility.

Perhaps because I'd been carving grids into the very landscape I was observing that morning, becoming more proficient and comfortable in manipulating linearity, that most civilized of obsessions, it was not difficult for me to imagine this future landscape presided over by the geometrical forms of a multimegawatt power plant and its many supporting players. After all, I had the example of the Navajo Generating Station I'd marveled at all summer, and the even more insistent example of Lake Powell I could see so clearly that morning. Part of my certainty was based on the kind of inertia I'd come to accept as inevitable in the march of human progress; part of it was the more immediate urgency driven by the threat of long lines at gas stations and the annoyance of power shortages. It was part human history unwilling to be slowed or redirected, and part American impatience when considering the looming specter of inconvenience. And it was in large part my conscience that forced me to place the otherworldly sized block of a power plant, and its twin pillars spouting pale white smoke, at that exact spot where I knew Nipple Bench awaited its fate as the theater stage for the next great epic human beings were capable of producing.

"Yep," Richard said again. "They'll build that thing. They always do."

We sat there looking, not saying much, just taking in the views, present and future. Finally, I said, "Did we really see those horses?"

"I'm pretty sure we did," Richard said.

We were wrong about the power plant. The ten-year interval Richard and I had imagined filled with construction proved to be peaceful; it turned out that the 1984 view would not have included a multimegawatt power plant contributing its cubes and smoke to the scene's overall effect. Development of the Kaiparowits was eventually postponed, not as a result of the environmental impact report, which pronounced the project environmentally permissible if certain conditions were met, conditions that look in retrospect pretty timid, actually pretty generous to the movers and shakers. And postponement was not exactly the result of the kind of epic battle between environmentalists and developers that culminated in legislation that spared Echo Park at the expense of Glen Canyon in 1955, or legislation that halted the Bureau of Reclamation's plans for a series of dams in Grand Canyon in 1968. Political opposition from such groups as the Wilderness Society and the Southern Utah Wilderness Alliance culminated in a series of courtroom skirmishes through the late seventies—prompting much official state-of-Utah indignation concerning delays and postponements won by environmentalists—and some debates were even heard on the floor of Congress; but finally it was the perceived end to the energy crisis, better relations with OPEC, and America's short attention span that ultimately had its way. Building the power plant finally wasn't perceived as necessary, or even profitable, given the economically daunting distance between the Kaiparowits Plateau and just about anywhere else.

Although newspapers would carry stories in 1991 about renewed interest in developing the coal reserves that still waited patiently for exploitation (European investors were mentioned, somewhat sinisterly), nobody got too excited on either side, and in 1996 the unthinkable happened. That year the Kaiparowits Plateau was included in a brand-new national monument, a category of protection only slightly compromised by the fact that the presidential proclamation was largely understood to be a transparently cynical gift the Clinton administration presented to the distant and vaguely green electorate of California, whose electoral college votes counted much more weightily in the presidential election that year than the few votes Utah could muster, and those solidly Republican no matter what Clinton did, or didn't do.

This is not to say that the view from Navajo Mountain didn't change. In 1974 Lake Powell was still filling, more slowly with each year as increased acres of impounded water were required to expand into ever broader inland seas, cresting above the vertical walls that marked the Kaiparowits's dramatic drop into what had been Glen Canyon, covering the broad sandstone shelves that stood on the brink of the lake that year, creeping farther and farther up the side canyons that still seemed that summer pretty dry, water evaporating from all that surface area at a rate close to the rate of impoundment, but still expanding with the kind of relentlessness portrayed in those fifties documentaries that mapped in leaking red colors the amoebic spread of communist infiltration and conquest. I could make out Rainbow Bridge that day, and although I can't be certain without returning to the summit, something I'd both love to do and worry about now with a kind of hesitation I didn't fully explore that summer, my guess is that today I would be able to see the reservoir water that fills the wash directly beneath the span of Rainbow Bridge, an incursion that calls into question the misleadingly reasonable assumption that national monument status can really halt the flood of progress. It was literally *illegal* for Congress to approve a project that would inundate a national monument, but in 1956 it did so nevertheless, a fact of history that those of us who have taken preservationist comfort in the establishment of Grand Staircase/Escalante National Monument might keep in mind.

Perhaps the most noticeable change that has taken place since that day in July 1974 involves Lake Powell's bustling shoreline. Since its filling in 1980, the reservoir has risen and fallen according to the many ups and downs that define a reservoir's usefulness, a response to the decades-long swings between the flood and drought cycles of nature, as well as the more immediate electrical needs of the urban Southwest and the best guesses of Bureau of Reclamation bureaucrats concerning year-by-year flood-control requirements, electrical power demands, and tourists' recreational needs. This has resulted in perhaps the most obvious statement of the reservoir's artificiality: a broad white band of bleached sandstone that rims the reservoir, a scabrous no-man's-land called with either horror or affection the "bathtub ring."

In examining the photographs I took in 1974, I've sometimes tried to answer the question honestly: can I *really* tell that Lake Powell doesn't belong there? What doesn't look—as opposed to *feel,* or to comprehend through the lens of logic or history or politics— natural? Pondering Lake Powell from the summit of Navajo Mountain today, I could answer that question easily: the whiteness of the bathtub ring, a shoreline rendered albino and strange, the result of what could only be the unnatural rise and fall of a body of water accountable to the rhythms of its cash register, the stark boundary between Glen Canyon and the unflooded world of the Kaiparowits, between erasure and survival, a boundary located by explorers, outlined by government surveyors, constructed by Bureau of Reclamation contractors, and reinforced by history and nature as enduringly as a section line in Iowa.

As I've thought about surveying over the years, what strikes me is how powerfully the rectangular survey has affected America, and how *quietly,* with so little of the debate and dissent that have defined the environmental movement. Having failed to stop the construction of Glen Canyon Dam in the late fifties, environmentalists rallied through the next decade to successfully forestall the construction of dozens of new dams. Today, several active organizations, populated by individuals ranging from the tie-and-blazer type to the monkey-wrenching sort, are even agitating for Glen Canyon Dam's disassembly, and the consequent restoration of Glen Canyon. We've finally come to question the necessity of applying the capable hand of man to every potentially useful landscape.

But no one is suggesting that we question our reliance on the grid, the straight line run according to the cardinal points of the compass, a much more powerful and pervasive historical force than any number of Bureau of Reclamation projects, of much more consequence because it is basically a *cause* rather than an *effect.* Conventional wisdom has it that Americans have gone through some profound changes since the 1700s in the way we perceive nature. Just as the Enlightenment determined that the crooked lines and irregular lots of the metes and bounds survey would be replaced by the arrogance of the straight line and the squared grid, the romantic revolution ushered in a new sensitivity to the integrity of natural landscape, which (as the romantics relentlessly pointed out) seldom carves *itself* into squares. Frustrated by the tunnel vision of linearity, the romantics encouraged us to search for correspondences with nature, to find ourselves in what pure nature presents to the eye, not what humans have placed there for it to find. They taught us that ultimate truth is accessible through intuition, not mathematics; in those "untaught sallies of the spirit" Emerson recommended to Thoreau and to the rest of us, not the narrow calculus of science and reason.

The procession of what one college text calls the "environmentalist tradition" describes a steady march into increasingly respectful attitudes toward nature: from Thoreau and Emerson through John Muir and Teddy Roosevelt to David Brower and Edward Abbey; from Thoreau's groundbreaking *Walden* to Al Gore's ho-hum *Earth in the Balance.* It's supposed to *mean* something that we live in an America informed by such institutions as the National Park Service, the Sierra Club, and the American suburb, whose more prestigious avenues curve gracefully according to the metes and bounds conventions of the English countryside. An evolutionary progression of legislation ever friendlier to the environment, including the American Antiquities Act of 1906, the Wilderness Act of 1964, even the routine national recognition of Earth Day, would seem to have rendered the tightass linearity of the Ordinance of 1785 not only quaint, but moot.

Nevertheless, as if occupying some kind of parallel universe that exists in blissful ignorance of all this cultural and ideological progress, the straight lines of Jefferson's vision have quietly extended themselves for over two hundred years. As artists, writers, and philosophers labored to revise and expand our attitudes toward nature, government surveyors have worked quietly in the background reinforcing the old lines, and scratching brand-new lines into those few remaining islands of unsurveyed American terrain, constructing a squared and gridded landscape that is so pervasive as to be considered unremarkable. The Ordinance of 1785 has had the effect of keeping Americans trapped in the smug assumptions of the Age of Reason, and as a result, post-Enlightenment insights sit uneasily on the American countryside. The square-mile section that serves as the starting point for all property boundaries, public and private; the state highway that runs due north until it disappears into the horizon; the rigid checkerboard expanse of the Midwest we observe from 40,000 feet—all these intersecting lines subtly direct our thoughts toward the mathematical equations of the Enlightenment, not the spiritual correspondences of transcendentalism. In spite of Earth Day celebrations and new national parks, we continue to orient ourselves in a lined and squared landscape that inevitably frames our relationship with the natural world.

What does it mean for a nation to assume its identity amid all these straight lines? Bigger thinkers than I am can take that one on. I only know what it meant for me that summer: chronic ideological confusion, occasional disorientation, and an unaccountable and unseemly pride. Working for the Cadastral Survey had the effect of bouncing me back and forth between paradigms, summers committed to imposing straight lines on nature, the rest of the year in eco-rehab, backpacking and cross-country skiing and basking in the innocent glow of the modern environmental movement's golden years. Even so, my awareness of the vast disconnect in my life between my gentler inclinations and the work I did each summer didn't prevent me from reaping the psychological benefits of ruling the world. Through each long summer I watched myself getting better and better at my job, eating and breathing linearity until it became part of me, until line became *personal,* and on those days when my equations came out right and Polaris confirmed my place in the universe, when line ran straight and true the only direction it could—in spite of the eloquence of Emerson, the burgeoning neopagan nature worship of the times, and my own all-too-predictable qualms and guilts—Jefferson's vision became my own.

CHAPTER TEN

Hiking In, and Hiking Out

One of the assumptions the teachers talked about the most and examined the least held that nature was good for troubled kids, and that's why we'd brought this assortment of high school students to spend spring break in the canyons of the Escalante wilderness, the drainage just north of the Kaiparowits Plateau I'd contemplated the summer before from my overlook on Navajo Mountain.

I had finally gotten serious about teaching. My graduation with a degree in English was looming ominously on the horizon, and that fall I had visited the school of education offices to complete the necessary application paperwork and found myself part-time employment the following spring in an alternative school-within-a-school for at-risk high school kids.

The program was housed in a wonderfully high-ceilinged and well-lit room, but we didn't spend a lot of time there, preferring hikes in the foothills and field trips to museums and parks, and each spring we'd scrounge backpacks and sleeping bags, pack ourselves and our gear into an assortment of student and teacher cars, and drive into the southern Utah desert for reasons we believed were more profound than merely recreational. Our hope for these students was that contact with what in the mid-seventies we naively called "pure nature," in combination with distance from the traumas and temptations of home and neighborhood, would prompt them to reconsider some of the bad decisions they were making. Even though my own approach was complicated by the very different kinds of experiences I'd been racking up during each summer, I basically agreed with the other teachers in the program that nature—especially wild nature, untainted by the appropriation and waste that define human use (which is another way, I suppose, of saying "unsurveyed")—had that kind of power to heal and transform. Even I operated on the assumption, if only provisionally, that when it came to transforming these kids, it was all in the approach: take nature on its own terms, open yourself up to what wilderness could teach you, and something good would probably happen.

I remember that it rained during most of the drive south, making us worry about the thirty miles of dirt road we'd have to cover to reach the Coyote Wash trailhead. We stopped for lunch at a cafe in Escalante, the small town that marked the end of the paved road, ran splashing from our cars through the rain, and rushed through the door into what was clearly a cafe for the locals, not the tourists.

My two summers' experience as a surveyor, living in small southern Utah towns like this one, had taught me the difference. Most of the customers who looked us over were men. Some of them were regulars, the usual gathering of farmers and ranchers who met over coffee to talk feed prices, rainfall, and politics. The rest had been driven by the rain from their work in the mountains and canyons to a place dry and warm and not so lonely: contract loggers, cowboys, post cutters, men who entertained even fewer illusions about the beneficence of nature than surveyors did.

Because Escalante was located at the base of the Straight Cliffs that marked the north boundary of the Kaiparowits Plateau, the locals sustained many of the same hopes for development and prosperity I'd seen in Warren Knowles, and I understood pretty well that many of the cafe's regulars who checked us out that day would eagerly leave their work under the sublime wide-open skies of southern Utah to become miners and welders and pipe fitters the moment work commenced on the power plant proposed for construction not so far away on Nipple Bench. During the years since it had been announced, the project had become a lightning rod for every possible land-use faction—environmentalists objected to the inevitable degradation of air and water, tourists such as ourselves wanted the scenery to remain pristine, and the locals needed the work—and the arguments had only gotten uglier during the months since I'd surveyed Nipple Bench. Its fate, and the fate of Escalante, and a number of other small southern Utah towns, was being decided in courtrooms and legislative chambers even as we walked through that cafe door.

Less than a year earlier, in the few weeks before we'd taken on the Kaiparowits Plateau and had worked to reestablish the boundaries of that school section just west of Koosharem, Utah, our crew had established a routine familiar to government surveyors. Each morning we'd leave our motel rooms in Richfield and drive east on State 24, the highway that conducted tourists to the recently constructed Hite Marina on Lake Powell. After a few miles crowded bumper to bumper with swaying motor homes and trailered houseboats, we'd turned south toward work.

On our first day, we'd left transits behind and did what we called "recon," spending the day finding out what was what on our new job: the general lay of the land, the condition of the roads we'd travel, the gates we'd need keys for, the accuracy of the USGS maps we'd consult, the trustworthiness of the survey markers we'd be starting from. On the Koosharem job, we ran into trouble right away. The only road into the northern, more mountainous end of the section started out pretty well, meandering easily up the broad floor of a wash. Although the wash was watered this particular morning by a narrow trickle of a stream, scattered remnants of tree trunks and boulders the size of kitchen stoves reminded us that a good rainstorm would flood the wash deeper than our truck's roof. After less than a mile, the road degenerated into two ruts that twisted out of the wash and onto a steep ridgeline. Our four-wheel drive whining in compound low, we climbed steadily toward Koosharem Peak, negotiated a dozen tight switchbacks, then leveled off on a sloping bench of aspen, spruce, and Douglas fir.

This was the first week in June, early spring at this altitude, even though the temperature was already reaching into the eighties; we crossed several small creeks and plowed our way through a series of foot-deep snowdrifts, stopping finally in a sunlit opening that upon inspection turned out to be more bog than meadow. The tracks disappeared beneath the dark surface of standing water broken only by the skinny shoots of new grass, reappearing on more solid ground a hundred feet away. Come back in August, the landscape seemed to say.

Larry walked around looking things over and thinking. We needed this road; parking our truck here would mean a lot of hiking, adding three or four more daily miles to what was going to be a couple of weeks of long days, carrying everything we needed—chainsaw, transit, lath, water—to the beginning point; later, when we'd be running the section's northern boundary, this long hike would leave us only a couple of hours of daylight to actually do our work. It was clear, however, that there was no way we'd get through the swamp, even with four-wheel drive.

So we raised a dam and dug a canal. Without benefit of civil engineering expertise or environmental impact report, and without even checking the land status map to determine whether we might be doing Bureau of Reclamation work on private land, we located the source of the water, a small snowmelt-fed spring. We spent an hour digging a narrow trench and mounding a dike, a miniature Glen Canyon Dam of mud and sod a foot high, diverting the water away from the road, forcing it to find another path to the Sevier River. When we returned a week later (we had modified our schedule to attend to the south boundary of the school section first, approachable by way of a road requiring only the usual four-wheel drive), we were happy to find that our reclamation project had been successful. The meadow was still pretty wet, but considerably more solid than it had been, and with enough speed and momentum, tires spinning just enough but not too much, and some elbows-flailing lock-to-lock steering, Larry managed to blast through the meadow without once bogging down.

During that second week—the week Williams had stopped sleeping at all and was spiraling in on the breakdown that was destined to make Friday so memorable—I had a close call with lightning. We'd begun running the section's northern boundary, which crossed a ridge just below the 11,000–foot summit of Koosharem Peak. I lined in a flag on the crest of the ridge, pounded it in according to Larry's instructions over the radio, then watched Larry and Williams measure a baseline from which to triangulate the distance, preparing for the hike up the ridge to join me for the next leg into a broad high basin that presumably held the northwest section corner.

With nothing to do but wait, I passed the time watching a storm front darken and spread, filling the eastern sky as it blew itself in our direction. Larry had also seen the storm but wasn't quite ready to call it quits—he didn't think the storm looked serious, and with all that hiking just to get to the job, he wanted to make the most of the time we had on line—so he radioed me to find shelter while they did the same. I scouted up and down the austere ridgeline, finally locating a rock overhang several feet deep that offered no protection from the wind, but promised to keep most of me dry when the rain hit.

It was the only time I would ever see Larry misread the weather. As the storm moved closer and made its strength known, Larry radioed a change of plans, explaining through the radio's crackling static that we'd better plan on getting the hell out of there, but that I'd best stay where I was until this first wave passed by. He was thinking of the swampy meadow we barely made it through each day, and what a good rainstorm would do to our meager reclamation project, and he was thinking about the wash we'd have to drive through; but he was also thinking that I'd be an excellent candidate for a lighting strike if I started down the slope right then to join them for the hike to the truck. So I hunched in my shallow cave and watched lightning strike the slope below me, each jagged bolt hitting closer than the one before.

Other than my fear, what I remember most is that the lighting strikes actually raised dust. The storm front was dry, too loaded with electricity to hold much water, and the mountains had gone a couple of weeks without any rain to speak of, so the bolts hit dry earth, literally shaking the ground and raising small explosions of dust and dirt, smoky mushrooms that blew away quickly in the wind. For a few minutes I was sure the lightning would climb the ridge and find me out; the crash of thunder grew louder and louder, a flash and an explosion, one atop the other, both right on top of me; the electricity was a tangible presence, buzzing steadily between the echoing explosions, thickening the air with ozone and stiffening the hair on my arms. I pulled myself deeper into the overhang, knowing that being cooked in my oven-sized shelter was a real possibility. It was one of the few times in my life I truly understood that nature could kill me.

At almost the last moment, the line of lightning strikes angled away to the north, finally passing over the ridge and into the basin

where we'd planned to extend our line that afternoon, and I relaxed a little, my heart slowing, the buzz in my ears fading. Larry
came on the radio, the clearer reception communicating a little of
his true concern under his banter; predictably, he first asked
whether the lightning had scorched that ponytail of mine. Then he
told me that if I was still alive, it was time to run for it. Behind the
dry overcharged front the storm looked like a lot of rain, so as soon
as it was safe for me to hightail it down the mountain, I did.
Slinging the equipment over our shoulders, we ran through an obstacle course of rock and sagebrush to the truck, then drove as fast
as Larry's skills would take us, slewing through the meadow minutes before the rain hit in earnest, making it through the wash just
before it flooded.

"Pie and coffee," Larry said as we turned north on the paved
road, a kind of code like "recon" that implied something slightly
euphemistic. It meant that we were doing something we hardly
ever did, which was calling it quits early for the day. We drove up
the highway through the cafeless town of Koosharem, and turned
west onto 24, the highway that sped ski boats to Lake Powell.

We drove past the first cafes we saw because they were the places
tourists went. They weren't exactly national chains, but they were
too well lit by neon and too thoroughly heralded by billboards. We
finally stopped at a small cafe in Sigurd, a tiny community just far
enough south of Salina to be spared the white dust that filters
down like fine snow from the gypsum mine that provided employment in this otherwise depressed corner of southern Utah. It
was dark, inexpensive, and there were the regulars, local farmers
and cattlemen having their afternoon coffee, and a few others,
men who, like us, had been driven by the elements into a place
that felt safe and communal. They watched us as we came inside,
nodded, and then went back to their quiet conversations, to their
pie and coffee.

I knew even before I opened the door and herded my students
into the Escalante cafe, before I saw the glares and felt the hostility, that we didn't belong, weren't welcome. It didn't help that our
cars were plastered with bumper stickers that praised the Sierra
Club and condemned the interests that would build mines and
power plants in the coal-rich plateaus—chief among them the

Kaiparowits—that surrounded this poor desert town, projects that offered employment beyond the usual for the cash-starved great-grandchildren of Mormon pioneers: cutting cedar posts, working seasonally for government agencies, and hauling hay during the brief growing season. We were in the wrong place at the wrong time, and once again I felt disoriented, confused about my place and where I stood.

Of course I was with my students. I felt the fierce protective connection that I recognized a few years later when I had children of my own; like any good parent, I was upset that anyone would look at these kids in a way that could hurt them. But I recognized the glares, and I couldn't lie to myself about the depth of experience that lay behind them, the enormity of the gap that separated them from us, the distance that separated me from the person I'd been the summer before, a person who had learned something important in that school section above Koosharem, Utah.

Although I'd been happy to have survived the lightning and found a dry safe place, and was looking forward to the warmth of coffee and the domestic comfort of apple pie, I hadn't felt entirely at home that afternoon in the Sigurd cafe. This was only my second summer surveying; Larry reminded me daily that my long hair was going to get me beaten up in one of the small-town bars and cafes where we spent most summer evenings (among the more coherent graffiti I'd read in men's rooms throughout southern Utah was "kill all hippies and niggers"), just as he reminded me that my questions were stupid and my prospects as a surveyor doubtful. I'd actually been surprised at the end of my first summer, when after weeks of embarrassing disorientation on that township north of Vernal I'd finally achieved some measurable insight into the theory and practice of running line, that Larry had let me know I'd be recommended for further employment with the BLM, crediting less the quality of my work than the effectiveness of his instruction. In fact, it wasn't until late in my second summer, when we'd surveyed the township on the Kaiparowits Plateau (which in addition to offering up coal for the future production of electricity provided the snowmelt for Coyote Creek, the tributary of the Escalante River that carved the canyon into which I'd eventually march my students), I began to feel more at home in those places like the one Warren Knowles ran, the bars and cafes that offered true community only to those who understand that nature is not necessarily your friend.

Although this process of acculturation, of finding myself more or less comfortable in the redneck bars and cafes of southern Utah, was gradual, it was punctuated forever by one August day that summer on the Kaiparowits, the hottest day of a long blistering summer, probably the worst day of my surveying career. It had been unbearably hot; we'd gotten used to temperatures in the high 90s, but this day was nearer 115, the third day of a heat wave that had left us wilted and exhausted. The helicopter struggled in the heat and altitude to take us where we needed to go: the heat drained the air of the density the rotor blades needed to beat effectively, and the helicopter's temperature gauge trembled near the boundary where the green gives way to red. Even the starter motor hesitated, whining more annoyingly than usual as it cranked over the engine to take us to the ten hours of difficult work we'd planned.

At first I blamed this noticeable decline in performance on the new helicopter pilot, a Vietnam vet named Roger who'd arrived at the scene barely five feet tall and congenitally speedy in a pissed-off kind of way to replace Alan, who had been rotated back to the cooler if more bug-ridden climes of Alaska. But if Roger (who we began immediately to call Roger Ramjet in recognition of his gung-ho-ness, then simply Ramjet) wasn't in the same league with Alan, he was reasonably competent, and it really wasn't his fault; it was the heat, and then, as it turned out, the helicopter, that slowed things down that week.

The heat was really something, so searing that I actually walked a mile that day at high noon to find shade. We were running line across a wide shale flat, a few miles north of Nipple Bench; the smooth light gray surface reflected sunlight as effectively as a tanning mirror and poured heat through the soles of our work boots. The dry landscape practically shouted sterility: there were no junipers, no piñon pines, not even the occasional clump of demoralized saltgrass or hostile cactus. And there was literally no relief to this landscape, no rock behind which you could find a little shade.

We'd just planted our final corner marker, our shovels cutting slowly through the brittle layers of shale. Because this landscape was so open and unobstructed, and because we'd wanted to get as much done as possible in the relative cool of the morning, we'd worked fast and hard, finishing the mile we'd assigned ourselves an hour and a half before the helicopter was scheduled to pick us up and carry us to another line on the other side of the township, so we waited, some of us more comfortably than others. One of the many things I envied in Larry—something I'd noticed about the other party chiefs, most of them, like Larry, natives of the same southern Utah landscape we surveyed—was his ability to create shade. He wore one of those narrow-brimmed hats golfers sometimes wear, yet he was able to gather himself into its shadow as he squatted to enter numbers and notes in his yellow fieldbook, somehow shaded by that meager brim so that only the tip of his nose and the bend of his knees caught the direct scorching rays of the sun. The way he was able to create shade out of nothing seemed to go against the laws of physics I knew anything about, and I knew that no matter how I contorted myself, no matter what sombrero of a hat I wore, I'd still remain a city boy, exposed as a turkey on a spit. I was usually stoic at times like this, but it was 115 degrees, and I was willing to do anything to get the sun off my back, even for a few minutes.

I announced that I couldn't stand it—I needed shade. I looked toward the only relief I could see, a wash that paralleled our line a half mile away, and I walked in that direction, telling myself that my movement at least stirred up the air around me as I walked, cooling me a little even as it encouraged more fluid loss and hastened the inevitability of heat exhaustion. I wasn't disappointed completely—there was no shady overhang, but I found a narrow side wash just about my size, and after checking for snakes and scorpions, I squeezed myself between the ravine's crumbling shale walls and luxuriated in what at least was not direct sun. I curled there waiting for the whap-whap-whap of the helicopter's rotor blades, fantasizing about the rotor wash the helicopter brought with it as it landed. However noisy and stinging with grit and stinking of exhaust and hot oil, it was nevertheless *wind,* moving air, the only thing we had to look forward to on a day like this.

But that wasn't what I heard. What I heard was Larry's voice on my radio telling me that the helicopter wasn't coming.

"Ramjet radioed the thing won't start," Larry explained. The pilot had shut it down while he waited for the other crew to finish

its work, and now the engine wouldn't even turn over. It had suc-
cumbed to that most banal of all infirmities, a dead battery, the
same thing that eventually had brought low every marginal car of
my high school years, its solenoid making the same impotent
clicking noise.

"Better get on back here," Larry said, his words finding their way
through the static all too clearly. "Looks like we're hiking out."

Hiking out, we all well knew, meant at least seven miles to the
nearest road, a graveled two-lane that ran alongside the Cockscomb, the high straight sandstone fin uplifted to the nearly vertical by the same forces that had raised the flatter strata of the
Kaiparowits Plateau, neatly marking the plateau's western boundary. The other crew had parked a truck there; they saved time
each day by meeting the helicopter on the Cockscomb Road after
our crew had been flown directly from Wahweap City. We had
been spared that drive every morning because our township was
closer by air, which meant that we had an easier commute but a
longer workday. Today, it meant that although both crews would
have to hike out, ours would be by far the longest hike.

Actually, were it not for the fact that we were nearly out of
water, carrying our surveying gear, and doing it all in the direct
blast of a 115–degree sun, it would have been an interesting hike,
the scenery spectacular once we'd escaped the shale flat, the kind
of terrain I'd have hiked through happily in my previous life as a
backpacker and climber, a tourist who'd periodically wrapped himself in the red rock and blue sky of southern Utah. In that other
life, the desert was a wonderful place, alternately healing and en-
ergizing, and seven miles was nothing if it meant putting some distance between you and civilization. But this was work, *hard* work.
Our hike took us past the stranded helicopter, where we both profaned at and commiserated with the new pilot. After making the
inevitable offer to push-start the helicopter by shoving it off the
cliff, we continued our forced march, our demoralized ranks now
including Roger, who looked wistfully over his shoulder at the lawn
chair he'd inherited from Alan, now abandoned in the shade of a
large piñon pine. "Now you get to see how the other half lives,"
Larry said to him as we took on the remaining miles.

Our route led us across the gradually swelling rise of a high
plateau, then around the head of a wash that drained deeply to the
east, eventually joining the Escalante River near Coyote Wash. We

had to make the decision hikers in the desert always have to make: is it better to walk around the various rises and fallings of topography, trading altitude for miles, across for up-and-down? I'd spent my life before I became a surveyor preferring to maintain altitude, walking longer distances to keep the height I'd attained, but I was hiking with surveyors now, and although we angled south a little to avoid the biggest ledges, we otherwise climbed straight up the ridges and plunged into and out of the washes and canyons as if we were still running line, losing and then reclimbing thousands of vertical feet. I focused on the inch or two of water that sloshed in my canteen, resolving to drink it only when the truck was in sight.

Our way was easy to see: the Cockscomb dominated the view to the west, a sharp spine of crags and blades thrust dramatically along a straight line for twenty miles in a northerly direction, aligned as if it had been surveyed by someone who had a pretty good idea of where north ran but hadn't based his bearing on a precise observation of Polaris. We were approaching the Cockscomb from its slightly less precipitous eastern side, climbing a long steep slope dotted with small junipers and clumps of desert grass. This would be a difficult climb under any circumstances, and we'd been hiking for hours now without rest, the temperature reaching its midafternoon peak, the sun hitting us square in the face as we raised our eyes to the jagged skyline of the Cockscomb. We were finally letting our lousy attitudes surface, moaning and complaining, shifting our packs and tripods from the painful ruts they'd worn in our backs, wringing our shirts of sweat as we neared the conclusion of all that unforeseen and unwelcome work.

Reaching the crest, we spotted the Carryall parked five hundred feet below us, and by scouting along the spine we were able to find a rock chimney we could squeeze into and down, making our way through the upthrust sandstone reef and slowly down the cliff band of the nearly vertical west side. Trading breathlessness now for precariousness, we handed tripods, packs, and canteen belts back and forth as we took turns negotiating the most difficult pitches, climbing carefully from ledge to ledge, gouging ourselves on sharp outcrops and sliding painfully on our stomachs across the cheese-grater surface of decomposing sandstone faces, eventually reaching the loose scree at the foot of the cliffs, where by alternately skidding and digging in the heels of our boots, we managed to ski our way down to the road, nicely graded so as to conduct tourists comfortably alongside the sublimity of the Cockscomb to the apparently photogenic rock formations of Kodachrome Basin State Park. We finally arrived at the truck to find that there was no water there either, the crew chief having neglected his duty this morning of all mornings.

So we raced to the nearest bar along the nearest highway. This was something we never did—on those days the weather made work impossible we'd go for actual pie and actual coffee, and we'd consume it in a respectable cafe, not a saloon. On normal days beer drinking would commence after hours, when we'd made it back to our motels or trailers, pulling the tabs even before our boots came off, then walking to the nearest bar. We understood what a row of BLM trucks parked outside a tavern looked like to the average taxpayer. The few surveyors who drank on the job did it circumspectly, submerging a six-pack beneath motel-machine ice in the five-gallon coolers we carried in each truck, later burying the evidence at the bottom of the deep efficient holes we'd learned to dig.

But we were angry, depressed, and *really thirsty,* and this was not a pie-and-coffee kind of day: we needed a bar. After a skidding race down the Cockscomb Road, we parked our truck in front of the first beer-serving establishment we could find, a dilapidated bar on Highway 89 that in more elegant terrain would have been termed a "roadhouse" but here was only a windowless tin-roofed cinderblock cube with an ancient swamp cooler that screamed its scant comfort into our faces as we pulled ourselves around a table and inhaled as many beers as we could get down. I alternated swigs from my beer bottle with gulps from a glass of the bar's alkaline tap water, barely cooled by a few anemic ice cubes.

I'm trying to remember now what we looked like as if it could help explain what happened next. We were soaked and rancid with the sweat that had poured off us through a long morning of hard work and a longer afternoon of unanticipated walking, hotter even for the half hour we'd spent crammed on top of each other in the non-air-conditioned Carryall, after all those hours hiking nonrecreationally across the desert. We were burned black by our weeks in the sun, our work shirts and Levi's grimy with the gray of the shale flat and the sand that filled our work boots and pants as we slid down the steep west side of the Cockscomb. We were just beginning to stop being pissed off at the whole mess, the breaking down of the helicopter, the unnecessary hiking, the lack of water at the truck.

We were just beginning the process of rehydration and forgiveness, our cells just commencing to reconstitute themselves with water and alcohol, starting to feel a little normal, whatever that was, when three tourists, two men and a woman, walked into the bar to ask directions and perhaps take a break from the heat of their own driving. They were my age, college students, wearing shorts, tucked-in T-shirts, their long hair kept in check by bandannas in a variety of colors and arrangements: rolled into a headband, tied into a cap, the woman's holding her hair back in a kind of babushka.

We had the advantage on them in every way. They blinked as they entered the dark of the bar, looking around them as their eyes adjusted, not knowing whom to ask for the directions they needed or where to sit for refreshment they might want, and so we had a chance to look them over and make our judgments, which is exactly what we did, taking advantage, as if they were the enemy, of their momentary blindness and our clear view. We stopped talking and turned in their direction, taking in their Vibram-soled hiking boots, their baggy shorts, the beads that hung around their necks, their long hair.

I'm still trying to figure out exactly how I was able to hate them so entirely, so purely. I was more *them* than I was *us;* I had in common with them their age, their long hair, and eight months out of the year, their reason for being in the desert. The months I surveyed—who knows who, or what, I was? I was dressed like Larry, like Craig Sylvester, and the Richardson brothers, the men who had grown up in the desert and become surveyors, men whose great-grandparents had been Mormon pioneers exiled to this hell of chaotic red canyons and dry springs. A century of accumulated desert wisdom enabled Larry and the others to understand nature as it really was: an enemy that must be defeated in order for the community to survive. Their ancestry and their upbringing led them directly to this most logical of professions, surveying, enlisting themselves as the sappers who lay out the lines, preparing the way so that the invasion can be carried out efficiently, with as few casualties as possible.

In spite of our similar clothing, however, these sons of southern

Utah continued to regard me with some suspicion. As I said, more than a few surveyors knew me only by my alternating nicknames "Ponytail" and "McGovern." Although I was feeling more at home in the small towns where we rented rooms or parked our bunk trailers, I was continually aware of the cultural and geographical distance that defined the way I spent my nonsurveying months— Mondays through Fridays in school, weekends backpacking and cross-country skiing—and the way I earned my tuition money each summer.

Any other day I might have been torn, not quite knowing whether I stood with the backpackers in their shorts and vacation days or sat with the men I worked with daily. On another day, I might have offered a friendly word or helped with directions, not worrying that I was marking myself as something alien to the purposes of the Cadastral Survey, something Larry and the others already knew. But that day I had earned, as we used to say, my per diem. I'd walked a half mile each way just for the gift of a half hour's shelter from the sun, and then dragged myself on a waterless, shadeless, unplanned-for seven-mile forced march to a truck that had no water either, and I'd joined the ranks of survivors, suffered and prevailed in something that felt just a little more serious— and hence more real—than tourism. At that moment, I thought I finally knew what nature was, what those rocks and plateaus and geological formations actually were once you peeled fancy names like the "Cockscomb" and "Kodachrome Basin" and "Coyote Wash" away from them, names that only existed on the map, weren't embedded in the actual topography the way trees, cliffs, and survey markers were.

That afternoon in that nameless bar along Highway 89 there was not a single molecule of me that was confused. I knew whose side I was on. I not only couldn't understand why anybody in his right mind would come out into all this heat and dust and unshaded sun for any reason other than to do battle; I held these people in contempt for their stupidity, for their incomprehensible wrongness concerning nature. Whatever good feelings we'd begun to conjure up vaporized the second they walked through the door, and we all glared at them, a kind of electrically palpable hostility it was clear they felt, a threat of insults and perhaps even violence: my mind played a quick preview of the inevitable escalation, the pushing and the fists, the sort of unfair one-sided fight I'd observed but thus far escaped in other barrooms throughout southern Utah, this time not a bit unsure whose side I'd take.

One of them mumbled a question about the Paria Canyon wilderness ranger station, where they hoped to find a particular trailhead. As we watched them look around nervously, fish thrown upon a dry unfriendly shore, the bartender gestured toward the door and said, "A few miles down the road," which may or may not have been true, and the three hikers awkwardly turned and escaped into the bare sunshine of late afternoon, any thoughts of having a quick beer evaporating in the dry anger of the room.

It would be too simple to say I identified with the regulars in the Escalante cafe, that day nearly a year later when I'd followed my students through the door for lunch, taking a break on our journey to Coyote Wash in search of spiritual rehabilitation. To some extent, of course, I did, but it had been months since I'd worked as a surveyor, and the thick angry silence rattled me a little. My students handled the hostility a lot better than I did, their expressions communicating the combination of boredom and disdain they practiced daily. They were used to glares and judgments, understood that offending people was not only the price they paid for being teenagers, but sometimes even a kind of affirmation of the choices they'd made. This is not to say that their feelings were immune to hurt; it's just that they'd been hurt by the best, by those they had trusted and loved. A bunch of farmers in a small Utah town were pretty easy to dismiss.

My students had another advantage: they were city kids. Our high school drew from a district that cut through the range of social classes that stratified Salt Lake City; a few of our students were the children of doctors and professors, a few more had been fed their entire lives by food stamps and welfare checks, and the rest were from families who lived from paycheck to paycheck. They had in common—in addition to their being in some kind of trouble, the only qualification a kid needed to transfer into our program—their urbanity, their sophistication in the ways of city life. They had no clue about the way the people of Escalante lived, what they valued, how they survived. More important, they didn't *want* to know. They'd learned that however crummy their own neighborhoods, cities were the future, the location of power and dominance, the place where decisions about coal-fired power plants and wilderness areas were ultimately made.

They understood that there was the city, and there was the landscape outside the city, the mountains and deserts that existed in order that city folks could charge their spiritual batteries when convenient. That people actually lived in this landscape was a fact too complicated to consider, so they didn't. Instead, they sat down at the various unoccupied tables, ordered their hamburgers, alternately returned and ignored the hostility that permeated the room as they talked about what was important to them, enclosing themselves in the small communities of their booths and tables, fortified outposts in a dangerous landscape. Later, walking to our cars, one student said "redneck *ass*holes," and almost everybody murmured agreement, the words simultaneously naming and dismissing the whole experience.

I kept quiet. The summer before, when my rehydration had been interrupted by something equally urban and recreational, there had been something deep and sincere in the hatred I'd felt for the three people who stopped on their way to the Paria Canyon trailhead. In contrast, what I felt in this Escalante cafe was so complex as to be unidentifiable. Other than my feeling protective and a little scared—I loved these kids, felt responsible for their safety, and I knew firsthand the accumulation of anger warehoused behind those stares, understood that the potential for danger was more real than they knew—I felt justly accused of having done something wrong, something serious.

What I mostly felt was mistaken, that I'd not only betrayed loyalty—I felt an unforeseen sense of connection with these particular redneck assholes—but knowledge. I felt for a moment that I had denied what I knew to be true, that I was guilty of some kind of profound dishonesty.

Working in a particular landscape enables you to understand things about the terrain, the trees and grasses, the sharp unforgiving rocks and the rare stingy springs, things you will never learn as a tourist. You learn, for example, that although you can carve your lines into just about any forest or rock formation that you'd been assigned, the landscape snaps back. It can kill you in any number of ways: snakebite, rockslide, lightning, dehydration. You set up your transit beneath a crumbling rock face you know could at any moment collapse on top of you; you look around at the house-sized remnants of the most recent catastrophe, and you know there will be no warning this time either. Or the tree you're cutting down to clear line will fall the wrong way, swung by a connection with a neighboring tree even the most experienced axman wouldn't have seen, pivoting in a direction that catches you dead center. When you spend dawn-to-dusk workweeks, a lifetime of difficult unshaded work, under it, that beautiful southern Utah sun can be seen for what it is: nothing less than your enemy, draining you of the water necessary for life, cutting into the tender layers of your flesh to burn you into something that almost glows in the welcome darkness of nightfall. You learn that in wetter and cooler seasons, other forces take their turn: the random lightning strike, the wall of water that crushes you beneath the weight of rain that fell on a mesa thirty miles away. Coming or going, nature is something other than your friend.

What about spiritual regeneration, then? Did I really believe what we told our students concerning the purpose of our yearly expeditions, bringing their troubled souls into contact with nature, pure and uncontaminated? Over the winter, I'd begun reading Emerson with more care, so I was beginning to understand the theory; and John Muir, who helped me by elaborating upon the application, telling me, for example, that the lightning is something to be known, not feared, that literally the best way to understand the essentially loving nature of a thunderstorm is to place yourself in the top branches of the tallest tree you can find. And I'd spent so much time climbing and backpacking in the deserts and mountains of Utah and Wyoming that I should have understood the ways I'd been personally improved, *re-created*. I'd also seen the way experiences in nature touched my students, prompting various degrees of transformation in character and outlook: I'd observed a clearer depth to one kid's glance, a more measured response to the horrors another student faced daily. I'd even read studies done on teenagers who'd survived those expensive wilderness experience programs, complete with numbers proving that the majority of their graduates were measurably improved by the time they'd spent in nature: better grades, better attitudes, better prospects.

Nevertheless, beyond what seems to *work*, beyond the anger of southern Utah ranchers, the relative desirability of wilderness areas

or coal-fired power plants, the longer attention span of a particular student—beyond the specific individuals and issues that hover
around the periphery of the most important questions—you might
believe exists the *truth* about nature. Having experienced both
sides, having served both as wilderness guide for my students and
as a huddled target for a line of lightning strikes, perhaps I should
have understood what that truth might be.

Instead, what I understood was placelessness, a variation on the
theme I'd gotten well used to, especially that spring. In spite of my
resolve to do something specific with my nonsurveying life—that
is, to become a teacher—my experiences in my various lives had
overwhelmed me with far more information about nature than I
could handle, resulting in a kind of paralysis, a loss of identity,
a feeling of belonging nowhere, least of all in the landscape we
planned to hike into, the canyons carved by water melted from the
Kaiparowits snowpack. I was learning too much in both lives, none
of it adding up to the kind of wisdom that might have allowed me
to understand and perhaps complicate the pure hatred I'd directed
toward the three backpackers that hot afternoon the summer before.

Part of the problem involved my background: like my students,
I was a city kid. Even though I'd spent a good part of my life in the
out-of-doors, and had learned a lot of what James Fenimore Cooper
called the "subtle crafts of the forest," until I began surveying, my
frame of reference was essentially urban. My childhood had been
spent on family vacations to national parks, pack trips into various
wilderness areas in Utah and Wyoming, a week each summer at
Scout camp, daily hikes into the mountains above my home. It was
a great way to grow up, but looking back on those experiences
from the perspective of a surveyor, they start seeming superficial
to me, my participation somehow lacking in sincerity.

Emerson pointed out the obvious. Although my confusion was
partly a problem of history and culture, it was mostly personal—as
he put it, nature "always wears the colors of the spirit." Basically,
I didn't know where I stood because I didn't know who I was. This
condition had long preceded my experience as a surveyor, but
those eight years of watching my two lives speed in opposite directions accelerated my anxiety to the crisis point. Each summer
when I'd return to surveying, with yet another academic year's
worth of ever more sophisticated insights into the great scheme of

things, Larry would hold forth on the inverse relationship between the increase in my knowledge of things academic and recreational, and the corresponding decrease in my already meager inventory of common sense. He'd make the same joke each June: he'd loudly enroll me in Shovel 101, reviewing for me the techniques of hole-digging and assigning me a week's worth of homework. By the time I'd entered graduate school—and, based on Larry's sense that I was at least learning the procedures of surveying, having advanced to the position of crew chief and transit operator—he was prescribing Remedial Shovel, so stupid had I become during the preceding school months concerning the essential nature of our work and of the landscape we labored in.

Even so, each township contains four school sections, and Larry helped me learn more from surveying them than he would ever know. It's true that in college I was mastering increasingly subtle and sophisticated ways to consider the relationship between human beings and the natural world, but I was learning a lot more each summer. I was not only learning to think like a surveyor, a worldview that frightened me a little as I considered it from the perspective of a university classroom; I was learning to think like a native, like the locals who, when summer arrived, allowed me to approach their watering holes. The months I spent each year as a student and teacher reinforced something more intellectually complex but less substantial and profound, a view of the world constructed upon something less than a firm foundation. In this world, I knew a lot of things, but I'm embarrassed to say that I knew nothing that was true. Each winter I skated on the hard surface of intellectual inquiry, and I could execute some wonderful scholarly and pedagogical maneuvers, circling in tighter and tighter spins around the complex truths to be found in nature, thinking so hard about the mechanics of spiritual regeneration that it was finally reduced to a paradigm, a teaching strategy, not a way of actually living in your body, let alone in the landscape you occupy. I was learning a lot, but I didn't know a thing.

That's what finally troubles me the most. My hatred for those three backpackers was the closest I've ever come to knowing something deep in each of my tired bones, in my soul, in the core of my actual identity. I knew it the way Emerson tells us you know the truth—it wasn't reason or science or cultural wisdom; I hadn't gleaned it from a book, or from a conversation around a cracker barrel *or* a seminar table. It was animal, it was instinctual, it was not complicated at all. That day the landscape had taught me its essence in a way that was profound and personal, and when those hikers walked into the dark of the bar, their eyes blinded by the late afternoon sun, I hadn't regained my wits sufficiently to start *thinking* about it, to begin questioning and contextualizing the experiences of the day. A year later, by the time I opened the door and followed my students into the Escalante cafe, I'd regained my wits, along with all the confusion and complexity that is the legacy of too much information, too much thinking, understanding less than ever what I needed to know about my place in the landscape into which we hiked.

CHAPTER ELEVEN

The Polygamist Holds Forth

I spent one weekend in Wahweap, neither catching a ride home—wherever *home* was—nor hitching in the direction of scenery prettier than Wahweap City's stark postdevelopment blend of desert and deconstruction. It was the conclusion to a horrible week, which included the day we'd hiked out over the Cockscomb and then glared down those tourists who'd wandered into our grim bar just off Highway 89. That had been Tuesday. Wednesday we were back to doing a lot of hiking, the helicopter having not yet been restored to health and returned to Wahweap until late in the day, and although Thursday saw us back in the air, it was still blistering hot, and the crews felt stalled, their momentum gone. We worked a longer Friday than usual to try to catch up; then flew in shifts back to Wahweap, where there was the hurried loading of cars headed north to families and lovers for the weekend, and so I was alone, not counting, of course, Warren and his flock.

It had been a hard week, but it had also had its bright spot, too, at the end of that long hot Thursday: Richard Nixon's not completely unexpected resignation. It had been Alan's habit over the summer to greet the surveyors when he retrieved us from line with a summary of the day's Watergate happenings that he'd gleaned from news updates on the radio, and there had been much to report—it seemed that every day through June and July brought momentous news, most of it inclining against Nixon's surviving this final crisis. But the new pilot didn't listen to the radio or even, as far as we knew, read the newspaper, so each evening when we'd gotten back to Wahweap, we'd pump folks for information, and there was always some new deadly revelation, a damaging court decision, an announcement by yet another formerly loyal Republican lapdog finally swimming away from Nixon's sinking ship. That afternoon the word was resignation—even the incurious Roger Ramjet knew *that* much; Nixon had been, after all, Roger's very own commander-in-chief during his tours of duty in 'Nam— and we all wanted the visuals, which meant a trip into Page: if there was a TV to be found in Wahweap City, we didn't know where it was. We drove quickly into town and watched through the display window of a closed-for-business appliance shop an expensive blondewood-encased color TV broadcasting repeated images of Nixon's sarcastic hunched-shoulder goodbye wave from the door of his helicopter, which unlike ours managed a dependable start and flew him away. Then we had a celebratory dinner at Page's lone Chinese restaurant, bought a cheap bottle of tequila at one of Page's many liquor stores, and headed back to Wahweap to celebrate some more.

My memory of that evening is compromised by that bottle of tequila, and by several more bottles of whatever other alcoholic beverage we managed to get our hands on. It's also compromised by the fact that within weeks of returning to the U. that fall and enrolling in yet another fiction workshop, I turned the resignation of Richard Nixon into a not very good short story. The point of view character resembled me to an embarrassing degree, and there's conflict with a not completely unfair rendering of our new helicopter pilot, the story making much of his feet not quite reaching the floor as he sat down at a table in the bar, and his memories of a Vietnam war that was defined for him by courage in the field and craven limpness at home mostly involving protest marches, which meant that the story ended up being more about Vietnam than Nixon. Warren Knowles had been replaced in the story by a menacingly right-wing World War II vet tavern keeper named Curley in ironic recognition of his total baldness, but the town looked a lot like Wahweap, complete with bats flapping atmospherically around the lone streetlight and the town's best-days-are-behind-it backstory.

One thing the story represented pretty well was the fact that I was discovering that evening unanticipatedly mixed feelings in celebrating the resignation of the man who had been the focus of my activist hatred for about as long as I could remember having a political belief I could legitimately claim as my own: it was *Nixon's* face I saw during those marches to the federal building in downtown Salt Lake City; *his* police-state leanings that had prompted those threatened tear gas counterattacks. I remember exploring this realization with Matt and Richard as we poured tequila into our water glasses in Warren Knowles's bar, a blatantly illegal mode of drinking we'd learned from Woody and Koerner, a practice Warren overlooked as long as we kept buying one-dollar-a-bottle beer chasers. The returned missionaries, most of them Republicans and sober to a man, held their own memorial service in the missionary trailer.

I left the table long enough to call Karen on the cafe's pay phone, and we were mutually ecstatic, seeing in the fall of Richard Nixon some compensation for the cruel defeat of George McGovern that had somewhat ominously brought us together in the first place. "I wish I was there," I said to her, completely honestly.

"I wish you were here too," she answered. "It's fun here. Everybody's getting together at your apartment. Jeff's making pizza. We'll get high."

When I rejoined Matt and Richard and another surveyor whose name I can't remember, I began shedding the smug happiness I'd picked up talking to Karen, and began grumbling about Vietnam and Cambodia, about the way Watergate was small potatoes—I mean, the bastard was a *war criminal,* and they get him on *coverup* charges? "It's like pulling a mass murderer over as he escapes the scene of the crime, and punishing him with a speeding ticket," I remember muttering, at which point in my soon-to-be-written short story, Roger the bitter Vietnam vet/helicopter pilot kicks my point-of-view character's ass, having earlier that day failed in his attempt to push me/character out of the helicopter as a way of either reliving former glories, or teaching me some kind of lesson about action and sureness; such was the murkiness of the story, it's difficult to say. What I was *trying* to say that night in the bar, and in the short story too, now that I think about it, was that I'd *miss* Nixon. I may not have known what direction my personal compass was pointing that summer, but I knew it swung 180 degrees away from that war-mongering, Kissinger-appointing, dirty-trick-politicking Richard Nixon.

So I can't remember why I didn't catch a ride home that week-end. I think I wanted to—I know I did while I was talking with Karen—but for some reason doing anything that weekend felt like work, so I didn't do anything. I felt more tired than I'd remem-bered being for a long time, forgetting for once the reasons that had led me to spend days alone off in the desert when I wasn't being paid to do it, feeling instead a little of the loneliness that I'd been distracting myself against. Maybe it was the heat; maybe I was in Nixon withdrawal, suffering the hangover of anticlimax. Maybe I was suffering an actual *hangover,* the predictable conse-quence of that long night of celebrating, too much cheap tequila complicated by the polygamist's mandatory beer chasers. What-ever it was, I didn't really *decide* to stay in Wahweap City that week-end; I simply failed to put into effect the weekend that had become routine, hitchhiking to a likely trailhead, observing by myself the beauties of nature, then hitching back. Which left me drinking coffee that Friday night by myself in the polygamist's cafe, continuing my project to read the F. Scott Fitzgerald books I'd only pretended to read spring semester in the Fitzgerald seminar I'd faked my way through.

Drinking coffee led into dinner—the usual chicken-fried steak, with grainy mashed potatoes, canned corn, and a generic dinner roll—through which I read *The Crack-up,* Fitzgerald's all-too-sober account of the end of the trail *he'd* hitchhiked himself to. I'd parked myself in the quietest corner of the cafe, but the place still de-pressed me. The walls had been painted an institutional green dur-ing the cafe's late-fifties golden age and hadn't gotten any homier with the years, and the blinds at the other end of the room sagged under the yellow of grease and decay. The booths themselves seemed older even than Wahweap, probably, I had decided, evac-uated from some earlier failed cafe. That night the waitress was my favorite of Warren's wives: tall, long brown hair, early thirties, beautiful in a polygamist-wife sort of way, and smart as hell. She had my number. Clearing away my dishes and filling my coffee cup, she said, "So you want to be F. Scott Fitzgerald, huh?"

"Sure," I said, thinking, *oh my god, what if she's* right?

I slept late Saturday morning, alone for the first time in the six-bunk government trailer, which suddenly seemed enormous, even luxurious, compared to the jostling, elbow-in-your-face, life-in-a-submarine crowdedness I'd gotten used to during the workweek. I took a long, indulgent shower, just me and all those fungus spores, then had breakfast in the cafe at 11:00, just in under the wire when they change the menu, more banter with Warren's wives, more reading afterward at the cafe table. It was hot outside, so I finished off F. Scott Fitzgerald back in my bunk, and then started another book—I think it was John Steinbeck's *The Winter of Our Discontent.* As part of my apprenticeship as a writer, I'd been advised to read the three big guys that loomed over my generation, Hemingway, Fitzgerald, and Faulkner, and I'd added Steinbeck in recognition of a life-changing experience with *The Grapes of Wrath* in high school (my reading list was about as gendered as my survey crew). So I lazed around the trailer until midafternoon, when I walked back to the cafe for a hamburger.

This was a new experience for me, spending the day in Wahweap City, and I was aware that I was seeing everything differently, watching the sun angle across the trailer park, noticing as if for the first time the acres of empty cement slabs, the only remnant of Wahweap City's more prosperous days during the construction of the dam, one slab, apparently, per trailer. This was something I'd never imagined: a ghost town of a trailer park, cracked cement porches for absent trailers, power lines leading nowhere, short gravel driveways tracing imperfect rectangles through sparse sage, tumbleweed, and clumps of grass browning in the terrible sun.

I took advantage of my weekend in town to indulge what had become a kind of hobby that summer, which was cataloging the wives. A different wife with each shift: ranging (it seemed to me) from middle-aged to teenage, fruitful to barren, barely literate to well educated. One of Warren's newer wives—and certainly the most rarely seen of the species—had been absent from Wahweap City most of the summer, attending law school in Salt Lake, preparing for Warren's inevitable clashes with the law. She showed up finally in early August, beautiful and shy, her face framed by lank dark hair and shadowed by glasses with huge black frames. I remember the night Warren introduced her to us regulars; she snuggled herself under his arm like a child, said little to anyone, looked up at him as if she'd known him, and *only* him, all her life. And Warren moving among all the wives, never lifting a finger except to light his cigarette, holding forth from his favorite table, the booth near the cash register, under which he kept his gun. He'd made a point several times that summer of showing us this particular weapon, partly as warning not to fuck with him, and partly to illustrate a point he was often arguing about strength, about power, about what it takes to build the city of god in this fallen world.

After my late lunch, I returned to the trailer, read for a few minutes, and fell sound asleep (*The Winter of Our Discontent* was no *Grapes of Wrath*), curled up in what had become a late-afternoon oven of a trailer, waking near sundown in a pool of sweat, tangled in my ripe, dripping sheets and completely disoriented. It took me a good five minutes to realize where I was, so unfamiliar was this piece of BLM property, this rectangular box parked on a rented space, a swamp cooler shaking the aluminum sides into scrap, an expanse of fake wood paneling delaminating before my eyes. I finally calculated time and place: an evening in August, a government trailer in Wahweap City, Utah, near Wahweap Creek, a tributary of the Colorado River for which the town was named, just off Highway 89 a few miles from the Arizona border. This was not a precise location; we hadn't shot Polaris from the bunk trailers, but it was close enough for a provisional fix from which I might close in on the exact point. The cafe was two blocks to the west. It was dinner time. Although I wasn't hungry, for the first time that summer I was forced to recognize that I was really *lonely,* and wanted to be with people. I thought about calling Karen, but didn't. Instead I grabbed my book and headed for the polygamist's bar and cafe.

To my surprise, I found myself ordering a beer with dinner, apparently not having been as traumatized by my Nixon-resignation binge as I'd thought, and then found myself having a couple more afterward with Warren himself, who seemed as lost as I was, wives either working or asleep or singing lullabies to the community's children or doing law-school homework, he with no real responsibilities, but no wish to hit the sack himself, it seemed, in spite of his reputation for sexual athleticism. He held forth, as he did generally; asked me a few questions about the way the job was going, admired the mobility the helicopter afforded (my tale of failed jump starts in a suddenly forbidding desert having zero effect), and told me his theological view of things.

I remember unevenly the details of the evening that unfolded. Warren was comping me beers that I normally found prohibitively expensive, and we eventually moved on to a subject that, it turned out, was a favorite for both of us: the relationship between truth, god, prophecy, and insanity. And power, and nature. Okay, it was several favorite subjects.

At one point, Warren was explaining, not for the first time that summer, that god had told him to take plural wives, in order to populate this empty desert country and to prepare for the last days. As usual, I explained that I didn't believe god talked to anybody, because (a) there was no god, and (b) how could anyone know if there was? Going beyond my usual argument, which generally remained safely intellectual, I told the story I generally kept to myself, the punchline being this: I'd been fooled once. I was raised to believe that god talked to the prophets of the Mormon church, but I'd really only known one prophet in my years among the faithful, a sweet white-haired man named David O. McKay, whom I once met, actually shook his hand. During that one moment I believed with some degree of certainty that god talked to him, and that David O. McKay answered god back. I even believed they argued sometimes, for example, concerning the church's unwillingness to admit black Mormons into the Temple, a policy that in the wake of the civil rights movement had become glaringly reprehensible, or at the very least, old-fashioned. My slowly dawning disbelief paralleled the prophet's own gradual descent into what looked a lot like senility; during each increasingly rare appearance, he seemed even less coherent and oriented than before. He finally died at the age of ninety-six during my senior year in high school, the year I started questioning things out loud, began actively protesting against the war in Vietnam, realized the true evil incarnated as the Nixon administration, stopped taking sacrament in church, and began arguing with anyone who would suffer my bluster and naïveté that humankind's only hope was to accept the fact that we occupied a world defined by uncertainty and chaos, and to begin from there to make a life.

"Faith is the biggest of the big lies," I pronounced.

Warren missed my point. "Of *course* you lost faith in David O. McKay," he said. "He was a fake, a false prophet." Warren explained that no man since Brigham Young had spoken the truth about anything; Brigham's successor, Wilford Woodruff, lost the keys to the priesthood when he capitulated to the U.S. government and banned polygamy.

"Maybe he left the keys in his *other* pants," I said, making the obvious joke.

"God didn't speak a word for a century, not until he started talking to me," Warren said, not laughing. "And when he did, it was as clear as Paul Harvey's voice on the radio." I almost made another obvious joke—maybe it *was* Paul Harvey, on the *radio*—but kept my peace instead, exercising the kind of control I should have extended into the rest of the evening. "'Listen up,' the voice said. 'Marry Selida, and then marry Susanna. Prepare ye the way for the establishment of the new Zion.' It was impossible to misunderstand that voice," Warren told me. "It was speaking plain English, and what it told me to do could not be denied."

I expressed my usual doubts. Beliefs I was short on, but doubts I had in full measure, and doubts were the cornerstone of my arguments with religion. I'd been expressing doubts and questions to believers for enough years that it was almost a reflex, and I assumed that Warren was at least as used to being questioned as the series of relatives and former Sunday-school teachers and childhood friends I'd been expressing doubts to, it seemed, every spare minute for the previous half dozen years of my life. I had only recently begun to understand that most of those to whom I expressed myself concerning religion were being polite because they were nice, and they loved me and were trying to help me find my way back; there was a strategic purpose in tolerating my heresy and my self-righteousness, in avoiding taking personally my attacks on the coherence of their own religious convictions. They believed that I was gone, but not *far* gone. They could stand to listen to me berate their faith because I was a lost sheep. Perhaps even a prodigal son. And until that evening, somewhere deep inside lingered the thought—not acknowledged, and certainly not large as deep thoughts go—that they might be right.

Warren, however, could not have cared less about the state of my soul. He wasn't really concerned about enlarging his flock by any means other than marriage and procreation; he understood my arguments about his own revelatory powers to be personal attacks, as well they were. I told him that I didn't believe that Joseph Smith saw god, so why should I believe that Warren did? What I told him, basically, was this: you're either a fraud or you're nuts.

My pronouncement of this second possibility brought to mind a vivid picture of Jim Williams, the last crazy person I'd spent much time with, charging off into the wilderness in search of his own version of eternal and transcendent truth, and I found the connection troubling and instructive.

Warren's first approach was to overwhelm me with the richness of his revelations, a strategy I recognized years later while plowing through the writings of Jonathan Edwards for my dissertation. While Warren didn't particularly care whether or not I believed him, he nevertheless enjoyed taking inventory, letting the record demonstrate his credibility and the millennial significance of his having been chosen, the secrets god had revealed to him personally. For example, he'd been shown the secrets of Jesus' missing years, which had been spent as a tin mining magnate in England, and not incidentally making a bundle.

"Jesus Christ wasn't any pansy hippie," Warren said, looking at my ponytail in derision (forgetting for the moment his own longish hair, braided into two pigtails that morning by one, or maybe two, of his wives). Warren believed in capitalism, he said; he believed in the Anglo-Saxon people; he believed in the inevitability of Jesus' rule on earth. And he believed that god meant Warren Knowles to be the instrument of that millennial revolution.

Warren took me by surprise. He could be tremendously articulate—his words were calm, well chosen, and clear. He spoke with an even, husky voice, more like a gifted teacher than a televangelist or a country preacher, and the distance between the intelligence of his manner and the banality of his truth affected me in a strange way. I became even more dismissive than I usually was. Maybe it was the beer; maybe I was tired of having the same conversation I'd had for years with uncles and cousins and former scoutmasters trying to bring me back with appeals based less on truth than on sentimentality, or even worse, love: don't you *miss* us? Do you really *want* to break up your family for *eternity*?

Maybe I was tired of being unsure, surrounded by men who seemed to know exactly what was what and precisely where they stood. I couldn't quite dismiss the quiet certainty of Larry, who every day acted on the not unreasonable assumption that a person could weave a net of straight lines and right angles into something that felt *right,* compensation for the sometimes troubling religiosity of his small-town Mormon life, and the bureaucratic absurdities of the central office, which required, for example, that he trade a good truck for a worse one because the good truck had crossed some arbitrary mileage marker. Even crazy Williams had been compensated for his inability to function in the world with that clear view—however brief—of his position in the universe. I wouldn't have traded places with Williams for anything, of course, and I knew his certainty was hallucinatory, or at least delusional, but I'd never really known exactly where I stood, and without that I was in no danger of learning who I was.

And everybody else seemed fine. Tim would have a perfectly nice, not-completely-unexamined life; Richard was a lot smarter than me, and knew more than I would ever know—not content merely to hike recreationally on weekends and take classes each semester, during his months walking through the Amazon rainforest he'd learned things about the world I could only envy—and yet he seemed pretty uncomplicated, and totally grounded, even when wild horses invaded our campsite on Navajo Mountain (an event I'd begun to doubt had really happened), or when the specter of our complicity in ruining the Kaiparowits Plateau appeared with such materiality before our eyes. Evil and damaged as he was, even Richard Nixon had enough confidence and presence of mind to rule the world for much longer than *anyone* would have predicted.

And I'd been feeling that summer the more distant influence of my grandfather Hales, partly because of the mathematical nature of my work, and partly because he loomed large on the shore of the continent from which I was sailing—it was his family in particular I was fragmenting for eternity. Grandpa was a physicist who for nearly fifty years at Brigham Young University taught generations of young Mormons that what they might have been told by their Sunday-school teachers back home was incorrect: the earth really *was* several billion years old, he explained; the universe began in a compression of matter and energy that erupted into the Big Bang, and the beauty and utility of the flora and fauna you see outside the lecture hall arrived courtesy of the processes of natural selection and evolution.

I had always admired Grandpa for his ability to look into the telescope and report honestly what he saw, and I especially admired him for his ability to accomplish what I'd failed at again and again: he was not only able to reconcile the world he studied with the world god had created; he was somehow able to reconcile the physical and the spiritual, what he studied with his instruments and what he felt in his heart. He'd not only taught his students in BYU's astronomical observatory the facts of the material universe, he'd introduced them in the Provo Temple to the immaterial secrets of eternity. The same man who told me stories of instruments that had allowed him to actually see electrons tricked from their orbits to reveal themselves as flashes of light also explained to me that the Temple had allowed him to look into eternity: he'd seen the veil open, the curtain parted by some otherworldly wind. He talked about spirits with the same reverence and straightforwardness he used when talking about planetary orbits. Whether or not he'd ever struggled with matters of faith—as I had, it seemed, every day of my life—he seemed to have resolved the split between reason and belief, if indeed he'd ever seen it as a split at all. I was alternately skeptical and envious: although I sometimes wondered whether such belief was really possible, I never doubted that my grandfather's view of the world was genuine and deep. What I envied most was that my grandfather understood exactly who he was and what he was made of. At any given moment, he knew his exact location on earth, in the universe, and in eternity. Me, I was lost.

And here was Warren Knowles, whose beliefs were at least as wacky as Williams's had been, infinitely dismissible, and *yet*. I couldn't help it: that night I felt a little intimidated by the power of a man who believed what he was saying with a total depth of commitment and truth, so I hit him where I assumed it would hurt. I asked him to question his own sanity, the trustworthiness of the ear into which god whispered.

"How do you *know* god speaks to you?" I said. "How do you know you aren't dreaming? Come *on*, Warren—how do you know you aren't *schizophrenic*?"

"John, John," the polygamist said calmly, trying a fatherly tack in hopes perhaps of winding this discussion down, but to no avail. We went back and forth for what seemed hours. Warren described to me in a multitude of ways the physicality of god's voice, the unmistakably concrete fact of his presence in the room when they spoke to each other. I told him every story I knew of certifiably crazy people who were equally sure of god's presence. I told him about Williams, and then I told him about Mr. Hofstetter, a man living in the neighborhood where I'd grown up, who, during long nights of prayer, routinely found himself traveling in time to witness great scenes from the Bible, and I described to Warren the silence that surrounded Mr. Hofstetter one afternoon in sacrament meeting when he'd stood up and explained in detail the way he'd hovered in the air above Christ as he walked on the stormy surface of the Sea of Galilee.

"I mean, we were *embarrassed,*" I said, not a little slurrily. "And we knew he was nuts, and to tell you the truth, Warren, sometimes you sound a little like Mr. Hofstetter."

I explained that everyone in that meeting knew this guy had crossed some kind of line into mental illness, yet everyone in that meeting also believed that a doddering old man, David O. McKay, entertained god from time to time in his rooms in the Hotel Utah across the street from Temple Square, only a couple of floors down from the Skyroom restaurant where Woody had treated us to lunch.

"How do you *know,* Warren?" I said. "How does *anybody* know?"

Warren went on to quote scripture, most of which I'd heard before. He kept coming back to "by my fruits ye shall know me," and explained that his own life as a prophet, the diligence with which he was acting on god's instructions and the success he achieved, was also testimony to the reality of god's voice.

"The world out there is chaos and ignorance. It's falling apart because it's being run by people like *you,*" he said, his voice rising, and he pointed his finger at me in a gesture just short of angry. "My family is ordered, true, and safe, as stable as a triangle. God's holy tripod: there's authority, there's obedience, and there's love. No question goes unanswered, no hand goes unheld. The universe holds no terrors for us, and the world of man is a mere annoyance, a handy illusion, a means to an end. You ask anybody in my family whether god talks to me. They haven't heard our conversations, but the perfection of our lives is ample proof for anybody. I've built something here that stands on its own. God tells me where to nail every board, what to put on the menu, how much to charge for soup. This place may not look like much right now, but it's built well, and it'll last."

For some reason this got to me. My own voice was rising, and my arguments were getting less coherent and more blustery. I had downed a lot of beer by then, and I was finally furious at Warren's certainty, burning-hot pissed that anyone could really stand on so firm a foundation. It was part disdain, and, I realize now, part envy. I thought Warren's arrogance was absurd, and yet it nevertheless seemed a pretty wonderful way to make one's path through life.

My own life was spinning out of control. I felt more at home in that steamy government trailer than anywhere else in the universe—which is to say that I didn't feel at home anywhere. The rich wilderness of doubt, of moral ambiguity, and the wonderful irony of the Heisenberg Uncertainty Principle were no match for believing in a god who told you whom to marry, what to do with your life, and how Jesus spent those mysterious missing years, including his twenty-second, the year through which I was staggering lost and alone.

"But how do you *know* god talks to you?" I kept saying, not as a question but as an accusation, half expecting him to crack the way Perry Mason's guilty witnesses always did, overwhelmed by their own sense of moral doubt and the relentless logic of skillful cross-examination, because at that moment I finally understood that I was exactly right, that there was *nothing* out there talking to *any* of us, that like all those other guys professing truth and pure faith, Warren was either deluded, or lying. "Warren," I said. "How do you know that deep down inside you aren't as fucked up as everybody else?"

I'd never seen Warren get very upset, but now he was shaking his head back and forth with a seriousness I hadn't seen before, and grinding out his cigarettes with unusual force. After all, he wasn't trying to make any converts, and he was understandably sick of being asked to defend his sanity, which, to his credit, he wasn't. He said, finally, "*This* is how I know," and stood up, walked calmly to the cash register, and pulled out his revolver, still the biggest handgun I've seen in my life.

He held the barrel lightly against my temple and said slowly, "If I pull this trigger, we both know that your brains will be all over this cafe. We both know that. That's what certain knowledge feels like. That's how I know that god talks to me, and that's how I know that my life is testimony to the undeniable will of god."

He didn't build it into much more of a scene. He put the gun away as quickly and calmly as he'd retrieved it, so quickly that I didn't even get a chance to feel terrified, let alone persuaded concerning whatever point Warren was making, my reflexes numbed by beer, my realization of what was happening expanding slow as spilled molasses. Of course, as that realization took hold over the next several weeks, as I considered what happened that night in the cafe, I'd dismiss Warren's pulling his gun on me as bad theater; and as I remembered that he'd pulled the gun on Richard earlier that summer in order to make a similar point, I realized that it wasn't even *original* bad theater. I'd come to understand Warren's gunslinging to be a kind of rhetorical last resort—the more you think about it, pulling a gun really doesn't demonstrate very much in the way of universal truth—and I'd eventually feel a degree of pride in the fact that his demonstration hadn't succeeded, that I'd actually missed his point.

But there were some complicated feelings swirling around this handy conclusion. I couldn't forget what I'd *felt,* which was actually closer to disappointment than either fear *or* triumph. I knew that part of me had wanted it to *work*—hoped that adrenalin, or the pure physicality of the barrel's hard steel against my head, might make the kind of impression only pure truth can make, might help me at least understand the sureness of death, and therefore by means of comparison or metaphor or intuition what truth *feels* like when it's in the room, pressed against your skin.

Pulling the gun had broken some kind of spell, and of course ended the conversation, but on a lighter note than you'd expect: "Thanks for not killing me," I think I remember saying, as Warren returned to the table.

"Don't mention it," Warren may well have answered, and I remember that we laughed a little at how serious things had gotten, and actually shook hands as I stood to leave. Warren unlocked the cafe's glass door and held it open for me, and as I walked outside past his dusty black Lincoln in the direction of the only home I could lay claim to, I found myself wishing that what Warren had said about my brains was true, that Warren's demonstration had been successful, that I'd known, if only for that one brief beat of time, what certainty feels like. I walked slowly and unsteadily to the trailer, my way illuminated to no purpose by every blazing star in the moonless night.

CHAPTER TWELVE

Shooting Polaris

By mid-August we'd finally finished the complete subdivision of our township into the square-mile sections required by Jefferson's tidy vision of America, and we were spending the last week surveying the odd mile here and there we'd put off because they were easier, or more accessible to our single lonely road, and therefore jobs to save for when the helicopter broke down. Some of our work involved moving corners we'd planted earlier in the summer. Because this was an original survey, we marked and placed section corners as we ran line, gambling that when we hit the township boundary, or a line we'd already run perpendicular to ours, the line we were running would intersect perfectly the one we'd run a week or two before. This usually proved to be the case. But if we were off even a little, which we sometimes were, we'd have to revisit each wayward corner, and nudge it into correct alignment.

Cadastral surveyors have always checked their work by closing individual sections, making sure the numbers they calculated matched the lines they ran. Although we seldom ran the lines around one section at a time, preferring, whenever possible, to run six mile lines straight from township boundary to boundary, it helped me to think of closing sections this way: run a mile, then turn ninety degrees. Run another mile, make another ninety-degree turn. Two more miles, two more right-angled turns, and if you've done everything right—measured perfect one-mile sides and turned precise ninety-degree angles—your last line would intersect perfectly the flag you started from.

Such precision is unattainable, of course, and surveying legislation has always allowed a margin of error—"acceptable limits of closure," in the vernacular of the *Manual of Surveying Instructions*—to account for the relative inaccuracy of the equipment and the inevitable lapses in technique. When our nineteenth-century forebears ran their four miles of section boundaries and returned to their original flag, they were allowed to be off by fifty links—half a chain, more than thirty feet. By the time surveyors had been issued transits and eight-chain chains, the margin of error was twenty-five links, but no surveyor I knew was content with so sloppy a gap. Larry was pretty upset on those rare occasions when we were ten links off, and was only satisfied with something less than a five-link closure.

So each night Larry would recalculate his lines, closing his sections on paper, and if he discovered a troubling closure, he'd decide whether we needed to run line again, or just shift corners enough to bring them into alignment with each other according to the tiny corrections he felt necessary, and that's how we spent our last couple of late-August days on the Kaiparowits Plateau. The adjustments were never more than a few links, sometimes only a couple of tenths, which meant basically setting up the transit over the nearest flag, reestablishing line, and kicking the brass cap the inch or two it needed to go, then rearranging the rocks in the mound to reanchor the pipe.

There was one significant difference that year. Because we were running an original survey, Larry was required to do math he'd never done before, to work those calculations necessary to make our lines compensate for the curvature of the earth. The first instructions to surveyors, those included in the legislation passed by congress in 1785, neglected to provide for the fact that we live on a spherical planet, and this flat-earth mentality resulted in some awkward moments in the field, and later in the central office. The problem was this: on one hand, parallel lines are defined by the fact that they never meet. On the other hand, survey crews twenty miles apart ran what they assumed were parallel lines that turned out to be not quite *parallel*. Even though they had begun running lines according to what their compasses told them was northward, because these magnetic lines converged steadily as they ran toward the magnetic pole, their lines actually inclined toward each other, ultimately resulting in some disconcertingly trapezoidal sections, determined by not-quite-perpendicular angles.

Of course, this came as no surprise to the surveyors themselves, who had studied solid as well as plane geometry, and even those who surveyed across the great plains knew that the flatness they traversed was an illusion; but this simple fact seemed to have slipped the mind of Jefferson, whose attention had by then proceeded on to other problems in need of solutions (final passage of the ordinance took place while Jefferson was sipping claret among the philosophes of Paris and, not incidentally, getting an up-close picture of what the beginnings of a *real* revolution looked like). The basic impossibility of drawing straight lines on a curved surface was not addressed by Washington, D.C., until 1804, when the updated instructions mandated principal baselines and meridians, and gave further guidance intended to work out a compromise— some might say negotiate a surrender—between Jefferson's squares and the curves of nature, which of course sounds like the story of Jefferson's life, and I guess mine too.

Reconciling surveying's linear ideal with the earth's curved reality is how I remember spending my last day on the Kaiparowits Plateau, returning to the first few miles we'd run two months earlier in order to make a correction necessitated by that essential conflict between line and circle—to renegotiate, in one small instance, Jefferson's standoff. There might have been another, less esoteric reason for the correction, but I remember Larry talking with Craig early that summer about incorporating curvature into the usual calculations, and as a result having to make some adjustments, and in my memory it was the quarter corner between sections 25 and 26—one of the markers we'd placed our first day on the township, the line that grazed the western swell of Nipple Butte—that occupied a point that was a little out of whack with the less apparent but ultimately undeniable curvature of the earth. The difference between a flat earth and the one we occupied measured at this point eight-tenths of a link—about six inches—and it became my assignment, the first unsupervised employment I'd been entrusted with that summer, to nudge the marker into a more accommodating position.

I'd been awarded this responsibility partly in recognition of my slightly improved surveying competence—it looked as though I'd be moving up the ladder next summer, and Larry had already begun teaching me about transits and chains, letting me turn redundant angles and record one-chain measurements—and partly default: everybody else, *every single surveyor* more competent or senior, was otherwise engaged. The survey was shutting down. The helicopter had left the day before strapped to the bed of a flatbed, Roger looking childlike and diminished sitting alongside the mechanic in the truck's cab. The other crews, having sewn up the loose ends on their own townships, were packing equipment and preparing their trailers for towing to various BLM yards throughout the state, and Matt and Larry were scheduled to attend a meeting at the regional BLM office in Kanab.

That left Tim and me, and because I'd re-upped for next year and Tim hadn't, planning instead grad school and more focused attention on the career in business he anticipated, and because I'd been learning some transit basics, Larry took me aside, gave me my instructions, and wrote down the specific numbers I'd be responsible for. Matt ceremoniously handed over the small magnifying glass attached to a lanyard that he'd worn around his neck all summer.

"Honorary party chief," said Larry, his voice only slightly mocking, as he and Matt climbed into a tan government pickup and took off toward Kanab.

The job was an easy one, an hour's work at most once we got there, so we'd basically have the rest of the day off, although we'd been instructed to spend that time away from Wahweap in order to discourage the popular civilian libel that the civil service spent most of its time leaning on shovels and swilling beer at government expense. As the bearer of the government driver's license, I was responsible for driving the Carryall, almost obscenely big with only the two of us and not much equipment, and the dirt road went in the only direction it could once we'd taken the Nipple Bench fork westward. We followed the route we'd driven the first week of the summer, up the dugway and onto the bench, and stopped at that familiar bend in the road that looped nearest to where line ran.

We inventoried what we'd need: the transit, which I carefully removed from its scratched mahogany case and screwed onto the coarse brass threads of the tripod, careful to keep the angle necessary to avoid jamming the threads, something easier to foul up than you might think; Tim packed the one-chain tape, and I pocketed the two small hardbound books, the yellow fieldbook, in which I'd write down the new bearings to the bearing tree, and the Department of the Interior/Bureau of Land Management's official standard field tables, the small red book that contained the equations and log tables I wouldn't need for the job we'd been assigned, but for which I'd made plans anyway. I leaned the Gurley over my shoulder, having remembered to unclamp the vertical axis so it could swing with the bumps, and we began hiking the mile or so in the direction of the quarter corner we'd be moving.

The walk was pretty easy compared to the scrambling we'd been doing all summer. We stayed on the bench, walking in a lazy half-circle around the rise of the butte. I could see the occasional flag I'd pounded in two months earlier, noticing the way they looked random from our perspective, but trusting that they'd fall into line when we set up over the flag closest to the corner.

The guilty quarter corner sat alone on a sagebrush flat, a short distance from a stunted juniper, the only tree for many chains (one of the first bearing trees Larry had allowed me to blaze), the marker itself part nature—it was supported by a medium-sized mound of stone one foot high and three feet in diameter; we'd been able to dig a foot and a half into the sand before hitting the shelf of solid rock—and part human artifact, a perfect iron post, still shiny with its galvanized coating, the brass cap sitting on top like a Special Forces beret, bearing the inscrutable lines and numbers that identified its place in the township, its position relative to Temple Square. I set up the transit over the nearest flag, a chain and a half away, and began the process of wiggling the transit into position over the flag.

Center and level are the two conditions that must be achieved before accurate surveying can begin; any off center and tilt will compromise even the most carefully attended survey that proceeds from off-kilter origins. Both depended on getting the tripod in the right spot to begin with, as close to center and level as possible, which was the procedure I was just beginning to learn. I spread the tripod's three legs, pushed each one hard into the sand until it looked close, which it didn't, so I repositioned the transit and tried again. Closer, but still more than an inch off. I pushed even harder on one leg, driving it deeper into the sand, which seemed to take the head of the tripod over the flag and, as a bonus, the base of the transit seemed to have wound up in the neighborhood of level, so I tightened the large brass wing nuts that clamped each leg to the tripod's base and dropped a marble-sized rock from the hook from which other surveyors would hang a plumb bob. From the exact center of the tripod, the pebble dropped within a quarter inch of the lath's head. I loosened a leveling screw, allowing the transit itself to slide sideways in the right direction, dropped another pebble, nudged the transit a little farther. I dropped two more pebbles, noted with satisfaction that each one bounced directly off the head of the lath a foot beneath, and declared the instrument centered.

A transit rises from two bases, two tea saucers parallel and two inches apart, kept in loose formation until tightened by four leveling screws. The lower saucer is connected firmly and unalterably to the tripod, and so its level or lack thereof reflected the skill with which I'd gotten the tripod close by means of planning and pushing. The upper saucer is the base from which all the transit's measurements arise: compass and scope and verniers, and pivots and bubble levels and knobs of adjustment, and so this saucer must be *level,* as exactly level as possible. The gap between the two represents the difference between close and exact, between the bumps of nature and the transcendence of level. As Tim assumed the position surveyors always assume when there is literally nothing for them to do, leaning back against the nearest tree that offered the most shade, and pulling his flag hat's brim to half-staff over his eyes, I leveled, which involved going back and forth between the two sets of knobs, turning the transit ninety degrees one way, turning knobs until the bubble centered between its black lines, then turning another ninety degrees and adjusting knobs until that second bubble found that ideal spot, part finicky response to turning screws, part connection with that broadest of earthly orientations, level.

Level means a couple of things. To begin with, it means parallel to the horizon. Not the horizon you see, unless you're on a dry lake bed, or the ocean, but an idealized horizon, one free of obvious mountains or less apparent, more gradual swellings of the earth's crust, for example those fifty-mile-wide alluvial fans that fill the space between the dozen mountain ranges that take turns running north and south through most of Nevada. The valley floor seems perfectly flat until you notice that your underpowered Fiat needs downshifting to third gear just to keep going, maybe even *second,* a reminder that regardless of how flat the terrain looks in the windshield, you're *climbing.*

Even the level that defines sea level can be misleading. The moon pulls water into continent-sized swells that mess with flat; but of course even an ideal ocean, one somehow able to maintain sea-level integrity in the face of a fickle random moon, is anything but level because we live amid the confusions of curvature. Our belief in the level horizon is a consequence of our puniness—a significantly taller species could see enough of the horizon to never doubt the true spherical, anything-but-flat nature of the well-rounded earth.

In reality, then, level isn't the horizon; level is an ideal, a construct, maybe even a concept. A concept will only take you so far in surveying, however, so I'd arrived at my own more workable definition, which was this: level is a flat baseline planted perpendicular to the perfectly linear pull of gravity, the starting point for a line that shoots straight downward, aiming directly toward the exact center of the earth, a line undistracted by magnetic fields, the pull of the moon, or the shifting of continents. As a small concession to my poetry-writing student and her *Harper's* readership, I'd grant that this may be the only straight line there is in the natural universe: a true tangent, line in the most absolute sense because it doesn't even *try* to conform to a curved surface. This line really *does* go where it goes, and it pulls the level's clear bubble after it, intimidating the bubble into freezing at the glass tube's centerline when you've turned your knobs just the right amount and no farther, making the transit a truly level place in a world of near invisible slant and horizon-to-horizon upheaval. I sometimes thought of my leveled transit sitting on top of a very long golf tee, the pointed end zapping straight to the actual center of the earth, the transit sitting on the tee's level head like a golf ball ready for a perfect swing. Other human beings might feel connected to the earth in contemplating the horizon; on those rare occasions I felt connected at all, it was by means of a straight unbroken line that tethered me to the exact center of the planet.

Level anchors the transit in the actual earth, providing a place from which the ideal can hold sway, an entryway into a world of Platonic forms, of math. It's a place from which to begin the sur-

veyor's work compromised neither by overly ambitious government legislation nor the distracting ups and downs of natural landscape. Most other surveying instruments—chains, clinometers,
laths, and chainsaws—belong to the real, but that six-inch circle of
level on which the transit sits, the circular foundation from which
rises the various verniers and levels and optics, occupies the landscape of the ideal.

I consider the job before me, reciting Larry's instructions to myself, comparing them against my own sense of what needs to be
done, then checking the notes he'd written for me before departing for Kanab. I'm new at this, after all, but not completely stupid,
so I find another piece of paper on which I've written my own
more detailed checklist, beginning with the most basic instructions: first, center the transit over the top of the lath, then level it,
then find line. This last part turned out to be pretty easy—as I expected, line was a series of flags, laths I had sharpened on one end
and then pounded in earlier that summer, the farthest one about a
mile away to the south still waving its pink flag halfway up the
voluptuous swell of Nipple Butte, and toward north a much closer
flag sticking straight up beside the brass cap. Beyond that one, I
could see only one more flag, the rest of them—dozens, one after
the other, I knew, straight from this point more than four miles to
the township's northern boundary—hidden from my view by the
convulsions of the more complicated terrain of the township's interior. But one flag was all I needed, two flags—one in each direction—plenty. If I'd centered and leveled correctly over the flag, I
should be able to flip the scope from south to north and find each
flag exactly centered, which they were, mute testimony to the consistency of Matt's line and the adjustment of the transit's collimation, witness to the respectful treatment Matt had given the transit
all summer.

Tim has meanwhile observed from the shadow under his stars-
and-stripes brim that I'm ready to line in the new position for the
flag. He pounds in a short lath a few feet from the mound as a reference point for maintaining the same distance—Larry's calculations told him the distance was exactly right; it was the bearing
that needed slight bending to the longitudinal—and he measures
the two links to the east we need, sticks in a chaining pin for reference, and starts taking apart the mound. Eight-tenths of a link

isn't much of a correction, but it's a little beyond the convenience of a kick.

I join Tim in dismantling the center of the mound, pulling the rocks closest to the pipe away and out, trying to keep the larger rocks that constitute a kind of outer wall in their place, and eventually we've cleared a space around the pipe so we can push the pipe back and forth until we've widened the hole in the sand, and pull it out. Measuring with our knuckles a couple of links to the east, we enlarge the hole in that direction, using our hands and, when the sand turns out to be more solid than we'd like, we take turns attacking it with chaining pins, two clutched together to form a kind of skinny-toothed trowel, until we've cleared an oblong hole a foot down to bedrock, bedrock being never too far below the surface on the Kaiparowits. We throw in the pipe, center it where we've guessed it'll go, make sure it's aimed the right direction—numbers to the north, the inscribed line oriented the same direction the actual line runs—then pile in some rocks to hold it while we line it in exactly.

Back at the transit, I line in another chaining pin on the old line, the one we're correcting, but the point from which we'll measure the adjustment. Tim holds a chaining pin over the mound level with the brass cap; I line him in, and he holds that position, the old line, until I join him with the one-chain tape and measure the eight-tenths from the pin to the brass cap's new position. We firm up the position with a few more rocks, then measure the distance from the reference point to the chaining pin, decide it's correctly perpendicular, then pile more rocks around the pipe, trying not to knock it out of the alignment we've just established.

From here on it's mound building, then one more check against line for bearing and against the reference lath for distance, then we throw sand over the mound of stone, having been instructed that over time the sand sifts downward between the rocks, filling the cracks and acting as a kind of mortar keeping ice and snow from widening the cracks and scattering the mound, which would make it hard for surveyors retracing our tracks to find the artifact we've worked so hard to place.

So we're done for the day. But we have some time to kill, and it occurs to me—actually, I began thinking about it the night before— to practice an observation of Polaris. It's the perfect opportunity.

We have plenty of time, and Tim's the ideal assistant; he's not interested in perfecting his own skills, seeing as how his career as a surveyor will be over for good in a week or so, but he's cooperative and curious.

Best of all, he has no idea how it works, so he won't really be able to see me screw up. Later, maybe this summer, certainly the next, I'll do it under Larry's experienced gaze, and I know he'll teach me what I need to know to get it faster and better. But my first time through, I wanted to take my time, make my mistakes, consult the Xeroxed instructions and folded-double ephemeris and my own penciled notes without suggestions or criticism. I'd practiced the equations the same way—of course I`d followed Larry as he'd calculated star shots, and he was great about explaining things unless he had to explain things more than twice, but I'd also spent a couple of evenings doing the problems myself in the privacy of my bunk, and I liked that he would be at least one large southern Utah county away when I tried it the first time.

I looked around for a foresight, a point on earth as far as possible from where I was set up, on which I could zero the transit and begin my calculations. Happily, there was Navajo Mountain, the best foresight I could imagine. Navajo Mountain had given me my most useful bearings throughout the summer, weekends as well as weekdays. In this landscape of flats and jags, of bare hard-angled rocks and cliffs and long toothed ridges, the mountain stood higher than anything for fifty miles, but gently rounded, a sudden swell of blue-green earth, high enough to capture and hold clouds that would otherwise have escaped eastward to the Rockies.

Before settling on a specific point on Navajo Mountain, though, I had to zero the transit. I turned the clamping screws, loosening the horizontal and vertical axes, then turned the knob freezing the transit's upper axis, keeping the scope on line while I turned the vernier plate with my fingertips, finding the approximation of zero degrees with my naked eye. I turned the knob that froze the lower vernier, then looking through Matt's magnifying glass hanging conveniently and yet somehow ritually around my neck like a secular crucifix, turned another knob, the size and feel of the dial you turned to tune in a car radio back when radios *had* dials, and centered the vernier on something even *closer* to zero, lining up the small and smaller lines until they looked dead centered to the second on every possible zero: zero degrees, zero minutes, and zero seconds. After double-checking for a third, and then a fourth time, not quite trusting my ability to line up those tiny scales, I swiveled the transit in the direction of Navajo Mountain, scanning the horizon's various plateaus that hide Lake Powell from view, encouraging the illusion not only that Glen Canyon still might exist as John Wesley Powell saw it, but that you could walk straight to Navajo Mountain, a pilgrimage difficult but possible, one long uninterrupted ramp to the base. A few weeks earlier, when I'd been at the summit looking toward Nipple Butte, the view was one of impossibility, the landscape between these two points chaotic, any trek made impossible by the blank cold moat of Lake Powell. But the view from here was welcoming and hopeful, the illusion of connection.

Scanning the gently rounded summit for something to turn toward, an easily recognizable feature to serve as a foresight, a point of departure, a kind of ground zero for the many calculations to come, I could make out the rounded tops of the ponderosa pines I'd hiked beneath, and of course the radio transmission tower rising slightly above the mattress swell of gently curving treetops, a hard straight contrast to all that roundedness, its individual antennas and dishes difficult to make out exactly, but its mission clear.

I decided against the tower, even though I knew it would make the best foresight, a kind of giant lath, an apotheosis of the hundreds of laths I'd pounded in all summer, propped up by that giant mound of stone called Navajo Mountain. Instead, I found the sharp-edged trunk of an otherwise invisible ponderosa pine, the final one outlined against the morning sky before the mountain falls away into what was left of Glen Canyon. Although at this distance the trunk was barely visible, under magnification still skinnier than the transit's crosshair, it was an easy tree to remember, and I liked the idea that I might have actually stood beneath its branches as Richard and I took in the entire breadth of the landscape I'd been tracing mile by unimaginative mile weekdays. Perhaps those wild horses had grazed past this very tree on their way toward surprising us in our sleep. The tree instead of the tower: pure sentimentality, perhaps even denial.

After rechecking my focus and hiding the tree trunk exactly behind the transit's vertical crosshair—you not only need to remember which tree you've lined in; you need to know exactly where line crosses that tree, what branch or scar (you need to be careful

with scars; sometimes a scar is a function of sun and shadow, and
mutates into something unrecognizable as the day brightens)—I
stood back, taking the pause I'd need before making sure I could
really find my foresight again, regretting for just a minute that I'd
passed over the stark unmistakably out-of-place radio tower. I
looked again, found I was still on the mark, and turned toward the
sun.

I knew we had an accurate bearing on line—it was Matt's bearing, after all, and he'd checked and double-checked it all summer—but this was practice. When you first start out, or if you're on
a broken, mistaken bearing, then finding Polaris is a problem. It's
daytime, after all, and if you can't turn the correct angles from the
start, you won't get Polaris in your scope, and if you don't get
Polaris in your scope, you're basically lost: the sky is too big, and
Polaris is too small, too far away, and too dim in all that daylight,
and your scope only covers a degree or two. So what do you do?
You figure out an approximate bearing, an angle that will get you
in the ballpark with Polaris so you can turn the angles, find the
star, and then read a new and more accurate bearing, a bearing
with context.

A compass bearing usually isn't close enough, even as an approximation. It's not impossible to find Polaris with a magnetic
bearing—with a good compass, adjusted perfectly for declination
(compensating for the difference between magnetic north and
true north), and with no distractions from a wristwatch or ore deposits—the vast iron ore fields in northern Michigan were discovered by surveyors who were having trouble following their
drunkenly swaying compasses—you might get lucky, at least if
you're able to calculate an accurate vertical angle so you'll know
how high to aim in the sky. But the later nineteenth-century surveys were run on solar bearings, with the help of Burt's wonderful,
if easily bumped, solar compass, and they proved to be pretty good
bearings, so modern surveyors use the sun as the first step, a dependable way to get to the North Star and a more accurate fix.

Not that shooting the sun is easy, with or without Burt's help.
The summer before, one crew's Gurley had a solar attachment,
and although the party chief swore it made solar observations easier, the transit operator—who actually turned the angles and read
the verniers—told me later that it didn't make *anything* easier, and

it made handling the transit that much more difficult. The solar attachment stuck out like Victorian gingerbread on the front porch of an old house, delicate lace on an expensive dress, and you had to be careful not to knock something that's just asking to be knocked. And there's that problem of Polaris's daytime dimness. Some crews took their astronomical observations at dusk, claiming that Polaris couldn't be seen with enough clarity through the transit during the day, but Larry's philosophy was of *course* it's more difficult, but once you learn it, it's *easier.* You're dependent neither on Burt and his fussy entrepreneurial device, nor on the time of day. It's you, the transit, your ephemeris and standard field tables, and the sun and stars.

I'd already written down the relevant numbers, and so I got down to it, handing Tim the watch I'd borrowed from Matt (I'd set it according to the radio in Craig's trailer that morning, listening to a station that broadcast the exact time from an atomic clock somewhere) and my notebook. I reminded myself to flip down the tiny green glass filter that slides over the eyepiece—you don't want to look at the sun directly under any circumstances, but to look at the sun greatly magnified by the transit's gauntlet of lenses is especially dangerous. I'd learned this lesson one day while watching Larry taking a sun shot; halfway through the sequence of three observations he suddenly yelled, and jumped straight up as if scorpion-stung—that was my first thought, that some dangerous insect or reptile had climbed the tripod, striking at his face from behind the transit—and rubbed his right eye with both hands, one over the other, yelling *"Jesus! Jesus!"* The solar filter—held in place by a screw that needed just the right adjustment, loose enough to pivot, tight enough to stay put—had slipped, and Larry had gotten an eyeful of sun for a split second, not long enough to actually blind him, but enough to put that eye out of commission for fifteen minutes or so, during which time Matt took over. So I remembered to set the filter, and I checked the friction of the pivot.

You can see the sun all day, of course. The presence of the sun sort of defines the concept of *daytime,* so finding it is no problem. But for the purpose of a sun shot, you need to shoot it by midmorning or in late afternoon—you can't point the scope straight up and still be able to look through it, but even if you could, the sun slows down at midday, or so it seems, muddying the data. Explorers, on the other hand, have traditionally preferred the midday solar observation, but they're looking at the sun angling off a mirror. Shooting at high noon offers a way to partially nullify the time problem because you can watch the sun pause for a kind of lunch break before it starts heading downhill, and you know exactly what time it is no matter *where* you are, your vagueness concerning your location being the reason for the sun shot in the first place. Surveyors prefer the sun in motion because it *registers,* and there's a useful difference in the three observations the calculations require. Today, it was still pretty early, around nine A.M.—we'd started out that morning at six-thirty—a good time for a solar observation.

Finding the sun might be easy, but centering it in the scope is difficult. The sun shines on us from a position more than ninety million miles away, but that's still too close for getting an accurate fix because the sun moves too fast in relation to where you stand on earth. After all, you can actually see shadows move, something my mother pointed out to me when I was a kid asking her about shadows. She gave me an assignment to watch a particular morning shadow in motion, to place rocks along its border, then hunch over, not taking away my eyes, and watch the way the line of shadow pulled away from the rocks I'd lined up. I thought I'd be bored—my attention span was even shorter then than it is now— but I *wasn't.* I could see the shadow creep along the ground, and I discovered that it required some effort to keep the fence of pebbles set against the line of dark, and this taught me something about the seemingly immovable universe. I had known that day could be depended on to eventually become night, of course. But somehow I'd imagined a sun that didn't move; it just was up, then it was straight up, and then it was afternoon for a while, and then there was a sunset, and then it got dark. I knew time, and I thought I knew about the sun. But until that day, I hadn't noticed that constant motion, movement that might be gradual, but was as traceable as the slowly swinging arms of a clock.

As a surveyor, I learned that you can center a transit's crosshairs on just about everything *but* the sun: the flag you're lining in, the tree on line that has to be chainsawed out of the way, even a foresight as distant as that one tree on Navajo Mountain. But the sun is too big, and it moves too fast: the sun fills at least a third of the scope, and you have to keep turning the adjustment knobs to keep up with it, to keep it in view, let alone centered. It's easier to take a bead on a rabbit running a hundred feet away than the one you've spooked at your feet, and in cosmic terms, the sun is right there at your feet.

Actually, *we* are right there, although it doesn't really help to remind yourself that the earth, the place you're standing, is doing all the relevant moving. Sometimes that fact only confuses; for the purpose of calculating bearings, a Dark Ages view of the cosmos works just fine, with the sun speeding dizzily by, the stars moving at a slow dignified strut, the planets traveling their own idiosyncratic circuits. Still, I felt a kind of moral imperative as a surveyor to remind myself whenever I could that earth is *not* the center of the universe, something I was able to do only during those moments when I wasn't caught up in the chase, turning the knobs or doing the math, when I'd routinely revert to the earth-centered model.

Besides being too close and too speedy, the sun, at least as it appears through the filtered green of the eyepiece, is too gassy and globular, as skittery and insubstantial as a birthday-party balloon. I couldn't imagine centering it in crosshairs, and neither could the surveying handbooks, which instead recommended procedures that made of crosshairs something more useful, techniques that involved corralling the sun in each of the four pie-slice subdivisions split by the crosshairs, catching it in the ninety-degree angle between two crosshair arms so that it just touches a line on each tangent. This approach required that you get various shots on the sun in each quarter, which meant more math. This seemed way too difficult for my level of competence, partly because of the extra calculations, partly because, in my experience at least, mixing lines and circles seldom worked out happily. As the earliest American surveyors discovered, eventually you had to do *something* to adjust your straight lines to fit the anything but straight nature of the earth's globe if you wanted to avoid embarrassing collisions between townships, but those math problems were tricky, and you'd want to put them off as long as possible. It seemed to me that fencing in the sun with right angles was a similarly flawed concept.

Fortunately for me, my Gurley was equipped with a relatively recent innovation, the solar circle, a slim black radius centered by the crosshairs of a diameter that matched exactly the circumference of the sun. Containing the sun for a moment within the circumference of the solar circle was pretty easy, and more than a little satisfying; not only was the sun a perfect fit, but it benefited from its containment, seemed to gain a little dignity. The sun always looks a little fuzzy around the edges, the way an egg looks when you drop it from its shell onto the griddle. It spreads in a circle, but an uneven and unpredictable one, so the fancier restaurants have those tin rings that contain the spreading white in a circle, and what's brought to your table is a fried egg made perfect, true to its circular essence, the kind of egg I'm sure Thomas Jefferson preferred, just as he preferred his gardens squared, his Constitution triangulated, and his women corseted. The sun looks better contained within the boundaries of the later-model Gurley's solar circle, restored to the dignity of its status as an actual star, fueled to perfection for billions of years of dependable service, not frowsy and unboundaried, sloppy to the point of being out of round, out of control.

I did this three times: I followed the sun with the lasso of the solar circle, and when I'd caught it perfectly within the circle's boundaries, I'd simultaneously (and dramatically) yell *"Time!"* to Tim, and stop turning the knobs, letting the sun escape. Tim would write down the exact time from Matt's watch, and wait for me to read out loud the vertical and horizontal angles, which he'd write down as well. Then I'd do it again: center the sun, ask for the time, read the angles. Then once more.

By then Tim had written in my notebook three sets of numbers. I sat next to him in the shade, got out my notes and books—the numbers and formulas I'd written down the night before, the ephemeris, and the red book of log tables—and did the math, relatively easy compared to what was in store for me when I'd take on Polaris.

After about twenty minutes of looking up various sines, cosines, and tangents and doing the calculations, I had three numbers penciled at the top of a clean notebook page: a horizontal angle, measured from the zero of Navajo Mountain; a vertical angle, measured from the transcendentally perfect disk of level I'd achieved earlier that morning; and a time, counted off from the Greenwich Observatory near London, England, and converted to mountain daylight time.

≈

To find Polaris at night, all you need is the Big Dipper, and the knowledge of which of its stars to line up. It's that easy, easy enough for a child: the Big Dipper was the first constellation I learned, and Polaris was the first star I knew the name of, although in those days I knew it by its homier, more colloquial alias, the North Star. I knew Polaris so well I'd grown up somehow believing it was the brightest star in the sky.

Larry broke the news to me: as famous stars go, Polaris is pretty dim. Its usefulness lies in its near-perfect northness, not its brilliance, and the star is as difficult to find in the daytime as it is easy to find at night. To locate Polaris without the visual aid of the Big Dipper, you need three things: first, a bearing accurate enough to get Polaris in the scope (the reason for the sun shot); second, a scope with clear optics and sufficient magnification.

And finally, you need perfect focus, which is much more difficult than it sounds. You need to focus on Polaris to get perfect focus, but you can't find Polaris without *first* getting perfect *focus.* You'd think that you could just twist the focusing knob all the way to infinity, right? I mean, how much farther than Polaris can infinity be? It turns out that infinity lies quite a long way beyond the opposite edge of the Milky Way where sits Polaris, at least when you're focusing through a Gurley transit. You have to find something else to focus on, and it's here you realize just how big the universe really is and, strange to say, how small.

If the distant horizon is distant enough—fifty miles; a hundred miles is better, if there's no haze or waves of heat distortion—that focus is close enough: you find a faraway point on earth, turn the focusing knob until the line of horizon reads sharp and distinct against the sky, and if your angles are correct when you turn them and aim the scope, you'll see Polaris. You might need to jiggle the knob a little bit more to sharpen Polaris the way you'd sharpened the horizon, but not too much: it's easy to lose the North Star and not get it back. You know it's there, in the seeming blank of magnified blue sky, but the plane of focus is unbelievably thin, and when you've missed it, the best thing to do is return to earth, focus on something you know for *sure* is there, and try again.

The best, the *very* best object of focus for an observation of Polaris is the moon. I'm not sure what it means that the moon shares focus with Polaris, but it does, and when it's there in the daytime sky it's a gift: once you get the moon sharp in your crosshairs, you know Polaris will jump right out at you. I was lucky this morning; a lovely crescent moon hovered not that far above Navajo Mountain to the east, and that's where I found focus.

All these connections. To earthlings, the moon might as well be the same size as the sun, which is miracle enough. What are the odds that perspective would work this way, a huge flaming sphere made small by distance, a tiny dead globe made huge by nearness, to the eye exactly the same size, to instruments pretty close? And like the sun, the moon offers its own locational possibilities; it's actually possible to get a bearing by shooting the lunar disc. When Brigham Young's chief surveyor and theological consultant, Orson Pratt, established the center of Zion—only a day or so after the saints had entered Salt Lake Valley, and in an elaborate ceremony that determined the point marked today by the sandstone monolith at the corner of the Temple wall—he did so by means of solar *and* lunar observations, but I've come to believe that Pratt was at least as interested in numerology as accuracy, and I can imagine that his tying the moon into connection with the center of Zion satisfied a need beyond the merely cadastral, a purpose that might eventually have culminated in the architectural details of the Temple itself, the waxing and waning phases of the moon carved into the Temple's granite columns.

The moon has motivated numerous other attempts to prove its usefulness in navigation and orientation. In an attempt that seems, in retrospect, as theologically ritualistic as Orson Pratt's, the British Admiralty kept a platoon of mathematicians shut up in a room for years and years doing the math necessary to write tables that would allow seagoing navigators to determine their longitude by observing the exact moment the moon would eclipse dozens of stars, a project made irrelevant and even ridiculous through the invention of a dependable chronometer, which allowed handier and more accurate astronomical observations.

And there was that more recent, if less well known, attempt at lunar orientation, Jim Williams's experiments with time and space that focused mostly on his well-studied map of the moon's surface. I never really understood Williams's attraction to the moon, except that it reflected perhaps his own sense of himself in the world— that he found in the moon a physical fact well adapted to the light and dark phases that defined his own bipolar perception of ultimate truth, a body both distant and accessible, undeniable as cold

hard rock and yet somehow malleable, mysterious, even transcendent, a vision of the cosmos I envied even as I understood him
to be tragic in his wrongheadedness, supporting aptly the judgment
of that famous Shakespearean lunatic Othello:

> It is the very error of the moon;
> She comes more nearer earth than she was wont,
> And makes men mad.

Williams taught me that the moon bore the same relation to the
sun and stars that his stopwatch bore to Greenwich mean time, a
source of location too close and too personal to be of any practical
use. Contrary to Williams's assertion that he'd finally arrived at
some point of clear placement and location, situating himself at
the center of intersecting lines of rocks and concentric circles of
sand determined by his too-close observation of the moon, and
dampened by the last of his canteen water—an assertion whose
certainty I still couldn't sometimes help but envy—the fact remained that he was just plain *lost,* wandering the landscape of his
own dark side.

The truth be told, Othello was *right* about the moon, as was another of Shakespeare's commentators upon celestial orientation,
Juliet. Although it's fair to say that in the balcony scene she was
basically trying to hold Romeo off by means of deconstructing his
choice of heavenly bodies upon which to swear his love, she sum-
marizes the moon's limitations pretty well. When Juliet asks him
to swear by something more dependable and distant than plain old
teenage lust, which was right there in front of her on her balcony
in the form of Romeo himself, Romeo enlists the moon, a heavenly
body with all the usual romantic associations, prompting Juliet not
to swoon—the usual rhyming response to moon invocations—but
instead to practice literary criticism upon poor Romeo's choice of
tropes, when all Romeo wanted to do was neck some more. "O,
swear not by the moon, the inconstant moon," Juliet says, "that
monthly changes in her circled orb." Although missing by a mile
Romeo's romantic point, she was nevertheless right on regarding
the moon's relative undependability, the inconstant phases it inevitably outgrows: an appropriate figure, if a little cerebral, for describing a teenager's quick heartbeat and short attention span,
especially this particular teenager's. Juliet might even have added

equally discouraging facts concerning the moon's less-than-ambitious dependence on merely reflected light, and the way it seduces the ocean into wildly swinging cycles of tidal attraction that are tumultuous, literally overwhelming, and always unconsummated.

Still, I sympathize with Orson Pratt's desire to include the moon in his ritual equations, and also with Romeo, and even Jim Williams, and all those anonymous mathematicians struggling to make useful sense of a celestial body with such well-recognized charisma. Of course the moon's orbit is funky compared to Polaris's, and it's even closer to the earth than the sun, and the math alone makes the moon more trouble than it's worth for navigators and land surveyors alike. Even so, I loved the fact that the moon fit the solar circle so neatly, but unlike the sun didn't *need* the boundaries; the moon is cold gray rock, static beyond redemption, and when focused through the transit is even sharper than the horizon it rises above, its features not blurred by heat waves and power-plant haze, perfect in its individual completeness, its *focus*.

So I'm happy this morning to add the moon to my astronomical calculations, even tangentially, deriving that necessary focus from what little I could see in that morning's narrow crescent of light and dark seas, craters large enough to be distinguished in the daylight even through such limited magnification, one crater spreading rays like survey lines, each with a bearing and distance, and a starting point, which I understood to be a distant version of the corner of South Temple and Main Street, and I catch myself thinking—not for the first time that summer—that maybe Williams had a point. This morning, the air is almost supernaturally clear, and the moon is right there in the scope, flat but distinct, and I turn the knob slightly back and forth, from clarity to the edge of blurriness, then back a little less each time, stopping when it pops, when the moon's outlines, its rills and ridges, craters and peaks seem even clearer, perhaps even more real, than the contours of Navajo Mountain that curve skyward.

This morning, the moon and Navajo Mountain are almost touching, of nearly the same hard-rock substance and round shape, each calling tidally to each.

It's almost ten o'clock, the time on which I'd based my ballpark calculations, the horizontal and vertical angles that connect my foresight to Polaris. As I've said, lines on earth require two relevant numbers: bearing and distance. The horizontal angle is the only one that's necessary for direction on the ground: vertical angles are required to convert the distance you measure up a hillside into the true distance, the perfectly level one that connects those two ideal points, so it's used and then discarded as merely a means to an end, kept in notes so that the math can be double-checked in the office, but not really relevant to the meaning of the survey.

Once you start aiming your transit *above* the earth, however, things get a little more complicated. Distance becomes a silent factor in the equation: the distance to Polaris is terrifying to ponder, or comforting, depending on your mood, but not exactly relevant to determining earthly position or direction. But for the purpose of shooting Polaris, bearing takes on a third dimension, requiring that I find another bearing, another angle, the vertical. And suddenly the fourth dimension, time, becomes critical.

To use the figures listed in the ephemeris—which tell you the exact position of Polaris at any given moment on any given day— you have to convert your local time to Greenwich mean time, the time the clock says it is in England, at the site of the Greenwich Observatory, and that's when I'm reminded that although my situation in Utah was determined in part by the theology of Mormon millennialism, and although my mission that particular summer was determined by Thomas Jefferson's prescient sense of American continentalism; the numbers that describe my position on earth is a lingering legacy of Manifest Destiny's strict father, British imperialism. Everything begins at Greenwich: zero minutes, zero seconds, zero hours of time; zero degrees, zero minutes, and zero seconds of longitude line up like those vernier lines I read with Matt's magnifying glass through the Gurley's tiny glass window. Before you can figure out where you are in Utah, you have to go through the somewhat anachronistic and somehow humbling process of determining what time it is in England.

Petty nationalistic concerns aside, something wonderful happened whenever I added this element to the equation: I realized once again the reason the language of distance, of *longitude,* is also the language of *time.* Like an hour, a degree is broken into sixty minutes, and each minute represents an accumulation of sixty seconds. As the earth turns, and the line of the earth's shadow creeps across the Kaiparowits Plateau, if you measure the distance and record the time, you'll learn that it takes the sun exactly one hour to traverse fifteen degrees of longitude. In four minutes of time, the sun will have traveled exactly one degree; if the time in Utah is 10:00 A.M., in Greenwich, England, it's 5:00 in the afternoon.

In order to fit the equations and find the right numbers in the ephemeris, it's necessary to jump through two more chronological hoops: convert A.M. and P.M. numbers to the twenty-four-hour clock (because it's morning, it's still 10:00), which I'm fond of reminding anyone who will listen is *Pentagon* time, so pervasively militaristic is our culture, along with the transit's crosshairs reminding me daily of the essentially military dimensions of our mission. I've also adjusted for daylight savings time, first imposed, by the way, during World War I and then reimposed during World War II, in order to wring a little more wartime productivity out of America's workforce.

Finally, I enter these figures into a long equation, parts of which make more sense to me than others; do the math; and at last arrive at the numbers that tell me where Polaris can be found at 10:00 this morning. Or rather, where *I* can be found, since I'm the one who doesn't know where he is.

Polaris is sometimes easy to see in the daylight sky, once centered in the transit and magnified by the transit's barely adequate optics. Most of the time it isn't. It depends on a lot of things, including the accuracy of your focus, or the angle of the sun, or the humid thickness, or the dusty graininess, of the air. On those occasions when it pops, when you can be certain it's the real thing and not some particle floating on the surface of your eyeball, or a tiny prick of light bouncing off an otherwise invisible ding in the transit's objective lens, or merely wishful thinking (as *Moby-Dick* teaches us, if you look into blankness long enough, you'll eventually see exactly what you're looking for); when Polaris is right there, Larry would often say, proud of the precision of his calculations and the keenness of his eye, that it's "bright as a diamond in a goat's ass." And that's what it was like this morning, my last day on the Kaiparowits Plateau, the star shot I was calculating for no practical purpose.

Polaris was there. Pure beginners' luck—the angles were the correct ones, the transit's focus on the moon was exactly right, and my eyes themselves were focused and ready. Focusing your eye on Polaris, even through a perfectly prepared scope, is sometimes like trying to focus in a totally dark room—the chair might be right in front of you, ready to trip you up, or it could be planted safely on the other side of the room; but without perspective, without being able to distinguish the alternating layers of objects that place you in relation to the world, your eyes search with an intensity that is almost desperate, and in doing a star shot, with so little to go on, it sometimes takes your eyes minutes to pick something out of a million light-years of near-total emptiness. But among other things, all those hours I'd spent peering into the microscopes of my youth at similarly obscure points of light had prepared me well for this moment, and the deep blue tunnel of sky guided me in the right direction, and that day the star appeared in my sight with a kind of physical presence I had never seen before, even at *night.*

That morning, Polaris actually seemed like an object, not merely a point of light. Larry was right: goat's ass or not, it looked like an actual jewel. I know it's an illusion, but in the daytime, through the transit, a star seems like an actual object, a body with surface area and sphericity, not the dimensionless pinprick in the cover of darkness you see at night. And it *moves,* not with the recklessness of the sun, speeding relentlessly beyond the scope's circle of light, or the goofy bounce of the inconstant moon, but with a slow intentional grace, skimming almost imperceptively down the side of the vertical crosshair as I watch, a fact of pure white light standing clear alongside the black of the spiderweb crosshair.

I understood that I wasn't seeing a rock up there, or the five-pointed object of my childhood imagination, a glittery cutout hanging from threads against a blue-black draped background, like a star in the American flag. A scientist would tell me I was seeing a point of light; more specifically, my eye was recording electromagnetic energy radiated by a thermonuclear process, transformed by my eye's own narrow perspective through some negotiation with my brain into a beam, a pinpoint by my own narrow view, the pinpoint I myself represented in all that time and space. I was viewing a distant emission from a star that might no longer exist, having long since consumed itself in forging that light; and I knew also that even if Polaris *was* still there pumping out light (as astronomers tell us is likely), it was no longer even close to being in the same place it had been when it produced the light gathered by my eyes that August morning twenty-five years ago, that Polaris had already assumed a position that would provide less help in determining which direction was north, and therefore in fact had already stopped being the North Star. To this day, I'm not even sure why it appeared before me that morning with such solidity and substance. Why it seemed to possess, even in its pinpoint size too tiny for actual shape, more hard substantial mass than my planet's own sun, which seemed as gassy and insubstantial as it was huge, filling the scope like a bubble gum balloon.

Part of this clarity had to do, I'm sure, with context, the frame—the dark tunnel of the scope, the straight lines of the crosshairs, all that deep turquoise blue. Even so, in years to come, on other days shooting Polaris, when the focus was off, or the numbers from the sun shot were reversed or just plain wrong, I'd stare into the deep blue of where the star should be, staring and staring until something would appear that by god *had* to be Polaris, but it would become apparent moments later that I was zooming in on a hallucination, an artifact of wishful thinking, or floaters swimming behind the lens of my eye, self-conscious in its failure. Polaris, when it's there, is really *there.*

This solidity, the unmistakable be-ness of Polaris, seemed that morning to offer me something I'd never felt before, let alone ever understood. I'd read books, and passed high school tests on astronomy. I'd long since grasped the relationship between planet, sun, and stars: I knew that regardless of what common sense led us to believe, the truth was that *we* were doing most of the moving in the universe. But deep down inside I suppose I still believed the larger, more apparent truth: I stood on earth, the center of everything, and the sun, the stars, everything whizzed past.

Until that morning. At the moment it struck me what I was seeing, I understood that Polaris was something real, an undeniable point of reference in relation to which the earth simultaneously rotated and revolved, the earth a globe upon whose curved surface I stood, having seen horizon and sun emerge in triangulation to define a point a person could literally count on. I saw myself standing on the shoulder of the northern hemisphere, looking up, then looking north toward the earth's own pole, feeling the world turn under my feet, watching the sun as we spun around it in an orbit erratic in its closeness, its intimacy. Hanging on with my feet, careful not to touch the delicate eyepiece of the transit in front of me, I felt all this movement reduced to a slow skip of a bright jewel along the crosshair's thin vertical line. Staring at the star that long made me dizzy, and I stood back, opened the eye I'd been forcing shut for minutes while all that light and distance poured through my good right eye, blinked in the morning sun until I could focus on the ground, the trees, and then, beneath one particular tree, Tim, whose amused smile told me I'd been talking to myself again.

At first, doing the calculations seemed anticlimactic. My primary goal had been to locate Polaris, not to double-check the bearing, which the sun shot had already reaffirmed, and the math looked like *work*. But as I lost myself in connecting the dots of the long equation, converting my numbers into the arcane language of sines, cosines, and, appropriately enough, *tangents,* I came to understand my connection in yet another way beyond the physical, an orientation based on something other than sight or sense. I'd seen Polaris, and I'd felt the earth's movement reflected in the star's precise dance along the crosshair, but the calculations seemed a kind of web that brought into the same sphere *everything,* the tangible and the intangible. There was a number in the equation that stood for each element of the morning's experience: the blazed tree, the crisp blue summit of Navajo Mountain, the nubbly highlands and round craters of the moon, the barely contained thermonuclear explosion of the sun, even the grid of straight lines bent slightly in acknowledgment of the curved earth, the neat right-angled intersections pinned to the dirt with brass-capped iron markers engraved with the careful language of the *Manual of Surveying Instructions,* my own slow understanding of each skill and detail of my work: it all added up.

I even felt the import of the obscure Mormon connection I'd discovered in tracing our lines literally back to the corner of South Temple and Main in Salt Lake City, understanding that there was one more triangle to solve, even if it wasn't explicitly required by the *Manual*. This triangle's baseline ran direct and straight between my specific point on the Kaiparowits Plateau and the point marked by the sandstone monument at the corner of Temple Square. From this base, one side of the triangle rose directly from my transit to Polaris, the line I'd just found and calculated, the one that told me exactly where I stood. The other side of the triangle rose more theologically, and perhaps more ambitiously, from the Temple Square obelisk to that same North Star, the line calculated with such devotion by Orson Pratt and eternally fixed by the Big Dipper constellation inscribed in the granite facade of the Temple's west wall. This triangle reminded me that, whether I wanted to be or not, I was located as firmly by means of Mormon ritual and belief as I was by the momentum of Jeffersonian continentalism, and by the specific calculations that had led me to Polaris and confirmed my position on Earth.

That day I felt connected in ways I hadn't felt before, and haven't since. I understood then just what it meant to stand on a small spinning planet moving through the universe; I knew where I was in the state of Utah, the distance I'd traversed from Temple Square, the direction I was headed on earth. I'd calculated my own movement against the dependable reference of a star a thousand light-years away, and I'd discovered that my movements were measurable, even in the unimaginable scale of the Milky Way, and therefore possibly significant. I'd completed a set of calculations that told me exactly where I was, and I'd marked that spot with a mound of stone and an inscription on a living tree. I knew *where* I was, and I had a momentary sense that it was therefore possible to know *who* I was. I'd gotten a glimpse of what Thoreau had longed for, what my grandfather saw every day of his life. I'd made contact.

EPILOGUE

The Opening to the Womb of the World

All seven teenagers stopped hiking at the same moment, turning to examine more closely the arrangement of sandstone slopes and clefts that marked the place where a dry streambed joined the broad sandy floor of Coyote Wash. "It's a sipapu," one of the students, a pale blonde girl, said.

They argued a little about this. One student said that a sipapu was man-made, a feature located in the floor of a kiva, the religious meeting place for Pueblo Indians. The blonde girl responded with some heat: she had recently been thrown out of her house, and was living week to week with a succession of equally unenthusiastic relatives, and was feeling aggressive. She said she *knew* about kivas. That wasn't the point: a sipapu was the opening to the womb of the world, to Mother Earth, she said, and they happen in *nature*, too.

As they walked up and down the wash, examining the sandstone formation from different angles and talking quietly, the group came to the conclusion that the blonde girl was basically right, if not exactly correct in her details. One boy said, with uncharacteristic delicacy, "It looks like . . . well, a *vagina*," and we looked again, taking in the contours, the steep, rounded banks, the narrow channel that emerged from a tangle of ledges and walls to fall ten feet into a round deep hole that melted like a funnel between two sloping sandstone thighs. There was no missing it.

"Let's meditate here," a girl said.

261

They paused, thinking: how do you meditate around a sipapu?

"Let's do yoga," another student suggested, and everybody agreed: yoga was the thing to do. Another group might have continued the argument concerning the exact definition of the sipapu, discussed the complexities of culture and religion, invoked the sciences of geology and anthropology. Not these kids. They slid their packs from their shoulders and walked from the sandy bottom of the wash onto a slickrock ramp that led to a kind of porch attending the opening, a flat triangle bordered by the angled walls of the thighs.

The opening, the hole, the *sipapu*—for that was what we now called it—was as round as a well, five feet in diameter and textured with circular ridges stained darker as the tunnel deepened beneath the level triangular space where my students arranged themselves, each one facing the opening, filling the narrow space bordered by the sipapu and the sandstone walls that echoed the form of a woman's legs folded and bent upward from the groin, the posture of a woman on her back in the midst of dutiful sex or advanced labor. They assumed the lotus position, sitting with backs straight, calves and knees bent and interlaced in a way that never failed to cramp me up, extended their arms straight from their shoulders, and began chanting: "om . . ."

A photograph hangs framed above the desk at which I'm writing now, nearly thirty years later. In the picture, seven teenage boys and girls, my students, long hair loose and tangled or tied in ponytails or bound in handkerchiefs, wearing Levi's, sweatshirts, and oversize flannel shirts with sleeves rolled to the elbows, sit crosslegged around a deep sandstone pothole. From the angle I'd chosen for the photograph, the indentation looked especially vaginal, tan thighs spread open to reveal what might be a channel spiraling deep into the earth.

I've framed this picture to remind me of a remarkable fact about history and about myself, irrefutable proof that at one point in the mid-seventies this actually happened: a group of twenty-five teenagers identified by school counselors as "at risk" walked with their several teachers into a winding canyon in southern Utah that eventually joins the Escalante River, which not many miles later empties into a murky arm of Lake Powell. One of my students (we'd divided ourselves that day into smaller groups) suggested that the rock formation looked like a sipapu, the passage to the earth's womb revered by native people who have occupied the American Southwest—long ago, the Anasazi; today, the Hopi and Zuni. This was an anthropological detail they'd learned in my class as we studied Native American religions as a way of—what? Broadening their horizons? Undoing their ethnocentrism? Trying to keep them from dropping out of high school? Regardless of the motivation, they knew a sipapu when they saw one.

I remember that no one suggested we identify the rock (a *good* student myself, I knew: Navajo sandstone. After all, I'd studied under the professor who had mostly unmixed feelings about adding his name to the wall of ancient petroglyphs, and I'd learned under his tutelage even more obscure terms like *laccolith* and *unconformity*) or discuss its formation (I'd learned the answer to that one, too: rare desert rainstorms send water coursing down the cleft, over the earth mother's thighs, eroding and deepening the opening, called by geologists not a sipapu, but a pothole). Instead, other students suggested we arrange ourselves around the sipapu and do yoga, which they'd also learned in my class, along with haiku writing and stained glass window making. A yoga instructor had come to class, taught us the positions, the breathing, helped us to say *om* without giggling, and if I remember correctly, there was no giggling as they surrounded the opening to the womb of the world and ritualized the moment in the best way they knew how. After three intervening decades of educational relapses and political backsliding that have taken us from the guerrilla teaching of the sixties and seventies through that cowardly retreat we called "back to basics" into our current obsession with measurable outcomes—from hope to accountability, from love to standardized testing—I need this reminder of what kind of teaching is possible, what perhaps could even happen again.

In addition to reminding me of what was possible in the twilight years of the sixties, the photograph tells me something important about the relationship between Americans and the natural world, about how useless Western culture is when it comes to connecting with nature as it presents itself, unrehearsed and unshaped by human hands. We didn't sing the Hallelujah Chorus, or recite the Pledge of Allegiance. We didn't quote Aristotle, and we didn't praise yahweh, or beg him for our lives.

Neither did we determine its location by measuring its bearing

and distance to the nearest section corner according to the rules
I'd labored under the summer before, and would the next summer,
and each summer to follow through the end of the decade, so en-
amored had I become of more Jeffersonian approaches to connecting with the natural world. Instead of a Gurley transit, my
students and I peered through a lens we'd borrowed from a people
whose presence here preceded ours by two thousand years, and
we saw neither line to the next flag, nor the archangel-guarded
gate to the Garden of Eden, but instead a birth canal through
which human beings found their way into a world that loved and
nurtured them. We chanted a sound, however compromised by
time and distance and cultural inauthenticity, provided by a distant people we assumed knew not the word *alienation.*

This photograph also reminds me that I use the word *we* too
loosely. So haunted am I by the picture and all it represents, I've
had a slide made, and I occasionally show it to my university students in courses ranging from English education to graduate seminars in the literature of nature and wilderness. The last time I did
this, I asked my students to probe the image for meaning, to gen-
erate questions about what they saw projected on the screen. After
they'd asked about the individuals, the location, what they were
doing and when, one student—doubtless a budding scholar of critical theory—asked a smugly rhetorical question: where were you?

Where was I? I had to admit I was taking the picture, framing
the scene through the lens of a camera. As my students meditated
upon their place in the universe, I pondered the meaning of my
students' meditations. Even then, I knew the word *alienation.* It
wasn't me who spotted the opening to the womb of the world.

When I began working in the STEP Program, the winter following my season on the Kaiparowits Plateau, it had been operating
precariously for a couple of years as an alternative school within a
school for students who were, one way or another, in trouble. In
those days you could find teachers, and even a couple of adminis-
trators, who cared about these kids. Some of us believed that any
teenager worth his salt would take one look at the typical assortment of high school teachers, read a few pages of the typical textbook, spend a day following buzzer after buzzer through crowded
halls from one spirit-sapping classroom to the next, and say *no*

way. By walking away, these students showed us they were especially worth saving.

Our students ditched most of their classes, but lacked the commitment it took to drop out completely, and their bored and listless wanderings had eventually brought them into the STEP classroom. Many of them had terrible lives at home, punctuated by screaming, often violent fights with parents, and at any given moment several of our students were living with relatives or friends, or in their cars, or on the street. Some were in foster homes. Nearly all of them were using drugs, wrecking cars, and having indiscriminate sex. Few of their romances lasted. Kids with safe and stable families, and even those with lasting teenage loves, did not find their way into that dusty classroom with the high ceilings and tall windows, the thrift-store couches, the silk screen table, and the rock-and-roll posters.

The faculty similarly lacked consistency and respectability. We'd found our way into the program because we were at risk as well: none of us could keep a job in a regular classroom, and we didn't meet even the minimal dress code of a mid-seventies urban high school. We wore our hair long, dressed ourselves in T-shirts and peasant blouses, beaded necklaces, Levi's with holes in the knees. We planned lessons concerned last of all with skills, first of all with helping our students understand who they were and where they stood in relation to the world. We believed that if we engaged their hearts, their minds would follow, which I still believe to be the only educational philosophy that makes sense.

STEP was an acronym, but I've long forgotten what words the letters represented. Sometimes we joked about the teachers being stepparents, the students our stepchildren, and the love we felt for these kids could best be described as parental, but we understood that we were all orphans: the teachers were nominally in charge, but there was a sense that we had all fucked up, were all lost and wandering. Like Ishmael, we had been rescued by Rachael, looking for her own lost children.

Take me, for example. The sixties had divided my family as surely as a fault line, and although my parents and I had managed to maintain a relationship based on an understanding that we loved each other and on a mutual willingness to avoid talking too much about the beliefs and assumptions that separated us, we understood that I had become the kind of orphan the times had produced in such numbers. And like many of my students, I *felt* homeless. Even though my summers working as a surveyor had me living in a succession of bunk trailers and small-town motels, those short three months sometimes felt more real, more *grounded,* than the months that elapsed in between, seminars in romantic poetry being no match for an observation of Polaris as a means of defining substance and truth, or even *home*; as if I hadn't felt dislocated enough when my summer on the Kaiparowits ended and I returned to the crowded apartment I shared with a fluctuating set of college-student roommates, I'd been relegated to sleeping on the living room couch for a month until the person who had sublet my room for the summer finally left. That year I was between degrees, between commitments, between everything that had given my life until then the illusion of structure.

And like most of my students, I was drifting unanchored by the kind of love that mattered most. That fall, after I'd returned to the couch in my apartment instead of to her apartment, Karen and I began talking—about how I felt, and about how she felt, and I learned not surprisingly that she'd come to the conclusion that I was no longer the person she'd fallen in love with either, and that was pretty much it. When I thought about Karen in the months that followed, it seemed a little like I'd wandered out of her life with the same studied aimlessness with which I'd wandered into the STEP program, where the seat-of-the-pants curriculum often seemed aimless as well.

On the other hand, there was at least one thing students and teachers in the STEP Program counted on. The curriculum might change from day to day, but spring break was spent in the desert, in the labyrinths of sandstone that drain seasonal desert rains into the Colorado River, the landscape surrounding the Kaiparowits Plateau and Navajo Mountain I'd pondered from so many different perspectives the summer before. In spite of my own lingering uncertainties about such transcendental assumptions concerning the spiritual benefits of nature, I didn't question this STEP Program tradition, and no one else did either; only years later did I wonder about such certainty in a time of such apparent indirection. Students attended school erratically through the week, but they all showed up at 6:00 A.M. on the appointed day for the drive south, and the kids who promised their cars were there with their cars.

We'd postpone, revise, and betray the most heartfelt of pedagogical intentions, but the members of the STEP community spent a week each spring in the desert. We did this because we somehow believed in the healing properties of nature.

After my students had completed their meditation around the sipapu, we continued our hike downstream, following Coyote Creek as it wandered in leisurely detours as if postponing its junction with the Escalante River. We were looking for two landmarks: we wanted to see Stephens Arch, notable for its skyscraper-window inaccessibility near the top of a tall thin blade of sandstone; and we wanted to contemplate the boundary where the freely running waters of the Escalante met the sluggish backwater of Lake Powell. We spotted the arch first, an opening through which we could see an isolated fragment of blue sky, its sandstone frame warmed orange by the sun, a distant tantalizing contrast to our own shaded and chilly viewpoint on the Escalante. The river was a foot deep and surprisingly swift—I'd seen it a mere trickle on trips I'd taken later in the year, but this was spring break, and the rainstorm that soaked us on our hike in had apparently lingered over the Escalante's high-plateau headwaters, swelling and accelerating the muddy water we waded through on our way to observe its submersion in Lake Powell.

I'm not sure what attracted us. Maybe it was simple curiosity, or the momentum that takes over when you start walking downstream, or perhaps a desire to read up close the morality tale narrated by this particular intersection of natural landscape and human ambition. Whatever our reasons, it turned out that we'd walked directly from the earth's womb to the most depressing expression I know of what grown-up human beings can construct out of the materials the world has given them. The brochures call Lake Powell the Jewel of the Colorado, but there was nothing gemlike or inspiring about the spot where river met reservoir. Chunks of Styrofoam, weathered plywood fragments, and other lost and forgotten objects we couldn't identify had been tugged here by some backwater reservoir current, slow and inscrutable. An oily film flashed rainbows of murky colors, contributing a thin dark line to the sandstone brim of the Escalante arm of the fetid bathtub that is Lake Powell.

I began to lecture my students on the evil before us—having

only months earlier floated the few miles that survived of Glen Canyon, and having taken in the whole complicated view from Navajo Mountain, I felt moved, not to mention qualified, to hold forth—but my students were way ahead of me. They'd actually communed with nature earlier that day, not merely observed the phenomena, as I had; they *knew* what this meant. They didn't like it.

"This is fucked-up," one student said, and the other students agreed completely. They had an innocent, almost instinctive reaction against dams and power plants, strip mines, even national parks. They wanted sipapus and sandstone overhangs under which to spread their sleeping bags and smoke their pot. They understood that this was not what they'd crawled from their mother's lap to behold.

We spent the next morning rappelling. Our students took a long time waking up—the deep sandstone overhang kept the rain from falling directly on our heads, but this was our third day camping, the high-desert mornings were damp and cold, and they emerged from their mummy bags reluctantly, childlike, yawning and complaining, grouchily reminding us that this educational experiment depended on the cooperation of the students, something we teachers couldn't take for granted. But rappelling was a sexy activity, and the students who had done it before talked about the combination of fear and exhilaration, the *rush,* that comes from backing one's body off a vertical cliff, trusting only a rope and yourself, defying gravity: one more defiance with which to counter the forces that directed their lives.

We located a good cliff, less than fifty feet down, no difficult overhang, an easy scramble up the back, then gathered our students at the base to review what they'd learned a few weeks before in the classroom: the ropes and knots, the vocabulary for communicating instructions, the final warning about the consequences of getting it wrong. We didn't lay it on too heavily about the dangers, but we didn't have to: our students knew better than we ever would the risks they were taking. They tied the thick climbing rope to an immovable sandstone boulder and lowered the rest over the edge, making sure it unfolded straight and untangled against the rock, and I assumed my position on the cliff's edge. It was my job to watch as my students backed one by one over the cliff, making sure they were leaning outward at the necessary angle, and offering encouragement as they eased themselves alone into empty space, ready to calm and reassure the ones who panicked, or forgot what they'd been taught.

As the sun passed from behind the morning's clouds, rising steadily into the bright blue of a stark spring day, one student followed another over the edge, grimacing at that transition from standing—a simple vertical line against the pull of gravity, the posture they'd spent their lives coming to trust—into that unnatural sense of being out of synch with the most uncompromising of the laws that governed their world, assuming a position that all their lives had meant falling, learning to trust something new: their own rope lifeline, a knot they'd learned to tie themselves, words of instruction and comfort from their teacher, an adult who might or might not be more dependable than the other adults in their lives whose routine betrayals had allowed them to fall into lives at risk. All this as the sandstone revealed itself as increasingly unreliable, grinding into sand beneath the friction of their boots.

I remember one student in particular, a slightly overweight brown-haired girl who was making her way through her teenage years giving herself to one boy after another, trusting none of them but placing forlorn hope in the act itself, the pressing together of bare skin that took her for a moment somewhere beyond her own sad anger and aloneness. I stood at the edge of the sandstone face as the girl moved slowly toward the point of commitment, my words promising that I was there to help her if her nerve failed, if she forgot the procedure through which her own body's friction kept her in control and moving slowly down the rock face. "Don't worry," I said quietly, *"we've got you."*

She was doing pretty well until she reached that point where you simply lean back against certain death and walk backward in a way you've never walked before, lying almost horizontal in the insubstantial air, legs spread and braced against whatever came next.

"I don't fucking know about this," she said in a quiet, trembling voice, like no voice I'd ever heard from this loud, tough, in-your-face girl. "It's slippery; I feel like I'm falling already."

"We've got you," I said again, a little disingenuously—she was on her own now, as she well knew. I gave her the information I thought would help, reminding her about the rope's dependable anchor, the rope's friction she controlled herself. "You're okay," I said. "Just back down a few more steps. It'll get easier, it'll feel less strange. It will be worth it."

The look she gave me was like nothing I'd ever seen before: she suspected I was lying; she understood she could die any second. At that moment she credited neither the strength of rock nor the power of human concern. All my calming talk was some kind of white noise, elevator music that had nothing at all to do with gravity and cables, the last thing you hear before your free fall stops at the bottom of the shaft. There was complete helplessness in her face, and complete abandonment, and complete acceptance. It was my job to tell her what I believed she needed to hear, and it was her job to lean farther and farther back, to stabilize herself against spinning by spreading her legs wider, to accept fully the tug of the rope as she slowly reclined alone into empty space, watching me looking down, my lips moving with words she was past hearing.

I thought I understood pretty well the meaning of Lake Powell. As I said, I'd loitered around its edges, had observed its cramped cement conclusion from the visitor center overlook and beheld its backed-up expanse from the summit of Navajo Mountain. I'd experienced firsthand what remained of Glen Canyon below the dam, sidestroking alongside my raft in the unnaturally cold water that only minutes earlier had spun the generators. I'd even walked the one side canyon that survived intact, but none of this prepared me for experiencing with my students the sad intersection where the Escalante River met Lake Powell.

My students' vocabulary may have been borrowed from the bumper stickers that decorated their STEP-classroom lockers and their beat-up cars, slogans they chanted at the Earth Day celebrations that were part of our curriculum, but the rock formation they told themselves was a connection with some safe place from which they'd been exiled—the Garden, the womb, childhood—was comforting and substantial, perhaps even real.

Where the dead waters of Lake Powell arrested the vital flow of the Escalante was real beyond question, ugly and defeated, an intersection my students seemed to recognize: it *was* fucked-up, and they knew it in ways I could only imagine. Their lives moved between appetites and consequences, dreams and abrupt awakenings; between what they needed and what they were given, sinking slowly from the weightless flow of childhood toward their inevitable submergence into what we jokingly in those days called the "real world," the postgraduation future of full-time employment and adult responsibility, the world of their parents and teachers. Their at-risk behaviors—their communal marijuana smoking and keg parties, their insolence and their defiance, their railings against the parody of motherhood their own mothers had become—all spoke of their need to make a home they could actually depend on, and all this effort took place against the insistence of the future, something imposed and artificial, something overwhelming and inevitable.

The STEP program classroom was illuminated by a large stained glass window the students had constructed themselves, a collection of fifteen square-foot panels of colored glass, each one designed and leaded by a student, soldered together and suspended just inside one of the room's high windows, and I remember the campsite with similar images of light and hope: a shelf of white sand lit by sunlight reflecting off a golden sandstone wall, the wind-drifted floor of an alcove carved by prehistoric scourings of the stream, sheltered from rain and safely above the rare but inevitable desert flood. The tents we'd brought stayed in our backpacks; kids rolled out their sleeping bags on the sand and arranged themselves according to patterns and agreements I could only guess at. Smaller groups went different directions each day, but the students all gathered together at night in a large irregular circle as if in preparation for an attack they knew was coming. The teachers also camped in the shelter of the sandstone alcove but a discreet distance away, laying out our bags a little farther apart from each other, arranging ourselves in a way that accommodated our students' need to be attended to yet left alone, our need to talk things over out of their hearing, and the desire for individual privacy we'd developed as we'd entered deeper into the crowded obligations of adulthood.

After four nights camped beneath the overhang that had insulated us from the storms blowing over our heads, we loaded our packs and hiked upstream, slowly winding our way up and out of the canyon, pulling ourselves onto the broad expanse of alluvial fans and flat sagebrush plains that eased the transition between the eroded canyons of the Escalante drainage and the formidable rise of the Straight Cliffs that punctuated the northern extent of the Kaiparowits Plateau, the comforting rounded swell of Navajo Mountain coming once again into view.

It was late afternoon by the time we reached the trailhead, where we'd left our cars just off the gravel road near a small log cabin, and rather than risk a late-night drive back, we decided to postpone the inevitable, camp one more night, and get an early start the next day. The cabin was unlocked and open, drifted with sand and dusty with age, but a kitchen table and a few unsteady chairs made it feel inside like someone's home, and the students decided to move in for the night. They found a broom and swept the floor clean, sweeping the corners of cobwebs and mouse droppings and wiping clear the small windows to gather the last light of day, finally setting up their backpacking stoves on the table to make dinner, to boil water for tea and for dishwashing, creating a crowded version of family life that moved me deeply as I watched from the doorway.

Occasionally my university students will argue in class about the authenticity of what happened that day in Coyote Wash, the sipapu, the yoga: is this deep or shallow? Can a person innocently pick and choose among the offerings of a variety of cultures and religions, appropriate this, make a tool of that, have a valid spiritual experience disconnected from one's own culture and history? As much as I love the conversation—this is, after all, a very good question, one that leads to more profound questions concerning community, personal identity, and the benefits of cultural pluralism, and ultimately to that very *big* question concerning a human being's place in the natural world, the specific manner in which a person occupies that part of the universe we see up close—I sometimes think that any classroom discussion that ensues is doomed to miss the point, and I continue to be troubled by my inability to articulate exactly where I stood that day, and why this photograph means so much to me. Over the years, as I've examined the scene hanging on the wall of my office, I've considered a number of interpretations, some profound, some dismissive; some of them mythic, others merely historical.

What I see in the photograph depends to a great extent on how I'm feeling, whether it's been a good teaching day or not, whether

I've watched over one of those rare moments in the classroom when individuals—some shy or unsure; others defensive, contentious, or simply angry—meld into a community, begin moving toward shared insights derived from the group's sincere acceptance of individual perspectives, understanding the value of each person's experience in life or in reading, for a brief moment absorbing even me, their teacher, into the indiscriminate whole the class has become. On those days, I don't worry so much about my position on the periphery, occupying that oddly separate place in the landscape of love and connection, the relationship between student and teacher Theodore Roethke could define only by what a teacher almost is, but finally is not: "neither father nor lover." I take comfort then in my role as a prod or guide, and I allow myself to feel that perhaps I've earned that day the enormous gift of my students' trust. I think then of the significance of that moment at the sipapu, the possibility for comfort, for transcendence, even for happiness. I think: my students have learned something that has changed their lives.

Other days, when I'm thinking of what little progress I've made since that time in my life, how many opportunities for insight or connection I've turned from or betrayed, on those days when I've merely battered my students over the head with Emerson's "Nature" or Hawthorne's concept of the isolatoe, I wonder about where those students are today. I worry about which ones didn't make it, which ones did; which ones have moved beyond lives at risk into a world made whole by the possibility for love and home they understood that day. What I understand then is that their lives have likely become as ordinary as my own. I know that a few are still at risk, the rest so lacking in risk their adult lives might as well be sleepwalking. At these times, the scene appears to me as something insubstantial and eccentric, even desperate, a story of children expelled from the womb after a long troubled delivery, thrown too soon upon the bare sandy shore of the world, fighting to hang on with everything they've learned.

As the sun set, and the students settled themselves into the cabin they'd reclaimed, the teachers found once again that appropriate distance, close enough to satisfy our supervisory obligations, far enough away for plausible denial concerning whatever illegal smoke might pass into the rising night wind. I made my own camp on a ridge above the cabin, close enough to hear but not quite make out the murmured conversations of my students when the wind fell silent. After nights of sleeping beneath the overhang—it had rained, or threatened rain, every evening—I was looking forward to a solitary night under what I hoped would be the cover of an open sky.

It didn't rain. The sky was absolutely clear, rinsed by the week's showers, burnished by a wind that blew steady and cold as the night wore on and the moon rose higher, full and larger than I'd imagined possible. The moon seemed to take up the whole sky, illuminating the Straight Cliffs of the Kaiparowits Plateau, the high bluff above the cabin, the sagebrush and sand, perhaps even the coyote I could hear howling not so far away. I snuggled in my mummy bag for warmth and wrapped my poncho around myself against the cold wind.

I don't remember getting much sleep. I remember feeling confined and comfortable in my sleeping bag, my face exposed to feel the steady powerful wind and smell the wet sagebrush, snug in the odors preserved in my sleeping bag, old goose down and a week of backpacking sweat. It wasn't quite as bright as day, but the land shone silver where the moon painted itself on cliffs and plateaus, white as phosphorous in the sky, a few stars but mostly a pale black emptiness, white moonshine almost too bright to look at directly, and a landscape that appeared snowdrifted and yet distinct, precise in every shadowed outline and detail. I watched the moon follow its transit across the sky, and finally fell asleep when it set behind the Kaiparowits Plateau, waking an hour later when the lightening sky outlined the Abajo Mountains to the east.

That night I felt perfectly alone, measuring the exact distance from my students, far from my family and friends, distant from the possibility of love and home, but welcome to view what nature had to show me, perhaps the only gift I was prepared to accept. This night had not been made by human hands. It was neither Bureau of Reclamation project nor soothing amalgam of Zen and shaman and Earth Day environmentalism, and it had nothing to do with straight lines and precise Enlightenment intersections. The moon hung there simply, erasing all but the brightest stars in the sun's reflected light, neither illuminating Williams's obscure truth nor focusing my own search for placement. Somehow it was enough for me to stay awake, unthinking for once through a night that wasn't warm, or exactly personal, nor anything more than the sum of its parts. It was the bare moon, the moonlit landscape, the steady scouring wind, and the dependable Straight Cliffs of the Kaiparowits Plateau.

ABOUT THE AUTHOR

John Hales was born and raised in Ogden, Utah. He earned his bachelor's and master's degrees at the University of Utah, and his Ph.D. in American literature and culture at the State University of New York at Binghamton. After working as a high school teacher, university instructor, and land surveyor in Utah, his East-Coast employment included directing the Basic Writing Program at SUNY-Binghamton and teaching literature at Vassar College. His essays have appeared in *Creative Nonfiction, Fourth Genre, Southern Review, Hudson Review, Ascent, Weber Studies,* and *Georgia Review,* and in the anthology *On Nature: Great Writers on the Great Outdoors.* His work has been cited numerous times in *Best American Essays* and in *Best American Science and Nature Writing,* and was awarded a Pushcart Prize. He currently teaches in the MFA Program in Creative Writing at California State University, Fresno.